The Inclusive Learning Center Book

Dedication

This book is dedicated to the newest members of our family: Bryan, Elizabeth, and Fisher. Each has brought new joys and experiences to our lives.
—Christy and Rebecca

Acknowledgments

Special thanks to the teachers who allowed us to visit their classrooms and take photographs for this book. Their help is greatly appreciated, as we strive to make *Learning Centers* available and appropriate for all young children.

Sarah Hackney

Deborah Miller

Leigh Scheuer

Bristol Tennessee City Schools

Debra Hughes

Beth Simms

Johnson City Schools

Darrellen E. Lodien

Brandy Shelton

East Tennessee State University Child Study Center

Special Thanks

Several people have provided significant help in the creation of this book.

Sheila P. Smith, our resident editor, who carefully attended to the details of this book. She made sure that the design, words, and appendix were technically correct. Her diligent work and special skills made our book better.

Sue Kell helped with selecting the supportive children's books. Her effort strengthened the literacy connection that is so important.

Michael O. Talley made the wonderful photographs that provide the examples of children working in centers. His willingness to take "just one more picture" is greatly appreciated.

Our Editor-in-Chief, Kathy Charner, is always a joy to work with on projects. She values our ideas and helps us create the best book possible. Thank you for being so supportive.

We also extend our gratitude to Leah Curry-Rood and Larry Rood, who continually encourage the development of quality materials that focus on the education of ALL young children. You treat all of us with such respect. We thank you.

The Inclusive Learning Center Book

for Preschool Children With Special Needs

Christy Isbell and Rebecca Isbell

Illustrations by Stacy Larsen and Kathy Dobbs

Photographs by Michael O. Talley

gryphon house
Beltsville, Maryland

©2005 Christy Isbell and Rebecca Isbell

Published by Gryphon House, Inc.
PO Box 207, Beltsville, MD 20704
800.638.0928; 301.595.9500; 301.595.0051 (fax)

Visit us on the web at www.gryphonhouse.com

Illustrations: Stacy Larsen and Kathy Dobbs

Cover Photograph: Straight Shots

Library of Congress Cataloging-in-Publication Information:

Isbell, Christy.
   The inclusive learning center book : for preschool children with special needs / Christy Isbell and Rebecca Isbell ; illustrations by Stacy Larsen ; photographs by Michael O. Talley and Sarah Hackney.
       p. cm.
   Summary: "A resource book for preschool teachers, containing information for creating an inclusive learning center classroom and adaptable activities for children with varying special needs"--Provided by publisher.
   Includes bibliographical references and index.
   ISBN 0-87659-294-9
 1. Inclusive education--United States. 2. Classroom learning centers--United States--Planning. 3. Children with disabilities--Education (Preschool)--United States. I. Isbell, Rebecca T. II. Title.
   LC1201.I73 2005
   371.9'046--dc22
                                    2005003163

Bulk purchase
Gryphon House books are available for special premiums and sales promotions as well as for fund-raising use. Special editions or book excerpts also can be created to specification. For details, contact the Director of Marketing at Gryphon House.

Disclaimer
Gryphon House, Inc. and the authors cannot be held responsible for damage, mishap, or injury incurred during the use of or because of activities in this book. Appropriate and reasonable caution and adult supervision of children involved in activities and corresponding to the age and capability of each child involved is recommended at all times. Do not leave children unattended at any time. Observe safety and caution at all times.

Table of Contents

Introduction

Chapter 2: Sociodramatic Centers

Chapter 3: Unique Centers

Table of Contents

Chapter 4: Observation and Evaluation

Chapter 5: Building and Creating Items for Children With Special Needs

Introduction

Overview

The Inclusive Learning Center Book: For Preschool Children With Special Needs is designed for teachers and directors who work with all young children. The content was developed with specific attention to children with special needs. Each center included in this book suggests adaptations for children with special needs. Each learning center can be used with children in an inclusive setting, a special education classroom, and with typically developing children.

Centers are designed to actively engage children in their learning, while building on individual interests and abilities. In a center, every child has the opportunity to select or to make a guided choice of the materials they will use. The centers are equipped with related materials and invite children to participate and develop their skills in personally meaningful ways.

Why Centers Work With Preschoolers Who Have Special Needs

All children, whatever their physical, cognitive, or emotional level of development, have their own interests. Learning centers are open-ended by design, allowing children to work at their individual levels and to succeed in the activity. The small number of children in each center offers each child many opportunities to talk, interact, and shape the play experience.

Centers provide an environment that allows young children with special needs the opportunity to follow their interests. Centers also facilitate learning through interactions with peers and adults. In learning centers, young children can practice sharing, using words with their peers, manipulating objects, using symbols to represent objects, and moving around their environment. Centers may be easily modified to address a child or group of children's special educational needs. For example, picture labels may be added to objects or storage areas to assist a child with speech and language problems in selecting items for play. To prevent a child with autism spectrum disorder (ASD) from becoming over-stimulated in a center, the teacher could reduce the number of materials or choices available.

The first five years of a child's life encompass a critical period of brain development when connections are made at a rapid rate. These connections are stimulated when children are exposed to a wide range of experiences and are actively engaged with their environment. Centers provide the active and expanding environment young children need for their development.

A Very Important Person: The Teacher

Teachers look for ways to create an environment that will support children in their development. Centers offer spaces that provide the "just right" challenge for each child, allowing children to be more independent in their learning and to match their activities with their interests.

Teacher and child share a special time with a book.

When teachers are nurturing and responsive, young children learn that they are capable. In a caring environment, children are willing to try new things and experiment in ways that are beneficial to their development. By carefully observing children, teachers are able to respond to individual needs and abilities. With the information gained in such observations, teachers can select centers and materials that will work for their classrooms and the children in them.

Learning From Play

Young children learn through manipulation of objects. As with all young children, children with special needs work best with objects that are real and concrete. These objects need to be safe and easily accessible, which varies with the individual needs of each child. For example, a child with physical challenges who is in a wheelchair will need objects placed at arm height, while a child with visual challenges may need objects placed on shelves covered with white paper.

Children are naturally motivated to play, and they enjoy the process. However, children with autism and other disabilities often appear to have no desire to play. These children may respond better to modeling of play behaviors or directed play activities.

The first level of play development is sensory motor. In this stage, young children bang, mouth, feel, and move objects in repetition. This kind of play helps children learn about the objects and their world. In the next stage, they begin to use symbols, which represent real objects in their play. In this beginning level of sociodramatic play, real objects, such as plastic cups and telephones, assist them in developing symbolic representation. Some children begin simple role playing at this stage. This type of play can be encouraged with centers such as Home Living or Doctor's Office. Children will pretend to be Mama, the baby, or the doctor giving a shot. These are events the child has experienced and, therefore, has developed an idea of how the roles are played.

Developmental Issues

Each child develops at his own pace. What is considered "typical" development covers a broad range of behaviors and skills. There are both environmental and genetic influences on development. Children tend to show more interest in or demonstrate greater skill in one or two areas of development at a given time. If a child is performing well below average in one or more areas, he may be considered developmentally delayed.

The following paragraphs briefly describe typical preschool development in the areas of cognition, language, gross motor, fine motor, social and emotional, and self-care. Some children will have already been identified to receive special education services before they enter your preschool classroom. In other instances, you may recognize that a child is not developing in a typical manner and may suspect that the child would benefit from special education services. In that case, you may request assistance from a professional who could assess the child further. Whether or not the child has been identified as having special needs, you may still use the adaptations recommended for each center presented in this book.

Cognitive Development

Many young children are in the pre-operational stage of cognitive development. In this developmental period, they have special ways of learning about their world. Their thinking is concrete, focusing on the real things they can see, touch, and manipulate. They gain knowledge from their interaction with objects and people in their world. They learn about a beach ball by feeling it and seeing it. They experiment with the ball to discover how it responds to throwing it in the air or rolling it on the floor. This experimentation helps them gather the information they want. Later, they will revisit the beach ball to replicate the information gained.

This exploring of objects, materials, and toys is essential to learning. Each new and meaningful experience builds connections in the brain. This thinking provides the foundation for current and future understanding. Several writers indicate that a child's attention span is longer when the child chooses the activity and is interested in the outcome (Sluss, 2005; Branscombe, Castle, Dorsey, Surbeck, & Taylor, 2000). Centers allow children to choose and follow through with activities and materials they find personally interesting.

Experimenting with water increases learning connections.

Language Development

The preschool period is a time of "language explosion" for many children. During these years, children learn labels for their world, building meaningful vocabulary and using sentences that are more complex. It is essential that young children have many opportunities to listen and interact with other children and adults as they develop language use. During these interactions, children learn about communication and how effective exchanges work. As children play together in centers, they use language and expand their vocabulary in language-rich environments.

Gross Motor Development

Gross motor skills include large motor activities where children use their entire bodies. As they mature, preschoolers become more coordinated in their gross motor activities. By the end of the fifth year, preschoolers should walk and run, in an adult-like pattern. Preschoolers learn how to gallop, hop on one foot, and eventually skip. They also explore more adventures on the playground by climbing, jumping, and swinging on play equipment. By age five, many preschoolers can catch a basketball with two hands and throw a small ball with one hand.

Fine Motor Development

Fine motor activities involve the use of hands and arms. Eye-hand coordination improves rapidly during preschool years. Preschoolers learn how to snip with scissors and to cut out large shapes. Grasp of objects becomes more refined; most preschoolers are able to hold a crayon or marker and draw on paper. By the end of the fifth year, many preschoolers can write their names. Most preschoolers enjoy using their hands to make creations with materials like yarn, beads, paint, paper, markers, glue, and scissors. They can string small beads, build with small blocks, and manipulate tools such as toy hammers and screwdrivers.

Social and Emotional Development

Social and emotional development expands during the preschool years. Young children learn how to interact with others. They also begin to learn about their own feelings and the feelings of others. During the preschool years, children learn to play together in groups and to share and take turns. Three-year-olds begin to show interest in friends, typically just playing beside one or two friends. Five-year-olds develop friendships, typically of the same gender, and can cooperate in play activities in groups. Preschoolers enjoy dressing up and acting out roles in play. Preschoolers also become more self-assured. Typical four-year-olds love to show off and are eager for adults to see what they can do. While preschoolers are growing in the awareness of their own emotions (and are much better at this than toddlers) they still need encouragement to understand the feelings of others.

Self-Care Development

Self-care skills include daily life activities such as dressing, feeding, bathing, toileting, and grooming. Preschoolers grow more independent in their self-care activities. As preschoolers develop eye-hand coordination, they learn how to snap, unbutton and button, unzip and zip clothing. Most preschoolers should be able to dress and undress independently by age five. By the time a child is five years old, he should be able to feed himself with a spoon or fork and to drink from a cup using one hand, with little spilling. Preschoolers can make choices of foods and serve themselves. Many three-year-olds are toilet-trained; most five-year-olds have achieved independence in the toileting process.

Cleaning up is easy with a brush and dustpan.

Safety Issues

Special safety considerations should be made to assure that the learning center environment is safe and healthy for all preschoolers. Federal and state regulations for child care facilities must be followed. Toy and furniture manufacturers also set safety standards for their products. However, teachers of young children are ultimately responsible for the safety of the children in their care.

Each preschooler with special needs will have his individual limitations and corresponding safety issues. For example, a child who is just learning to walk with braces will need stable furniture and a clear walkway in the center. An occupational therapist or physical therapist can assist in determining appropriate environmental modifications for the child with special needs. The following list includes safety guidelines for all preschoolers:

- Ensure that strings, ropes, and cords are no longer than 12 inches.
- Provide materials that are washable, nontoxic, and nonflammable or flame retardant.
- Check for food allergies before using any edible products or foods.
- Secure toys that are suspended and keep attached cords short.
- Avoid toys with rough edges or sharp points.
- Cover unused electrical outlet covers.
- Store cleaning products and any hazardous material on high, out-of-reach, locked shelves.
- Use good hand-washing principles and teach them to the children.

Matching the Environment to Preschoolers With Special Needs

For the purpose of this book, disabilities and special needs that are often found within a population of young children have been organized into the following categories: Physical Challenges; Speech and Language Problems; Autism Spectrum Disorder; Developmental and/or Cognitive Delays; Behavioral Challenges; and Visual Challenges. In each center, adaptations are suggested for specific categories of disabilities. For easy reference, an icon is used to represent each category of disability or special needs. A description of the categories and icons follows.

Physical Challenges

Children in this category have a condition that influences their motor development and the use of their bodies. These children may have no learning problems. Children with diagnoses of Cerebral Palsy (CP), Spina Bifida, Traumatic Brain Injury, Muscular Dystrophy (MD), or burns fit into this category.

Speech and Language Problems

Speech and Language Disorder is one of the most common diagnoses found in the early childhood special education population. The majority of children are able to communicate verbally by age three. Children with Speech and Language Disorder have problems with the oral production of language and/or lack an understanding or use of language.

Autism Spectrum Disorder

This term includes a broad range of diagnoses such as autism, Pervasive Developmental Disorder, Asperger's Syndrome, and Rett Syndrome. Children in this category manifest delays in social skills and language before age three. Some of the children in this category also have cognitive delays. They may resist change in their environment and have limited play skills. Children with autism spectrum disorder may be overly sensitive to sounds, light, and touch.

Developmental and/or Cognitive Delays

These children will learn skills more slowly than others. Children in this category may have mental retardation. Some are slow learners who will later be identified as having learning disabilities. Common diagnoses included in this category are Down Syndrome and Fetal Alcohol Syndrome.

Behavioral Challenges

This category includes children who have behavioral difficulties. The most common diagnoses in this category are Attention Deficit Disorder (ADD) and Attention Deficit/Hyperactivity Disorder (ADHD). Children appear to be in a constant state of movement and cannot attend to activities long enough to complete a task. ADD and ADHD are not typically diagnosed until after five years of age. Typically developing children in preschool will sometimes demonstrate characteristics consistent with this diagnosis.

Visual Challenges

This category includes children who have problems with vision. These children may have visual acuity problems requiring corrective lenses. Children who have a diagnosis of Amblyopia (lazy eye) and are under treatment by a doctor have severe vision problems at the outset. During treatment for lazy eye, the child will need large print and pictures, good light, and participation in gross motor activities. Blindness also fits in this category. Vision varies with lighting, time of day, and even weather. It is common for these children to be overly sensitive to touch and sounds.

Evaluating the Individual Child in the Learning Center

No matter what the child's disability or challenge, it is useful for the teacher to be a careful observer of each child in the center. While you observe the child, think about what is hindering his successful learning in the environment. Effective learning occurs when a child has the "just right" challenge. A child who is given a task that is well above his skill level may give up or develop low self-esteem because he cannot complete the activity. If the challenge is below his skill level, he may become bored and leave the area. Each child has individual interests and needs. Matching your expectations to the child's expectations and skills will lead to successful learning.

In this book, each center has a section labeled "Evaluation of the Individual Child." This section is designed to help determine if that particular center is effective with a specific child. The evaluation section includes questions to guide the observation and consideration of each child. Teachers may use these questions to guide the writing of objectives for the child's Individualized Education Program (IEP). A list of typical developmental milestones for three-, four-, and five-year-olds is located in Chapter 4, Observation and Evaluation. These milestones can be used in the evaluation and goal-setting for a child with special needs.

How Learning Centers Work

Management of Centers

An essential element of learning centers is that they provide children with choices: which center they will work in, what materials they will use, and how they structure their play. Some children with special needs may require assistance in making choices. To make the choice of centers more concrete, take a photograph of each child, laminate the picture, and attach a piece of Velcro to the back. Place a board, with the appropriate number of Velcro spots, for attaching pictures next to the centers. Perhaps a child will be offered a choice between two centers that are open—Home Living or Doctor's Office. The child will choose a center with an open spot and attach his picture to that spot, indicating his

selection of center. A child with special needs may also need help getting to the center selected and help in getting started with play. Co-playing with the child at the beginning and slowly moving out of the center may be effective. Pairing a child with a typically developing peer or with one who is able to make choices may also assist with the transition.

Centers may vary in the number of children who can use them. Two to four children will work in most centers. You may want to have centers open for 15 to 20 minutes of time at the beginning of the year and increase that time as the year progresses. The length of time in centers will vary, depending on the composition of children in the classroom.

Predictable Sequence

Providing a consistent pattern with center time will guide young children in understanding and moving into this environment. A suggested pattern would include:

1) Identifying the centers that are open that day on a chart with pictures and a brief statement describing what is happening in each area.

2) Allowing children to make choices and indicate with their names or pictures where they will go that day.

3) Scheduling center time at the same time each day.

4) Using a consistent signal to prepare children for the end of center time and cleanup in the centers where they played.

5) Regrouping to talk about what children did in the center they chose. Following this sequence consistently will help children learn their responsibilities and understand how centers work.

A choice board helps children make decisions.

Children plan their time in centers.

Traffic Flow

When placing centers in your classroom, make sure that quiet areas such as the Books/Library Center or Fine Motor Center are out of the way of classroom traffic. If there are children using mobility devices (such as a wheelchair or walker), the entrance and space in the center must be sufficiently wide to accommodate their movement.

Noise Level

Some children are very sensitive to loud sounds or crowd noise. Make centers and the classroom quieter by including sound-absorbing items such as rugs, pillows, and display boards. Another possibility is sound boards, which can easily be constructed and attached to walls to contain the noise. See page 315 in Chapter 6 for directions in constructing a sound board.

Lighting

A variety of types of lighting should be included in centers. Soft light can be produced by using floor lamps, clip-on lights, and strip lights. It is also helpful to have dimmers on the light switches so lighting can be changed to match specific needs. The brightness, flickering, and humming sound of fluorescent lights is over-stimulating for some children with Autism Spectrum Disorder or Attention Deficit Disorder. At the same time, fluorescent lights may be helpful to children with Visual Challenges. Consider the children in your classroom and the lighting options that will work well for them.

Labeling

Use word and picture labels. During the preschool years, it is helpful to label storage areas and toys with both words and pictures. This matches different levels of understanding and encourages the transition to a higher level of literacy understanding. A child with Autism is particularly attracted to pictures and words.

Visual Boundaries

Each center should be clearly separated from the other. Low bookcases and substantial dividers work effectively to provide visual boundaries for centers. This management technique will assist child in determining where centers are located and what materials are found in that space. It will also assist the children to understand the type of play and interaction that is appropriate for the specific center. In addition, these visual boundaries will help young children with special needs to keep object and materials in the centers where they belong. Limit items in centers, store others, and rotate various items into the centers to stimulate interest. This will assist children with special needs in the selection and use of materials.

Adapting the Environment for Preschoolers With Special Needs

The centers described in this book are designed for use with all preschoolers. Each center has a list of suggested activities that may be used with that center. For each activity, there is a corresponding list of adaptations. These adaptations are recommended with special consideration for children with the following special needs: physical challenges; speech and language problems; autism spectrum disorder; developmental and/or cognitive delays; behavioral challenges; and visual challenges. The following section contains general adaptations for children with special needs. Refer to the adaptations section for specific suggestions for each center.

Once it has been determined that a child will benefit from an adaptation, then determine the type of adaptation to make. Some adaptations are easier to carry out than others, depending on the nature of the activity and the center. Environmental modifications involve changing the physical, social, or temporal environment; for example, using pictures on shelves to demonstrate where toys are kept. Materials can be adapted by using squeeze, big-loop scissors for cutting in the Art Center. Assistive Technology (AT) such as computers or electronic devices may be utilized to modify the environment or adapt materials. Adapt the activity, making it easier for the child by reducing the number of steps in the task. Peer assistance is another means of support. For example, a peer can help a child change into dress-up clothes in the Home Living Center. Finally, there is adult assistance. For example, the teacher may model a way to make snakes out of clay while verbally describing the process.

 Children who have a physical challenge may benefit from adapted positioning that provides support to enable them to complete fine motor activities. A health professional may recommend adapted positioning devices such as floor sitters, chair inserts, or standing aids. Preschoolers with a physical challenge may use mobility devices such as wheelchairs, walkers, or scooters to help them move freely in the environment. Switch-controlled devices may assist with learning cause-and-effect relationships. These children may have had limited interactions with other children; peer support can help them to learn how to share and take turns. Preschoolers with physical challenges may have limited fine motor skills. A modification includes providing board books that are simpler to turn and manipulate. Each center includes an Essential Literacy Connection, which suggests books that relate to the theme. Board books are indicated by an asterisk.

 Preschoolers with significant Speech and Language Problems may need symbols, communication displays, or word processing tools to provide them with independence in expression. These preschoolers tend to do well with peers and adults who can model more advanced language use. They also learn from songs, touch and visual experiences as well as verbal descriptions of their actions.

Children who have a diagnosis that falls under the category of autism spectrum disorder may need adult support to help them learn how to interact appropriately with their peers in centers. Many of these children learn best from visual images such as symbols, pictures, and word labels. They may respond best to directions given as a song. Hand-over-hand support can help children interact with fine motor activities. Many children with Autism are easily over-stimulated by cluttered environments, bright lights, and noise. Making your centers less cluttered and letting them wear sunglasses or earplugs may decrease this reaction.

Children with cognitive or developmental delays work best when their teachers maintain consistent expectations and consequences for their behavior. These children may benefit from peers who can assist them with activities and model appropriate social interactions in play. Breaking down an activity into a few simple steps may help the child succeed. Assisting the child in completing the first steps and then allowing the child to complete the last step of an activity may also be helpful. These children learn well through repetition and a multi-sensory approach such as visual, tactile, and auditory inputs. Communication aids, such as symbols and pictures, may help children with cognitive disabilities to make choices in centers. Board books often contain a simplified text that may be useful for children with Cognitive or Developmental delays. Board books are identified by an asterisk in the Essential Literacy Connection for each center.

Children with behavioral challenges need to move around at regular intervals throughout the day to improve their attention. Allowing the child to sit on a therapy ball or foam egg-crate pad in a chair while completing fine motor activities will provide opportunities to move and stay on task. Decreasing noise and visual distractions in the environment will help these children maintain focus. It is a good idea to get the child's visual attention before speaking to him, and then to use simple instructions. Provide the child with positive feedback when he demonstrates appropriate play in the centers. Using realistic rules and consequences and following a daily routine may also improve behavior.

Most children with visual challenges will benefit from a well-lighted environment and the use of bright-color objects in centers. High-contrast materials using black, white, red, and yellow in combinations or individually, are easiest to see. These children will benefit from activities that involve touch and sound. Because fine motor activities are challenging for these children, provide more gross motor experiences. A professional may recommend enhancement of visual information with screen readers, screen magnifiers, and/or Braillers to assist children with visual challenges.

Valuing and Displaying Children's Learning

When children work in centers, they sometimes create pictures, make books, or build a structure. Each of these activities demonstrates a child's learning and his involvement in the process. The products of this learning, whatever the level, provide valuable examples of children's work. They should be displayed in the center where they were produced or in another part of the classroom where the children and parents can enjoy them. Digital cameras provide another way to document what the children are doing in centers (see pages 306 and 312–313 in Chapter 5 for directions in making a documentation panel and Plexiglas display area). Photographs of children playing in centers, building props, or working together clearly demonstrate their learning with concrete evidence of the process that is occurring. The children can use these photos to talk about their work or to revisit their activities later.

Documentation panel of experiences making bubbles

Book Organization

This introduction includes information about the use of centers with young children and the importance of including children with special needs in nurturing environments.

The centers in this book have been selected for use in early childhood classrooms with children with special needs or classrooms that serve children in special education. Each center design offers components that assist the busy teacher in designing, setting up, and evaluating these spaces. Other components are objectives for children with special needs, a letter to parents or guardians about the learning that occurs in the center, teacher- and parent-collected props, and a literacy connection that includes both books and other literacy materials. Each center offers a number of activities with suggested adaptations for children with special needs.

Chapter 1: Traditional Centers

Many frequently-used centers will remain in the classroom for most of the year. The materials and props can be changed, while the main theme remains the same.

Chapter 2: Sociodramatic Centers

These centers focus on a specific theme that encourages role-play and the use of materials related to the topic. Teachers can rotate the use of these centers for a period of two to three weeks or keep them in use until the children's interest declines.

Chapter 3: Unique Centers

These unusual centers will provide different materials and play opportunities that extend the children's thinking. The teacher should determine the selection and use of these centers, after matching the center's possibilities with the children in the specific classroom.

Chapter 4: Observation and Evaluation

Chapter Four will address the issue of evaluation of centers and the young children who use them. How can centers be used to document the learning and skills of young children who are working in these areas? This chapter includes information about using center observations to support Individualized Education Programs (IEPs).

Chapter 5: Building and Creating Items for Children With Special Needs

Chapter Five will focus on building and creating items that will be especially useful for children with special needs. The items are easy to build and offer low-cost ways to enrich the classroom environment.

This book concentrates on using centers with all children. It addresses specific ways of including children with special needs in these appropriate and challenging environments. Working and playing in effectively designed centers can nurture the development of young children—an opportunity all children should have.

References

Branscombe, N. A., Castle, K., Dorsey, A. G., Surbeck, E., & Taylor, J. B. (2000). *Early childhood education: A constructivist perspective.* Boston: Houghton Mifflin.

Sluss, D. J. (2005). *Supporting play: Birth through age eight.* Clifton Park, NY: Thomson Delmar.

Traditional Centers 1

Introduction

Traditional Centers have been used in early childhood programs for many years, providing a play environment that matches young children's level of understanding, while stimulating their thinking. Some of the centers will be set up in the classroom for most of the year; props will be changed throughout the year.

Centers included in this chapter:

Home Living Center
Block Center
Art Center
Sand Center
Water Center
Books/Library Center
Gross Motor Center
Fine Motor Center
Pre-Writing Center

Cooking and stirring in the home living center

Home Living Center

Overview

The *Home Living Center* has a long history of use in early childhood classrooms. This center provides an important connection to the home and the activities that occur in that environment. The center and props inspire young children to use play as they dramatize and talk about things that are important to them, and try out familiar roles and materials. This popular center is often the first center that children use. When children are dealing with difficult issues or trying to solve personal problems, they will often play in the *Home Living Center*. This safe and familiar center provides a nurturing environment for young children's meaningful participation.

Learning Objectives

The child with special needs will:

1. Try out roles she has experienced.
2. Use language to accompany her play.
3. Develop skills that are used in the home.
4. Match food and tools to develop visual discrimination.
5. Begin to consider others in her play.

Time Frame

This center will remain in the classroom for the entire year. Make changes and additions, including seasonal clothing, cooking items, and materials that relate to a curriculum focus or to different appliances to maintain the interest of the children.

Letter to Parents or Guardians	Dear Parent or Guardian, One of the most popular centers in our classroom is the *Home Living Center*. This center allows children to play and dramatize in the place they know best, the home. We have included a kitchen area with an eating place and a section for dressing up. These props encourage children to pretend that they are preparing meals, taking care of babies, and dressing in special clothes. In this play, they learn about the important work that one does to make a home. They pretend to do the things you do, such as grocery shopping, cooking meals, and cleaning up. We would like to include pictures of our families in this area. If you have a family photo that we can display on our Family Board in the *Home Living Center*, we would appreciate your willingness to share it with us. Be sure to send pictures that can be touched and admired by our children.

Layout of the Home Living Center

The *Home Living Center* should include a kitchen area with a table and chairs for eating, an area with a baby bed, a rocking chair, and a dress-up area with a mirror that will extend the type of play that occurs in this center. It is also helpful to place the *Home Living Center* next to the *Block Center*. Often, children will bring blocks into the *Home Living Center* to symbolize something (for example, a block will be a loaf of bread or a carton or milk), or they will build an addition to the home in the *Block Center*.

Vocabulary Enrichment

baby	father
brother	food
clean	home
cook	mother
dishes	pet
dress up	sister

Teacher- and Parent-Collected Props

- dress-up clothes (male and female clothing, and seasonal items)
- empty grocery items, such as cereal boxes, milk containers, cookie/cake mixes, cans of vegetables, and other items that are familiar to the children
- cooking utensils, such as pots, skillets, cookie sheets, muffin tins, and large wooden and plastic spoons
- tableware, such as plastic plates, cups, glasses, knives, forks, spoons, tablecloth, and artificial flowers for the table
- furniture, such as table and chairs, stove, refrigerator, sink, high chair, baby bed, and rocker
- other items, such as telephone, mixer, sweeper, broom, mop, feather duster, pot holder, and sponges

Web of Integrated Learning

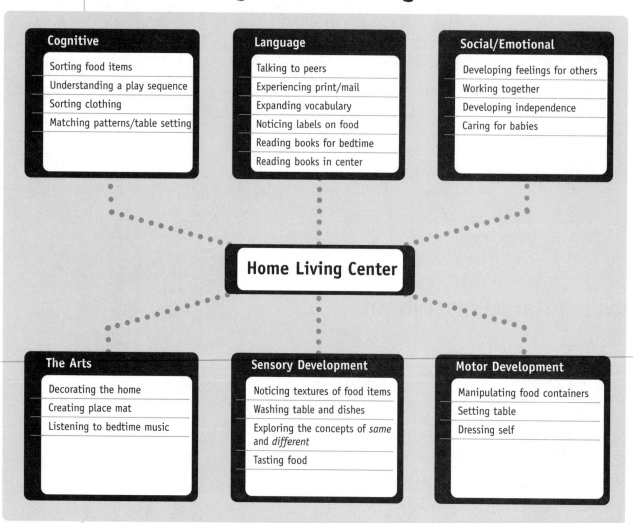

Cognitive
- Sorting food items
- Understanding a play sequence
- Sorting clothing
- Matching patterns/table setting

Language
- Talking to peers
- Experiencing print/mail
- Expanding vocabulary
- Noticing labels on food
- Reading books for bedtime
- Reading books in center

Social/Emotional
- Developing feelings for others
- Working together
- Developing independence
- Caring for babies

Home Living Center

The Arts
- Decorating the home
- Creating place mat
- Listening to bedtime music

Sensory Development
- Noticing textures of food items
- Washing table and dishes
- Exploring the concepts of *same* and *different*
- Tasting food

Motor Development
- Manipulating food containers
- Setting table
- Dressing self

What's for Dinner?

Materials

- colored sheets of construction paper
- plates, forks, knives, and spoons
- black marker and other color markers
- clear contact paper or lamination
- plastic container

Procedure

1. Select two to four sheets of brightly colored construction paper.
2. Place the plate, fork, knife, and spoon on the paper (in table-setting pattern). Add the children's names to the place mats.
3. Trace around the utensils with the black marker.
4. Offer children the option of adding decoration with markers.
5. Cover the mat with clear plastic or laminate.
6. Place plates, forks, knives, and spoons in a plastic container on the table.
7. Invite children to set the table by matching the pattern on the place mat.

Adapt "What's for Dinner?"

 Name the plate, knife, fork, and spoon when creating and using the place mat.

 Put word labels on the corresponding utensils on the mat.

 Create a mat that has only a plate and a spoon.

 Using a white piece of paper, fill in the eating utensils with a black marker, or trace the outline of the eating utensils with colored glue so the child can feel the outline.

 Ask the child to describe verbally where to place the appropriate utensil.

Activities

Bedtime Music

Materials

- baby dolls and bed
- rocking chair
- bedtime items for the center: blankets, pajamas for dolls, slippers, soft toys, low-light lamp, and bedtime books
- CD or cassette player and recordings of lullabies or bedtime songs

Procedure

1. Add bedtime items to the bedroom area in the *Home Living Center*.
2. Play bedtime music on the CD player.
3. Suggest that the children "read" the books to the babies.

Adapt "Bedtime Music"

 Talk with the child about her bedtime routine or sing her favorite bedtime song.

 Place pillows, cushions, or a beanbag chair on the floor.

  Suggest that the child read a book to the baby before bed.

Stocking the Kitchen

Materials

- shelves or cabinet for storage of food
- four or five large grocery bags
- collection of empty grocery containers (Make sure that you have two matching items of a number of containers. The size, shape, and labels of the matching items should be exactly alike.)

Procedure

1. Allow the children to empty the grocery bags and put the groceries away.
2. While they are doing this, encourage them to put identical items together. For example, two boxes of macaroni and cheese or two milk cartons that are the same size.
3. Provide shelves or a cabinet where they can view their groupings.
4. Point out products that are the same.

Adapt "Stocking the Kitchen"

 Use the vocabulary "same" or "different" during the process.

 Use a smaller number of grocery items that match.

 Give the child a small box to put in her lap, or a canvas tote bag to fill with groceries.

  Give positive feedback for making matches. "You are doing a great job putting those groceries together."

 Line the shelves or cabinet with white contact paper and use brightly colored grocery items.

Dressing Yourself

Materials

- collection of clothes that are easy to put on and fasten, such as jackets with large buttons, shoes with Velcro, knit hats, skirts that wrap, stretch tops that pull on, shorts/pants with elastic waistbands, and stoles (These clothes work best if they are slightly larger than the normal size the children wear.)
- pieces of interesting fabric, 1' to 2' pieces work well
- unbreakable mirror mounted at children's height or sitting on the floor
- camera

Procedure

1. Hang easy-to-wear clothing on a knob hanger (see page 307 in Chapter 5 for directions).
2. Let children select the items they want to try on and wear.
3. When they have dressed themselves with several items, take photos.
4. Make a photo display of the children labeled, "I can dress myself" and arrange it next to the clothing display.
5. Mount a label at the bottom of the photo and write the child's name and the date on it.
6. Document these skills in the child's portfolio or file.

Adapt "Dressing Yourself"

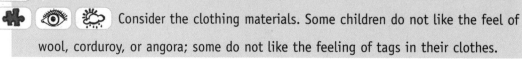 Talk about the pieces of clothing the children are wearing.

Add long beaded necklaces, scarves, and baseball caps for the children to try on.

Add a floor lamp or table lamp to enhance the light in the center.

Consider the clothing materials. Some children do not like the feel of wool, corduroy, or angora; some do not like the feeling of tags in their clothes.

Laundry Sort

Activities

Materials

- three plastic baskets
- clothing for women, men, and children

Procedure

1. Place a picture and the word "man," "woman," or "child" on the side of the corresponding basket.
2. Children can sort clothing for washing into the different baskets.

Adapt "Laundry Sort"

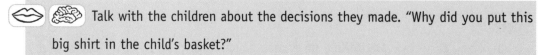 Talk with the children about the decisions they made. "Why did you put this big shirt in the child's basket?"

Before beginning, give children a few simple instructions on how to do the activity.

Place baskets on the table in the *Home Living Center*, so the child can sort while standing, sitting in a chair, or using an adaptive seating device.

Use dark colored clothes and white baskets for more visual contrast.

Mailbox

A mailbox encourages children to write letters and retrieve mail.

Materials

- box designated as a mailbox
- collection of junk mail
- trash can
- tools, such as pencils, pens, envelopes, stamps, paper, scissors

Procedure

1. Place a mailbox at the entrance to the center.
2. Put a collection of junk mail in the box.
3. Children can open and examine the mail.
4. Provide tools for dealing with mail, such as a trash can; checks, pens, and a calculator for paying bills; and stamps for stamping the envelopes.

Adapt "Mailbox"

   Make an assembly line for sorting mail. One child can open mail, another child can stamp the envelopes, and another child can throw them away or recycle them.

  Give the child two simple instructions for the process. Use simple sentences, such as, "Open the mail," or "Stamp the mail."

 Use large pieces of mail with large print. Place red tape around the outside edge of the mailbox and trash can.

The Essential Literacy Connection

Books

Cabrera, Jane. 2000. **Dog's Day**. New York: Orchard Books. *Dog imagines all day that he goes on adventures with his stuffed animals. When all of his animals are tucked away, he likes to play with his Daddy.*

Keller, Holly. 1988. **Geraldine's Blanket**. New York: HarperCollins. *Geraldine is no longer a baby, but still she does not want to give up her worn and torn blanket.*

Leopold, Niki Clark. 1999. **Once I Was...** New York: Putnam. *Rhyming text shows children the exciting changes that go along with growing up.*

Merriam, Eve. 1989. **Mommies at Work**. New York: Simon & Schuster. *Mommies are portrayed in many professions.*

Rockwell, Anne. 2000. **Career Day**. New York: HarperCollins. *Children introduce the occupations of individual family members, depicting men and women in non-traditional roles.*

Shott, Stephen. 2002. **All About Baby**. New York: DK Publishing, Inc. *Simple text takes the reader through babies' daily activities.* *

Ziefert, Harriet. 2002. **Toes Have Wiggles, Kids Have Giggles**. New York: Putnam. *The author uses rhymes to talk about many different events in a child's everyday life.*

Zolotow, Charlotte. 1985. **William's Doll**. New York: HarperCollins. *Everybody teases William because he wants a doll more than anything. His father will not buy him a doll, so his grandmother buys him a doll and explains to his father that William is just practicing to be a good father someday.*

(*Indicates the book is available as a board book)

Other Literacy Materials

- cookbooks and recipe cards
- labels on furniture and storage areas with words and pictures, such as "food," "pots," "plates," and "cups"
- newspaper with a children's section, if available
- paper and marker, for writing a grocery list
- telephone book

A phone encourages language development.

Layout of the Block Center

The *Block Center* is a noisy place because knocking down a structure is as important as building it. Therefore, this center should be placed in an area of the room where noise can be contained. Carpeted areas and sound boards (see page 315 in Chapter 5 for directions) absorb sound. It is helpful to have a table where children can build while standing or sitting. A wall or secure room divider provides a strong surface to build against.

Vocabulary Enrichment

big	little
blocks	stack
build	tall
help	

A variety of blocks encourages children to build complex structures.

Teacher- and Parent-Collected Props

- aluminum cans of different sizes with taped edges
- cardboard and cereal boxes in various sizes
- carpet remnants
- disinfected egg cartons
- dry sponges
- fabric
- milk cartons
- phone books
- sandpaper

Web of Integrated Learning

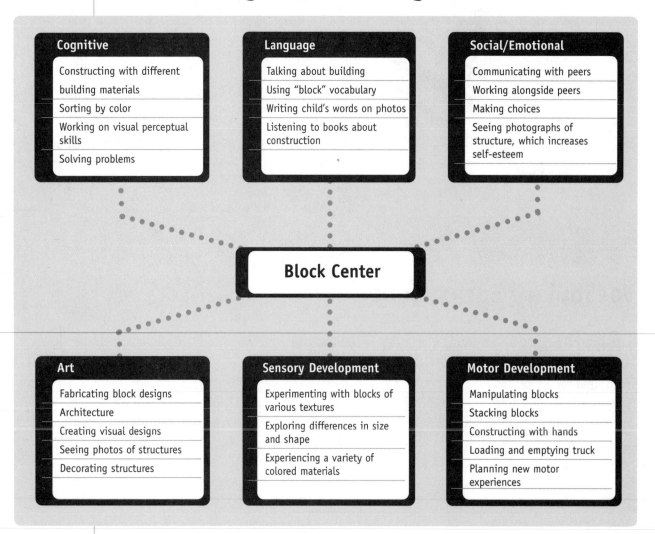

Cognitive

Constructing with different building materials
Sorting by color
Working on visual perceptual skills
Solving problems

Language

Talking about building
Using "block" vocabulary
Writing child's words on photos
Listening to books about construction

Social/Emotional

Communicating with peers
Working alongside peers
Making choices
Seeing photographs of structure, which increases self-esteem

Block Center

Art

Fabricating block designs
Architecture
Creating visual designs
Seeing photos of structures
Decorating structures

Sensory Development

Experimenting with blocks of various textures
Exploring differences in size and shape
Experiencing a variety of colored materials

Motor Development

Manipulating blocks
Stacking blocks
Constructing with hands
Loading and emptying truck
Planning new motor experiences

Activities

Milk Carton Blocks

Materials

- 10 half-gallon cardboard milk cartons
- 10-15 individual cardboard milk cartons
- masking or electrical tape
- contact paper

Procedure

1. Wash milk cartons thoroughly and let dry.
2. Fold the tops down flat.
3. Tape the tops securely down to the sides.
4. Cover the cartons with contact paper.

Adapt "Milk Carton Blocks"

 Use red, yellow, black, or white contact paper to cover the milk carton blocks.

 Attach Velcro strips to blocks for easier stacking and building.

 Use material such as felt, metallic contact paper, or sandpaper for added texture.

 These lightweight blocks can be knocked down.

 Talk about different kinds of blocks and how they are used in building.

 Provide the child with a few blocks initially and then add to the collection as she becomes more skilled.

Stacking and Sorting Cans

Materials

- empty aluminum cans, large, medium, and small in size
- empty aluminum cans with plastic lids, such as coffee or potato chip cans
- electrical tape
- nontoxic paint and paintbrush or contact paper

Procedure

1. Wash and dry the cans and lids.
2. Apply electrical tape around all sharp edges of aluminum cans that do not have lids.
3. Paint or cover the cans.

Adapt "Stacking and Sorting Cans"

 Paint same-size cans with the same color nontoxic paint or cover with the same color contact paper. This will assist in sorting by size or color.

 Provide child with boundaries and a good background for building. Place a light-colored sheet, towel, or carpet square on the floor of the *Block Center*.

 If a child is mouthing the cans, give her something more acceptable to place in her mouth such as a drinking straw or nontoxic plastic tubing.

 Use simple vocabulary words, such as "big" and "little" to make distinctions.

Activities

Look What I Built!

Materials

- camera
- scrapbook or poster board
- tape
- markers

Procedure

1. Observe the child building in the *Block Center*.
2. Take a picture of the structure, both in progress and completed, with the child or children who built it.
3. Include child or children's names on the picture.
4. Post photographs by:
   - Placing the photograph on poster board for display at the children's eye level in the *Block Center,* or
   - Placing the photograph in a scrapbook that is kept in the *Block Center* so that children can reflect on their work.

Two children build cooperatively with blocks.

Adapt "Look What I Built!"

To develop children's self-esteem, tape a photograph of the builder to the structure so both the child and her peers can admire the construction.

Enlarge photographs; use black or red tape around picture edges.

Ask the child to describe the structure. Write down her words to place under the photograph of the building. Read her words back to her.

Texture Blocks

Materials
- 10 shoeboxes
- masking tape or electrical tape
- glue
- metal pie or cake pan
- 2 or 3 medium-size house-painting brushes
- fabric with interesting textures, such as corduroy, satin, burlap, and felt

Procedure
1. Invite children to help create texture blocks.
2. Use shoeboxes as the base.
3. Tape or glue box tops closed.
4. Pour glue into a pie or cake pan.
5. Invite the children to use paintbrushes to put glue on the box.
6. Press a piece of textured fabric on the glued side of the box.
7. Continue to work on blocks over several days.
8. Allow to dry thoroughly.
9. Blocks can be used for textured construction in the *Block Center*.

Activities

Adapt "Texture Blocks"

 If the child is not strong enough to manipulate a house-painting brush, try a small watercolor brush.

 This activity is excellent for children with visual challenges.

 Do not force the child to touch particular textures. Provide children with several choices of texture and see which ones they like.

 Talk about the feel of the different blocks. "This one is fuzzy." "This one is rough."

Dump Truck

Activities

Materials
- large laundry soap box or sturdy cardboard box
- piece of rope or macramé cord
- scissors
- art materials
- glue

Procedure
1. Remove the top from the box.
2. Cut a 12" length of rope.
3. Make a hole in one end of the box.
4. Insert the rope and tie a large knot in both ends.
5. Children can decorate the truck and use it to move things or to make deliveries in the *Block Center*.
6. Provide foam or wooden blocks to be transported.

Adapt "Dump Truck"

 Say, "Pull, pull, pull," as the child pulls the load around the *Block Center*.

 Cut a longer piece of rope and make a loop at the end for the child to hook around her arm for easy pulling.

 Load up the truck with heavier blocks and encourage the child to pull it; this will increase the child's body awareness and calm and organize her.

The Essential Literacy Connection

Books

Hutchins, Pat. 1987. **Changes, Changes**. New York: Aladdin Library. *In this picture book, many different things are built when two wooden dolls rearrange blocks.*

Lillegard, Dee. 1989. **Sitting in My Box**. New York: Dutton Books. *A cardboard box gets too crowded, as many large animals join a young boy inside. No one wants to leave until a flea jumps in.*

Rau, Dana Meachen. 1997. **A Box Can Be Many Things**. New York: Children's Press. *Two children show their mother that a box she says is trash can actually be used for many things.*

Russo, Marisabina. 2000. **The Big Brown Box**. New York: Greenwillow. *A boy goes on an imaginary journey in the box the new washing machine arrived in.*

Stevenson, Robert Louis. 1992. **Block City**. New York: Puffin. *A boy builds a village by the sea while playing with his blocks.*

Stevenson, Robert Louis. 1998. **Where Go the Boats?** San Diego: Browndeer Press. *Children use their imaginations as they play and build with various objects.*

Other Literacy Materials

- blueprints
- home improvement advertisements
- labels for building materials

Adding Spark to the Block Center

Use flat fabric sheets to make a canopy over a section of the *Block Center* (see pages 304–305 in Chapter 5 for directions). This creates a special place for the children to play, while also providing boundaries and adding to a feeling of security. Hang fabric over fishing line that has been secured to the ceiling or attach it to tops of shelves in the *Block Center*.

Evaluation of the Individual Child

Is the child:

1. Manipulating building materials?
2. Attempting to vertically stack blocks or building materials?
3. Communicating with adults or peers while in the center?
4. Beginning to work alongside peers or cooperating with peers in construction?
5. Constructing and identifying structures?

Art Center

Overview

The *Art Center* provides opportunities for developing creative abilities and for experimenting with a variety of materials and tools. This center supports the participation of young children as they investigate the way things work and see materials respond to their interaction. Many of the activities included in this center are open-ended and can be done in different ways. These varied possibilities inspire young children to think and solve problems as they work in the *Art Center*. Young children are more interested in the process of creating than they are in the finished product.

Learning Objectives

The child with special needs will:
1. Explore a variety of art materials and tools.
2. Improve small motor coordination.
3. Value the artwork she completes.
4. Use vocabulary that relates to art projects.
5. Demonstrate problem solving during the artistic process.

Time Frame

The *Art Center* is included in the classroom for most of the year. Many materials will remain the same, although new ones can be added periodically to expand interest. The combination of open-ended and planned activities allows independent work and also provides guidance to children who have trouble thinking of an idea.

Letter to Parents or Guardians	Dear Parent or Guardian, When you visit our classroom, you will see children creating in the *Art Center*. This area is popular with our children, and they are fascinated by the work they can do. Here, we have a variety of paper, paints, clay, and markers, which the children can use to cut, paste, and construct. Although the primary goal of the *Art Center* is to develop an interest in art, many kinds of learning are also taking place. As your child uses art materials and tools, he or she develops small motor coordination and visual discrimination. Your child also learns about colors, textures, and sizes. This is a messy area where the children get their hands and other parts of their bodies into their creations. We ask that they wear a smock or a big shirt to help protect their clothing. Of course, in our active learning environment, washable play clothes work best. Remember to display and talk about the artwork your child brings home. They love to have their work appreciated. We will display their artwork in our classroom for both you and your child to enjoy.

Layout of the Art Center

The *Art Center* should have a sink or water source. If this is not possible, plastic tubs or buckets with water can be used. This area needs a large display board, a place to dry work, and a storage area for art projects that the children want to revisit. Art materials should be clearly visible to the child and at a level that encourages independent selection. Tools, such as scissors, markers, glue, and brushes, can be set on the table for easy access. Tables and working surfaces should be surrounded with plastic, newspapers, or washable materials. Cleanup items, such as sponges, paper towels, and spray bottles should be available to encourage children to clean up after their artwork.

Vocabulary Enrichment

art

artist

brush

chalk

colors

create

glue

paint

paper

scissors

water

Teacher- and Parent-Collected Props

- junk items, such as foil, plastic bubble wrap, small boxes, fabric scraps, trim, ribbon, yarn, macramé rope, Styrofoam pieces, plastic beads, and straws
- paint smocks that are commercially made or homemade, or old large button-front shirts
- paper, including butcher, construction, computer, brown wrapping, shelving, newspaper, and cellophane
- roll of plastic or clear shower curtain liners
- serving trays
- tools, such as scissors, paintbrushes, hole puncher, and washable markers

Web of Integrated Learning

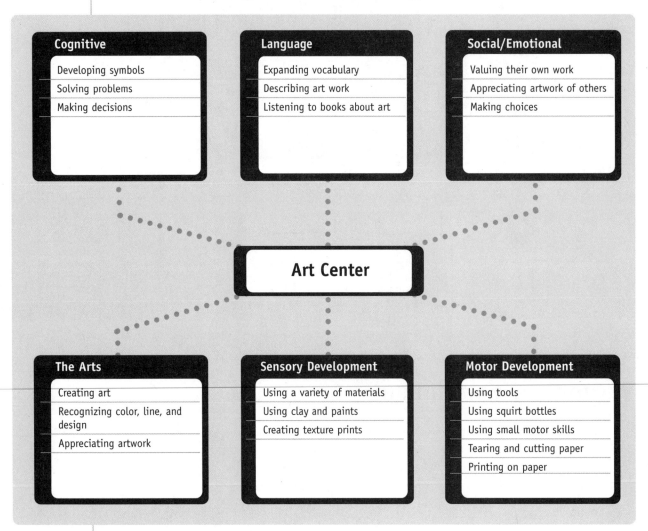

Cognitive	Language	Social/Emotional
Developing symbols	Expanding vocabulary	Valuing their own work
Solving problems	Describing art work	Appreciating artwork of others
Making decisions	Listening to books about art	Making choices

Art Center

The Arts	Sensory Development	Motor Development
Creating art	Using a variety of materials	Using tools
Recognizing color, line, and design	Using clay and paints	Using squirt bottles
Appreciating artwork	Creating texture prints	Using small motor skills
		Tearing and cutting paper
		Printing on paper

Prickly Building

Materials

- Styrofoam pieces or balls
- plastic container
- toothpicks
- straws
- small dowel rods
- glue
- twigs
- serving tray or lunchroom tray

Procedure

1. Place pieces and balls of Styrofoam in a plastic container.
2. Include a box that has a collection of items that can be stuck into Styrofoam.
3. Each child can attach items to her piece.
4. Use small dowel rods to hold several pieces together.
5. Display the growing structure on a serving tray or lunchroom tray in the *Art Center*.
6. Children can return to the *Art Center* to add others parts to the three-dimensional structure.

Adapt "Prickly Building"

  This activity is not appropriate for children who mouth objects.

  Demonstrate how to stick objects into the Styrofoam.

 Talk about the prickly and sticky items the children are putting in the Styrofoam.

 Use a black marker to trace the edges of the Styrofoam base and give boundaries to the base. This will help the child see where to place the straws and toothpicks.

Activities

Real Clay

Materials

- block of clay from art or craft store (see pages 311–312 in Chapter 5 for directions for making other types of clay, such as playdough and play clay)
- plastic containers
- trays
- clay tools, such as rolling pins, plastic knives, plastic forks, and pie servers

Clay responds to children's touch.

Procedure

1. Store clay in a plastic container with the lid closed.
2. Remove three to four pieces of clay and place them on lunch trays.
3. Provide a plastic container of water on the table.
4. Invite children to explore the clay and add water as needed.
5. As they experiment, children may want to use tools to cut or make designs in the clay.
6. At this stage, children are more interested in the properties of clay than in producing a product.
7. Encourage children as they enjoy the learning that is occurring.

Adapt "Real Clay"

  The child may need to kneel or stand at a taller table or other surface.

 Ask the child to use words to describe what she is making. You may label the completed object with the child's words.

 This task is good for children with visual impairments and mild physical disabilities because clay is so responsive to touch.

Strip Art

Materials

- large sheet of black paper
- construction paper in a variety of colors
- crepe paper in colors
- tissue paper in colors
- scissors
- plastic container
- glue

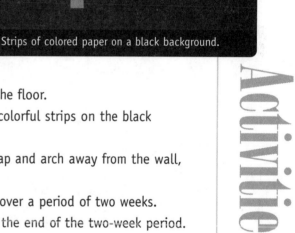

Strips of colored paper on a black background.

Procedure

1. Attach a large sheet of black paper to the wall of the *Art Center*.
2. Cut strips of construction, crepe, and tissue paper.
3. Place the strips in clear plastic containers on the floor.
4. Start the design by gluing the ends of several colorful strips on the black background.
5. Encourage children to glue strips so they overlap and arch away from the wall, giving it a three-dimensional effect.
6. Children can add to this three-dimensional art over a period of two weeks.
7. Revisit and discuss design, colors, and form at the end of the two-week period.

Adapt "Strip Art"

Label the colors the children use in their design. Talk about gluing the ends of the paper.

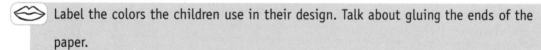 Use tape instead of glue. Pre-tape the ends or let the child use a tape dispenser.

Use a large sheet of sandpaper instead of black paper so the child can feel where to place the paper.

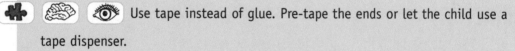 Tear the paper instead of cutting strips.

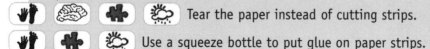 Use a squeeze bottle to put glue on paper strips.

Activities

Printing Abstracts

Materials

- poster paper or a roll of construction paper
- art trays or lunchroom trays
- scissors
- plastic containers containing thick tempera paint in blue, red, green, and yellow
- collection of items that will produce interesting prints, such as a potato masher, variety of sizes of jar lids, comb, wheel, cookie cutters, and cups

Procedure

1. Cut sheets of paper to fit inside the tray.
2. Place containers of paint colors on the table.
3. Provide a wide variety of items that will make interesting prints.
4. Children can select items and colors they wish to use to make prints.
5. During the process, children will experiment with and learn about color and design.

Adapt "Printing Abstracts"

  Put paint in pie pans for easier access.

   Provide sponge letters, shapes, or numbers for printmaking.

   Categorize things to make prints into small containers to organize space.

 Give children only two or three choices of materials.

Squirt Art

Materials

- collections of empty and clean plastic squirt bottles, such as catsup, mustard, and salad dressing
- tempera paint
- fingerpaint paper, shelving paper, or pieces of cardboard

Procedure

1. Fill squirt bottles with a variety of colors of medium thickness tempera paint.
2. Let children mash and squirt the paint onto thick paper.
3. Allow children to use several colors or just one color.
4. Place creations in an area where they can dry.

Adapt "Squirt Art"

  Let children use large handle paintbrushes, or put a small amount of paint in plastic measuring cups with handles for children to use to apply paint to paper.

  Place paper on a lunch tray or cookie sheet to provide boundaries.

  Use the words "squirt" and "squeeze" as the child makes art.

  Give the child a choice between two colors of paint. "Would you like to use blue or green?"

The Essential Literacy Connection

Books

Carle, Eric 1992. **Draw Me a Star**. New York: Philomel Books. *A young boy creates an imaginary world of his own, drawing the stars, the sun, and other things.* *

Catalanotto, Peter. 1995. **The Painter**. New York: Orchard Books. *A young girl waits patiently to spend time with her father, while he works. After dinner, he rewards her by taking her to his studio where they paint together.*

Jay, Alison. 2002. **Picture This**. New York: Dutton Books. *Beautiful artwork, labeled for the beginning reader, portrays the seasons and nursery rhymes.*

Moon, Nicola. 1995. **Lucy's Picture**. New York: Dial Books for Young Readers. *While Lucy's classmates are painting pictures, she is making her art out of different textured elements that she finds around the school. At the end of the story, Lucy gives the picture to her blind grandfather.*

Reynolds, Peter H. 2003. **The Dot**. Cambridge, MA: Candlewick Press. *A teacher uses wit and encouragement to inspire a young girl who insists that she cannot draw.*

Walsh, Ellen Stoll. 1989. **Mouse Paint**. San Diego, CA: Harcourt Brace. *Three mice find three jars of paint—red, blue, and yellow—and discover new colors.* *

(*Available as a board book)

Other Literacy Materials

- posters of the works of famous artists that relate to children, such as those that feature children, animals, families, and landscapes
- tools that are used for writing— paintbrush, markers, crayons, and chalk

Paper glued to a board for writing and drawing

Adding Spark to the Art Center

Framing the Masterpieces

Make cardboard frames that will fit over standard size construction paper or art paper. Cover the frames with interesting paper or fabric and place the beautiful frames in a large art portfolio in the *Art Center*. Children can select the frame they want to use to display their masterpiece. Provide unfinished frames for children who want to create their own frame covering. Nothing is as beautiful as the framed and displayed artwork of children.

Evaluation of the Individual Child

Is the child:

1. Effectively using art tools, such as a brush, crayon, marker, glue, and scissors?
2. Participating in creating art?
3. Making choices related to materials?
4. Enjoying or showing appreciation while working in the *Art Center*?
5. Using language that relates to artwork?

Sand Center

Overview

The *Sand Center* provides responsive, natural material for young children to explore. Sand play is focused on the manipulation and use of this intriguing substance. Many opportunities are provided in the center to answer questions about sand. What are the properties of sand? How does it move? What tools can you use with it? The answers to these questions and many more can be found in this center, allowing children to explore at their own pace and select the questions that interest them. Problem-solving challenges enhance children's thinking and lead them to discover answers.

Learning Objectives

The child with specials needs will:
1. Explore the properties of sand.
2. Develop small motor coordination through pouring, digging, and sifting.
3. Use problem-solving abilities in meaningful ways.
4. Build attention span while using natural materials.

Time Frame

This center can be used many different times throughout the year. It is usually set up for one or two weeks at a time and then stored away for later use. Props can be cleaned and stored in clean plastic containers and labeled so they are easily found for future use.

Letter to Parents or Guardians

Dear Parent or Guardian,

Next week, we will add a *Sand Center* to our classroom. Sand is a natural material that fascinates young children. They love to examine how it feels, how it moves, and how to dip and pour. Their curiosity about sand leads to interesting exploration and learning. We will be adding plastic tools, bottles, and tubing that will invite children to make new discoveries while using their investigative skills.

Another ability developed in this center is fine motor skill. This essential skill is used to manipulate objects and to write. When your child pours sand into a plastic bottle, he or she is using his or her eyes and hands during the process. This enjoyable learning will build abilities that are useful now and in the future.

Layout of the Sand Center

The sand table is the central feature of the *Sand Center*. This table confines the sand and experimentation to this place. This center should be in an area that is easy to clean, such as a space that has tile flooring or is covered with heavy-duty plastic. Prop boxes, with related items, should be periodically rotated in and out of the *Sand Center* to provide opportunities for scientific exploration.

Vocabulary Enrichment

bottle	pour
dig	sand
feel	shovel
funnels	sift
observe	tube

Teacher- and Parent-Collected Props

- clear plastic tubing
- collections of shells, plastic animals, cardboard tubes, combs and hair picks, sticks, and gelatin molds
- large and small spoons
- plastic cups and bottles of various sizes
- shovels
- sifter/colander
- small handheld vacuum cleaner or broom and dustpan
- small pails
- spray bottles
- watering cans

Web of Integrated Learning

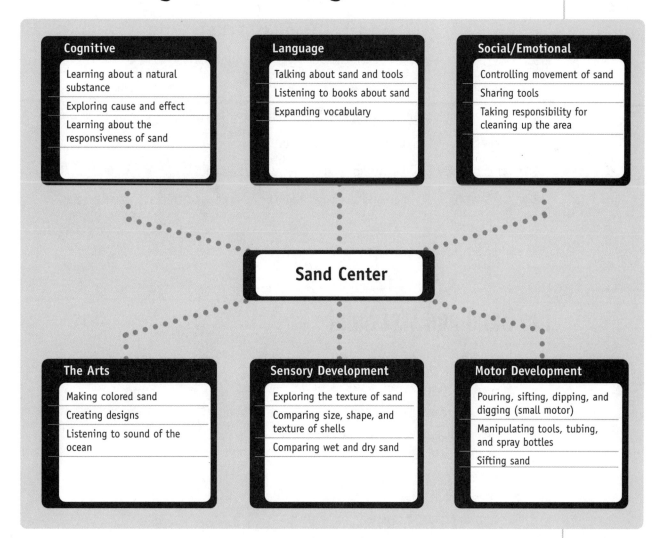

Cognitive
- Learning about a natural substance
- Exploring cause and effect
- Learning about the responsiveness of sand

Language
- Talking about sand and tools
- Listening to books about sand
- Expanding vocabulary

Social/Emotional
- Controlling movement of sand
- Sharing tools
- Taking responsibility for cleaning up the area

Sand Center

The Arts
- Making colored sand
- Creating designs
- Listening to sound of the ocean

Sensory Development
- Exploring the texture of sand
- Comparing size, shape, and texture of shells
- Comparing wet and dry sand

Motor Development
- Pouring, sifting, dipping, and digging (small motor)
- Manipulating tools, tubing, and spray bottles
- Sifting sand

Finding Shells

Materials

- variety of sizes and types of shells
- shovels
- plastic basket
- two large sifters

Procedure

1. Hide various shells in the sand before the children come to the *Sand Center*.
2. Children can find the hidden shells.
3. Provide plastic baskets to hold the found treasures.
4. Demonstrate how a sifter can be used to separate the sand from the shell.
5. Children will often re-hide the shells so they can find them again.

Adapt "Finding Shells"

 When you introduce the *Sand Center*, announce one or two "rules." For example, "The sand stays in the table." Post these rules in the *Sand Center*.

 Limit the number of children in the *Sand Center* to two or three at a time, especially if a child is easily distracted.

 Use brightly colored (red or yellow) tools in the sand.

 If the child does not like the feel of sand, replace it with small pebbles.

Dry Sand and Wet Sand

Materials

- spray bottles
- watering cans
- shells, cups, and plastic molds
- small plastic bottles
- shovels
- large spoons
- cups and plastic glasses

Activities

Procedure

1. Provide spay bottles and watering cans for children to use to add water to the sand.

2. Include shells, cups, and plastic molds for investigating new properties.

3. Make a chart that includes "Dry" and "Wet." Ask the children to identify the differences and include their words on the chart.

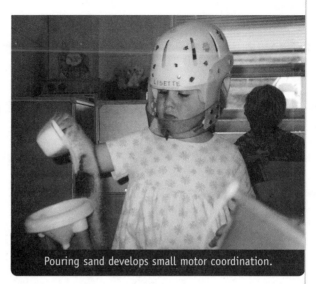

Pouring sand develops small motor coordination.

Adapt "Dry Sand and Wet Sand"

 Label spoons, shovels, glasses, and cups.

  If the child does not want to touch the sand, introduce it gradually.

Encourage the child to use the tools provided, rather than her hands.

 Provide two of each tool to limit arguments over toys.

 Provide two-handled cups, spoons with large handles, or child-size spoons.

Sifting Sand

Materials

- several aluminum pie pans of different sizes
- tool for punching holes (adult only)
- sifter with turn handle, colander
- shovels
- spoons
- cup or plastic container with a hole in the bottom

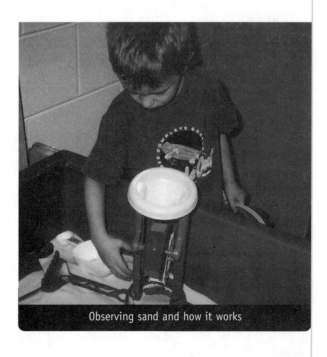

Observing sand and how it works

Activities

Procedure

1. Punch holes in the bottom of four to six aluminum pie pans. Vary the number and sizes of the holes in different pans.

Safety Note: Smooth any rough or sharp edges.

2. Remove other items from the sand table.

3. Place the different pie pans in the sand. Demonstrate how to sift or simply allow the children to make the discovery.

4. Add other sifters, such as colanders and sifters with handles that turn.

Adapt "Sifting Sand"

 Put the sand table in a well-lighted area of the room.

 Model ways to sift the sand, while using the corresponding words such as "sift," "fill," or "pour."

 If the child is unable to stand and play, place sand in a shallow plastic container and either place it in the child's lap or on the floor for easier access.

 Praise children when they are playing with the sand and tools in an appropriate manner. "Wanda, I like the way you are keeping the sand in the table."

The Essential Literacy Connection

Books

Beardshaw, Rosalind. 2004. **Grandma's Beach**. New York: Bloomsbury. *Emily and her grandmother spend the day at an imaginary beach.*

Jones, Lara. 2003. **Fun on the Beach**. New York: Barron's Educational Series, Inc. *In this unique puzzle book, items found on the beach are explored for their shape, color, and texture.**

Mathers, Petra. 2001. **Lottie's New Beach Towel**. New York: Aladdin Library. *Lottie's new beach towel has many uses during her day at the beach.*

Roosa, Karen. 2001. **Beach Day**. New York: Clarion Books. *Join this family as they spend a day at the beach.*

Selby, Jennifer. 1995. **Beach Bunny**. Orlando, FL: Harcourt Brace & Company. *When Bunny and his mother go to the beach for a day, they go swimming, look for seashells, and have a picnic.*

(*Available as a board book)

Other Literacy Materials

- brochures about beach trips
- chart of "Wet" and "Dry" sand properties
- labels on tools and storage
- sand writing

Adding Spark to the Sand Center

Take some sand out of the table and put it in a plastic container. Use a spray bottle filled with a thin solution of tempera paint and water to change the color of the sand. Place the tub with colored sand on the table in the *Sand Center*. Children can experiment with colored sand to see how it compares to the white sand in the table.

Evaluation of the Individual Child

Is the child:

1. Experimenting with the sand?
2. Using tools in her play?
3. Developing small motor skills, such as pouring, dipping, and digging?
4. Identifying different properties of wet, dry, and colored sand?

Water Center

Overview

The *Water Center* capitalizes on young children's interest in this natural liquid. The focus of the center is the water table or plastic tub that contains water for the activities. Here, children will become scientists as they determine the properties of water and observe how it responds to their actions. Water provides immediate feedback to their dipping, pouring, and stirring, inviting children to actively participate in meaningful learning.

Learning Objectives

The child with special needs will:

1. Explore the properties of water.
2. Develop small motor coordination while exploring water.
3. Use language to describe water and activities.
4. Discover cause and effect using water and tools.

Time Frame

The *Water Center* will rotate in and out of the classroom. The center can be set up for one or two weeks at a time and return later. Each time the center is reintroduced, children will demonstrate their continuing interest in water and related materials. All the props and tools used in water play should be kept in clear plastic containers so they can be selected and returned after each session. This organization will also assist in storing the materials for future use.

Letter to Parents or Guardians	Dear Parent or Guardian,

Children are fascinated by water. To build on this interest, next week we will set up the *Water Center* in our classroom. In this area, your child will experiment with water in a safe and supervised way. In the center, there will be tubes, funnels, plastic glasses, spoons, and cups for the children to use as they become young scientists exploring the properties of water.

The *Water Center* provides a place where your child can discover how a liquid responds to different actions. Here, he or she can pour from a plastic container, dip with a large spoon, and make waves with his or her hands. In this play, your child is making important connections between his or her actions and the way the water responds. These experiences will help them learn about cause and effect: "If I do **this**, then **this** is what happens." This is an important confidence-building lesson.

Layout of the Water Center

The water table or large tub contains the water used in this center. It is helpful if the center is located near a sink so the water can be emptied at the end of play. A large tube or hose can be used to drain the water from the table. Cover the floor of the area with plastic or use shower curtains to confine the spills. Plastic containers of materials for water play should be displayed so they are easily accessible for children to select to use to extend their play.

Vocabulary Enrichment

bucket	pour
color words: blue and green	same and different
dip	spoon
full	tube
funnel	water
hole	wet
pipe	

Teacher- and Parent-Collected Props

- clear tubes of various sizes
- eyedroppers or medicine droppers
- pieces of plastic pipe
- plastic shower curtains or a roll of plastic
- plastic buckets, cups, glasses, and spoons
- set of nested measuring cups and spoons
- small spray bottles
- sponges
- Styrofoam trays
- turkey baster

Web of Integrated Learning

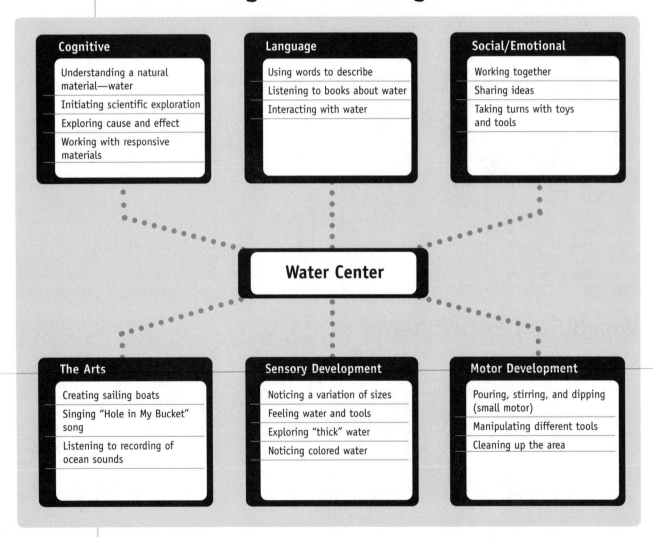

Cognitive
- Understanding a natural material—water
- Initiating scientific exploration
- Exploring cause and effect
- Working with responsive materials

Language
- Using words to describe
- Listening to books about water
- Interacting with water

Social/Emotional
- Working together
- Sharing ideas
- Taking turns with toys and tools

Water Center

The Arts
- Creating sailing boats
- Singing "Hole in My Bucket" song
- Listening to recording of ocean sounds

Sensory Development
- Noticing a variation of sizes
- Feeling water and tools
- Exploring "thick" water
- Noticing colored water

Motor Development
- Pouring, stirring, and dipping (small motor)
- Manipulating different tools
- Cleaning up the area

What Color Is Water?

Activities

Materials

- food coloring in blue and green

Procedure

1. After a week of experimenting with water, add a few drops of food coloring to the water.
2. Pose questions about the change, such as "How is the water the same? Different?"
3. Include the same objects and tools they used when the water was clear.
4. Develop a chart that helps the children compare and contrast.
5. After several days with blue food coloring, change the water to green.
6. Again, make comparisons with different colors and ways the water responds.

What color is water?

Adapt "What Color Is Water?"

Help the child use specific words to describe the water and tools. A one-word label or two-word pattern will assist in using language during play. For example, "water," "pour," or "blue water."

Gently introduce water to a child who is afraid to touch it. Let her observe others playing in the water or put a favorite water-safe toy into the water.

Place water in a washtub or large plastic container on the floor or on a table for easier access.

Review the items in the water for play; use only a few items. Allow the child to touch these before placing them in the water.

Activities

A Hole in the Bucket

Materials

- three plastic buckets of the same size
- screwdriver or tool to punch holes in plastic (adult only)

Procedure

1. Select three small plastic buckets that are the same size.
2. Punch a hole in the bottom of one of the buckets.
3. Place all of the buckets in the water table.
4. Let children in the center discover the secret: one of the buckets has a hole.
5. Allow sufficient time for exploration.
6. Replace the bucket that has a hole with one that does not.
7. Encourage observation and predictions.

Adapt "A Hole in the Bucket"

 Sing the song, "There's a Hole in the Bucket."

 If sharing is a problem, have a bucket available for every child.

 Make sure the *Water Center* is in a well-lighted area of the classroom.

 Use simple one-step directions such as, "Hold the bucket."

   Give all the children a small cup to help fill the buckets with water.

Sailing Boats

Materials

- Styrofoam meat trays or plastic salad plates
- tongue depressors or wooden twigs
- white shelf-lining paper (not adhesive-backed)
- glue
- floral wire (plastic-covered)
- scissors
- small electric fan or hand-held fans

Procedure

1. Provide a collection of meat and fruit trays.
2. Children can experiment with the trays in the water.
3. Demonstrate the addition of a sail to the "boat."
4. Let the child select the sail and figure our how to attach it to the base.
5. Children can create, decorate, and name their sailing boats.
6. Turn on the fan or use hand fans to create wind for the sails.

Adapt "Sailing Boats"

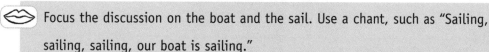 Focus the discussion on the boat and the sail. Use a chant, such as "Sailing, sailing, sailing, our boat is sailing."

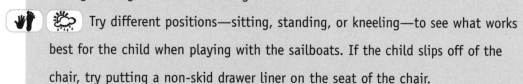 Try different positions—sitting, standing, or kneeling—to see what works best for the child when playing with the sailboats. If the child slips off of the chair, try putting a non-skid drawer liner on the seat of the chair.

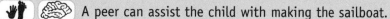 A peer can assist the child with making the sailboat.

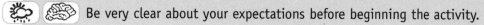 Be very clear about your expectations before beginning the activity.

Thick Water

Materials

- large plastic tub
- 2 boxes of plain gelatin
- water (according to gelatin recipe)
- large spoons
- plastic measuring cup

Procedure

1. Let children add the gelatin to water and stir.
2. Pour mixture into the plastic tub.
3. Refrigerate the tub.
4. The following day, place the plastic tub with hardened gelatin on a plastic-covered low table in the *Water Center*.
5. Let children feel and play with the gelatin.

Exploring the properties of water

Adapt "Thick Water"

   Place a small piece of the gelatin into a plastic plate or pie pan, so child can experiment with it.

 Use words to describe the movement, such as "wiggle" and "shake."

The Essential Literacy Connection

Books

Barner, Bob. 2000. **Fish Wish**. New York: Holiday House. *A little boy imagines what he would do if he were a fish.*

Cowley, Joy. 1998. **Mr. Wishy-Washy**. New York: Philomel Books. *Mr. Wishy-Washy is the best dishwasher in Washington until he accidentally washes the cat, who breaks the dishes and makes a big mess. He and the cat are much more careful after that.*

Degen, Bruce. 1995. **Jamberry**. New York: HarperCollins. *Follow this boy and bear as they go on a berry-picking adventure where they fill a canoe and make a waterfall of berries.* *

Dodds, Dayle Ann. 2001. **Pet Wash**. Cambridge, MA: Candlewick Press. *Two boys open a Pet Wash. When a friend brings his baby brother to be washed, they close the Pet Wash.*

Gorbachev, Valerie. 2002. **One Rainy Day**. New York: Philomel Books. *Pig explains to his mother why he is drenched, even though he had an umbrella. All of the animals took shelter from the rain by standing under the same tree. When the rain stopped, pig was so excited that he jumped in all the mud puddles on the way home.*

Gray, Kes. 2003. **Billy's Bucket**. Cambridge, MA: Candlewick Press. *When Billy fills his special birthday bucket with water, a deep-sea world emerges.*

(*Available as a board book)

Other Literacy Materials

- chart of similarities and differences in clear and colored water
- chart of words for "A Hole in the Bucket" song
- eye-hand coordination: pouring, sifting, and dipping
- visual discrimination of different watercolors
- writing name on sailing ships

Adding Spark to the Water Center

Place a collection of shiny stones or rocks on the bottom of the water table. These will not float and can be moved in the water with the children's hands or with tools.

Evaluation of the Individual Child

Is the child:

1. Participating in water play?
2. Pouring water into a large container?
3. Using words to describe the water or tools? If so, what are the words?
4. Imitating another child in play?

Books/Library Center

Overview

The *Books/Library Center* is an essential area in the early childhood classroom. This center makes the important connection between young children and books and other literacy-related materials. If effectively designed, this center will draw children into the space and capture their interest in books and printed materials. Studies show that this area is most appealing to children if it includes items that invite active participation rather than being a quiet place. With the addition of a few simple items, the *Books/Library Center* becomes an interesting place that includes many different opportunities to "read" books and hear and create stories, while enjoying the process in a comfortable environment.

Learning Objectives

The child with special needs will:

1. Explore books and other printed materials.
2. Identify personally interesting books.
3. Listen to stories being read, told, and recorded.
4. Share favorite books with others.
5. Attend to illustrations and printed content.

Time Frame

This center should be in the early childhood classroom throughout the year. The content of the center may change, but this center should be an available and predictable place to enjoy books.

Letter to Parents or Guardians	Dear Parent or Guardian, When you visit our classroom, you will see a special area called the *Books/Library Center*. In this space, we have included many books, tapes, and activities that relate to literacy development. We believe it is very important that children develop an interest in books and other printed materials during their early years.

You can help your child develop an interest in books and reading at home by reading to him or her each day, taking your child to the library or bookstore, and letting him or her see you read the newspaper, books, or recipes. These experiences relate to our *Books/Library Center* and will encourage involvement with books and words. At this time, we are nurturing an interest in books and reading, so that when children are developmentally ready, they will become readers.

A special feature in our *Books/Library Center* is a weekly guest reader. We invite you to visit our center and read a favorite children's book. You can sign up on "Our Library Center Readers' Schedule," posted on the parent information board.

Layout of the Books/Library Center

The *Books/Library Center* should be located in a highly visible area of the classroom, demonstrating that literacy is valued in this environment. The center should be warm and inviting; this can be accomplished with rugs, pillows, and attractive posters related to reading. A portion of the *Books/Library Center* should contain 15 to 20 children's books that the children can "read" by examining the illustrations. These should be displayed so the cover is visible for making selections. A space for listening to tapes and looking at books should be provided. Make sure the center has sufficient light, including lamps or clip-on lights. The most popular *Books/Library Centers* have a unique feature within the space, such as a mattress with a polka dot sheet, a beach umbrella, a small boat, or a dome tent for reading.

Vocabulary Enrichment

author	library
big book	magazines
books	read
favorite	story
illustrations	tapes

Teacher- and Parent-Collected Props

- area rug
- books recorded on tape or CD
- large pillows and beanbag chairs
- posters and pictures of book covers and children reading
- selection of 10 to 15 children's picture books (select books children can "read" by looking at illustrations)
- stand-up rack for displaying books so covers can be seen
- tape player or CD player

Web of Integrated Learning

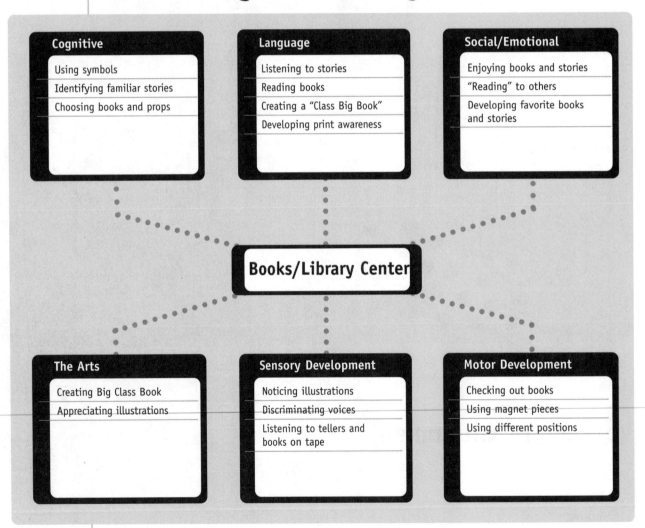

Cognitive

| Using symbols |
| Identifying familiar stories |
| Choosing books and props |

Language

| Listening to stories |
| Reading books |
| Creating a "Class Big Book" |
| Developing print awareness |

Social/Emotional

| Enjoying books and stories |
| "Reading" to others |
| Developing favorite books and stories |

Books/Library Center

The Arts

| Creating Big Class Book |
| Appreciating illustrations |

Sensory Development

| Noticing illustrations |
| Discriminating voices |
| Listening to tellers and books on tape |

Motor Development

| Checking out books |
| Using magnet pieces |
| Using different positions |

Activities

Check-Out Area

Materials

- low table
- props, such as index cards, pens and pencils, stamp and stamp pad, and card box (to file sign-out cards)
- title list of books in the *Books/Library Center*

Procedure

1. Place a low table in the corner of the *Books/Library Center*.
2. Place library sign-out props on the table.
3. Children can select a book they want to read, and sign out the book.
4. Find a comfortable place in the *Books/Library Center* to enjoy the book.
5. When children finish, they must return the sign-out card to the box.

Adapt "Check-Out Area"

 Include books that are related to children's experiences and home environment.

  Provide board books with easy-to-turn pages, simple pictures, and labels.

   Pair a child with a peer who can assist her in checking out a book.

 Provide a clip-on book light for the child to use.

Familiar Voice Tapes

Materials

- 15-minute or short cassette tapes
- tape recorder
- several popular children's books
- photographs of the teacher, aide, director, and custodian
- lamination machine or clear contact paper

Procedure

1. Record the teacher, aide, director, and custodian reading a story.
2. Place the tape and book they read in the *Books/Library Center*.
3. Make a scrapbook that includes copies of the covers of the books read.
4. Laminate or cover with contact paper the pictures of the readers.
5. The child can place the reader's picture with the book they are listening to on the tape.

Adapt "Familiar Voice Tapes"

  This activity is good for children with visual challenges or speech and language disorders.

 Physically assist the child with turning on the tape recorder and turning pages of the book.

 Select a short, interactive story for the child to read, such as *Five Little Monkeys Sitting in a Tree* by Eileen Christelow.

Reading Chair

Materials

- fancy or uniquely decorated chair
- basket filled with children's books
- light or floor lamp
- large doll or stuffed animal
- blanket

Procedure

1. Introduce the Reading Chair during Circle Time.
2. Place this special chair in the *Books/Library Center*.
3. A child may decide to sit in the Reading Chair while in the *Books/Library Center*.
4. In this chair, she can read to a doll or to a large stuffed animal.
5. Guest readers in the *Books/Library Center* may also use this chair.

Adapt "Reading Chair"

  Include picture books with very few words, or wordless picture books.

  Provide board books that have easy-to-turn pages.

  Offer books with textured pages.

 The child may need an adaptive seating device to sit comfortably.

  A child-size rocking chair may help a child stay attentive to the book.

Magnetic Story Board

Activities

Materials

- familiar children's book
- copy machine or scanner
- clear contact paper
- magnetic strips with adhesive on one side
- clear plastic bags
- magnetic board (metal that magnet will adhere to, such as cookie sheet)

Procedure

1. Select a book that is a favorite in your classroom.
2. Photocopy important characters and events.
3. Cover these copies with clear contact paper.
4. Attach a magnetic strip to the back.
5. Put pieces into a clear plastic bag.
6. Display the book and the magnetic pieces next to the magnetic board.
7. Children can retell the story using the magnetic pieces.
8. The children can create different stories using the same pieces.

Adapt "Magnetic Story Board"

  Create magnet pieces that accompany a three- or four-sequence story.

  Glue characters to cardboard and cover with plastic to make them more durable and easier to hold.

  Start the story for the child and let the child fill in missing pieces, for example, "Once upon a time, there was a little girl named Little Red Riding Hood. She lived with her..."

Activities

Class Big Book

Materials

- camera
- large sheets of construction paper
- markers
- clear contact paper or lamination
- 3 metal rings (to hold pages together)

Procedure

1. Take photographs of children with their favorite book or involved in a classroom activity.
2. Create a "Big Book" using these pictures.
3. Label the photographs with the names of the children and describe what they are doing.
4. Read the "Big Book" during Circle Time and place it in the *Books/Library Center*.
5. Every time a new activity occurs in the classroom, take a photo and add it to the "Big Book."

Adapt "Class Big Book"

 Attach photos to a piece of poster board and place in the *Books/Library Center*. Children who cannot turn the pages can still "read" the "Big Book."

   Enlarge pictures to 8" x 10", label them, and place them in the book so each page is one picture.

 Ask the child to describe what is happening in a specific picture. Label the picture with the child's words.

"[Young children] begin to learn about their own feelings and the feelings of others."

The Essential Literacy Connection

Books

Barner, Bob. 2000. **Fish Wish**. New York: Holiday House. *A little boy imagines what he would do if he were a fish.*

Barrett, Judith. 1982. **Cloudy With a Chance of Meatballs**. New York: Aladdin Library. *Food is raining and snowing in the town of Chewandswallow. What happens when the wrong foods fall or too much food falls?*

Craig, Paula M. 2000. **Mr. Wiggle's Book**. Grand Rapids, MI: Instructional Fair. *This story demonstrates the importance of taking care of books.*

Martin, Bill. 1996. **Brown Bear, Brown Bear, What Do You see?** New York: Henry Holt. *Discover what each animal is looking at in this book of pattern and rhyme.*

Schaefer, Carole Lexa. 1996. **The Squiggle**. New York: Crown Publishers. *While on a walk with her class, a girl finds a string, which takes the form of many different things.*

Shaw, Charles G. 1993. **It Looked Like Spilt Milk**. New York: HarperCollins. *The white mass on a blue background looks like many things, such as spilt milk, a rabbit, or a bird. In the surprise ending, children discover that it is actually a cloud.* *

Stephens, Helen. 2003. **Blue Horse**. New York: Scholastic. *Through her imagination, a shy little girl goes on adventures with her stuffed blue horse and learns how to make friends.*

(*Available as a board book)

Other Literacy Materials

- book catalogs
- books on tape
- check-out props
- children's magazines
- magnetic storyboard and books

Adding Spark to the Books/Library Center

Invite special readers to visit the *Books/Library Center*. Possible readers are teachers, aides, parents, grandparents, director, principal, repairperson, custodian, cook, and groundskeeper. Have appropriate books available so guest readers can make their selection if they did not bring a book.

Sharing a favorite book in the library center.

Evaluation of the Individual Child

Is the child:

1. Choosing to go to the *Books/Library Center*?
2. Manipulating and examining literacy materials?
3. Demonstrating a favorite book? How?
4. Displaying literacy behaviors, such as selecting a book, holding the book, and turning pages?
5. Saying words or making sounds related to the book content or illustrations?

Gross Motor Center

Overview

The *Gross Motor Center* is recommended for all young children, both with and without special needs. This center offers preschoolers the space and experiences necessary to develop their ability to move in the environment. Through movement activities, a young child learns about her own body and the relationship of her body to the environment. Movement experiences also stimulate language for many children. In the *Gross Motor Center*, preschoolers can practice gross motor skills such as walking, rolling, and jumping, which are useful in school and life activities.

Learning Objectives

The child with special needs will:

1. Actively engage in the physical environment.
2. Demonstrate new gross (large) motor skills.
3. Develop body strength and flexibility through activity.
4. Participate with other children in movement activities.
5. Demonstrate body awareness.

Time Frame

The *Gross Motor Center* should be available throughout the year. Basic center materials such as a floor mat and balls will remain in the center through the year. Other materials should be changed occasionally to increase the children's interest levels and add variety to their movement experiences.

Letter to Parents or Guardians

Dear Parent or Guardian,

It is so important that your child be encouraged to interact with the environment by moving his or her own body. In our *Gross Motor Center*, your child will experience a wide range of movement activities. These activities will improve balance, coordination, and strength. Large motor activities also encourage your child to learn skills that are useful throughout life, such as walking and moving around obstacles.

Each child has a unique potential for learning large motor skills such as walking, running, jumping, or catching a ball. In the *Gross Motor Center*, we will provide fun materials and the space necessary for your child to expand his or her own skills at his or her own speed.

Layout of the Gross Motor Center

Gross motor experiences can encourage lots of noise from the children and the objects they play with. This center should be placed in an area of the room where noise is acceptable and more easy to contain. You may be able to place the *Gross Motor Center* in a different room of the building, such as an empty storage room or a therapy room that is not used at all times. However, if you do not have an empty room in your building, that should not stop you! Place your *Gross Motor Center* in a space in the room that is large enough to include a floor mat and a place where children can move on the floor. An unbreakable wall mirror will allow the children to watch themselves as they move.

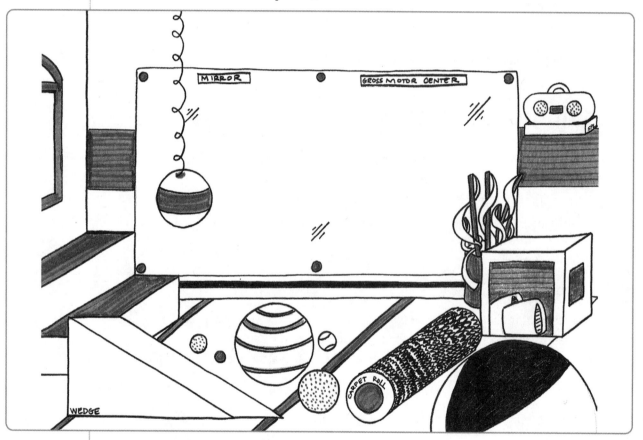

Vocabulary Enrichment

arms

body

catch

dance

jump

kick

legs

move

throw

Teacher- and Parent-Collected Props

- beanbag chair
- blankets
- cardboard boxes
- carpet rolls (see page 305 in Chapter 5 for directions)
- plush carpet or floor mats
- rocking chair or rocking horse
- sand pillows (see page 314 in Chapter 5 for directions)
- soft balls of different sizes
- wall mirrors, unbreakable
- wedges (see page 316 in Chapter 5 for directions)

Web of Integrated Learning

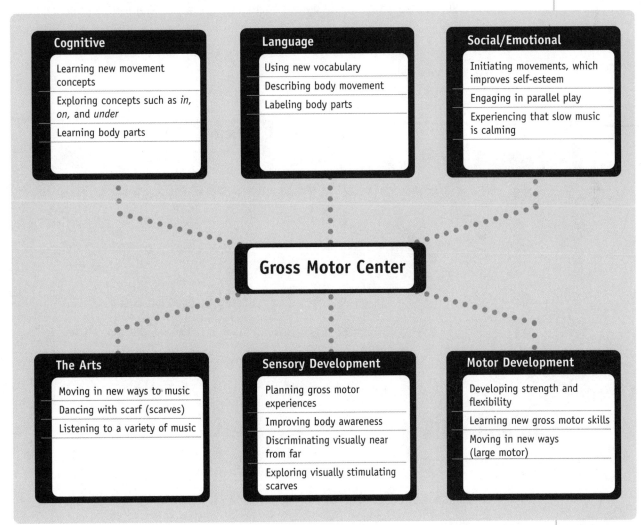

Cognitive
- Learning new movement concepts
- Exploring concepts such as *in*, *on*, and *under*
- Learning body parts

Language
- Using new vocabulary
- Describing body movement
- Labeling body parts

Social/Emotional
- Initiating movements, which improves self-esteem
- Engaging in parallel play
- Experiencing that slow music is calming

Gross Motor Center

The Arts
- Moving in new ways to music
- Dancing with scarf (scarves)
- Listening to a variety of music

Sensory Development
- Planning gross motor experiences
- Improving body awareness
- Discriminating visually near from far
- Exploring visually stimulating scarves

Motor Development
- Developing strength and flexibility
- Learning new gross motor skills
- Moving in new ways (large motor)

Scarf Dancing

Materials

- scarves made of a variety of materials, opaque and transparent—long, short, thin, square, with or without tassels
- container or box to store scarves
- recorded music and tape or CD player

Procedure

1. Invite children to choose their own scarf or scarves
2. Select music that will promote a wide range of movement: slow, fast, rhythmical, or arrhythmical, such as country, classical, jazz, easy listening, and pop.
3. Demonstrate different ways to dance with a scarf.
4. Imitate the children's dancing styles.
5. Describe the movements you see for each style of music. "Caroline is swaying to the slow music."
6. Ask the children to put the scarves on different body parts. "Can you put your scarf on your head?"

Adapt "Scarf Dancing"

 Use metallic material to make scarves.

 Glue or tape material onto the end of a dowel rod so the scarf will be easier to grasp.

 Use soft, slow, rhythmic music if children are easily over-stimulated.

 Label body parts as the children move or use them.

 Play a video of children or adults dancing to different music.

 If the child cannot move her body to the music, she can be the disc jockey or director with responsibility for turning the music on and off.

Animal Walk

Materials

- books about animals, such as *Pretend You're a Cat* by Jean Marzollo, or pictures of animals

Activities

Procedure

1. Introduce this activity to the children by reading a book about different animals or showing pictures of animals.
2. Demonstrate how to walk like an animal.
3. Let the children imitate your animal walk, assisting them, as needed.
4. Animal walks that you might demonstrate include snake, monkey, duck, frog, cat, dog, horse, elephant, bear, or kangaroo.
5. Use words to describe the way the children are moving. "See how Michael crawls like a bear."
6. Ask the children if they can walk like any other animals.

Adapt "Animal Walk"

 Children may sit in their seats and do arm movements if their balance and coordination are not good.

  Move children's bodies into the animal walking positions if they cannot imitate your movements.

   Describe body movements by using simple phrases. "Swing your arms."

 Use animal sounds to accompany movement.

 Some children with physical or developmental disabilities may fall more frequently. Have the child wear a protective helmet while participating in the *Gross Motor Center*.

Riser

Materials

- see pages 313–314 in Chapter 5 for directions on how to construct the riser

Procedure

1. Place a carpeted riser on the floor of the *Gross Motor Center*.
2. Children can climb over and around the riser.
3. Children can walk across the riser like they would a balance beam.
4. Place toys on top of the riser to encourage play while standing, or place toys on the opposite side of the riser to encourage crawling over the top.

Adapt "Riser"

 Use the riser to assist children with standing, sitting, or cruising.

 Place red, yellow, or reflective tape along the borders of the riser.

 Identify the toys that are being used on the riser. "Elizabeth is rolling the car."

  Verbally praise children for appropriate participation in this activity.

 A peer with good motor skills can assist a child who is having difficulty with this or other movement experiences.

Obstacle Course

Materials

- large therapy ball
- mini-trampoline
- several Hula Hoops

Procedure

1. Demonstrate how to sit on the ball and bounce (with feet on floor), jump on the trampoline, and walk or jump through the hoops.

2. Assist the children in completing the obstacle course in the order it is set up.

3. Use fewer or more obstacles to decrease or increase the difficulty level of the course.

Crawling through a tube in the obstacle course

Adapt "Obstacle Course"

  Use fewer or more obstacles to decrease or increase the difficulty level of the obstacle course.

 Use reflective tape to outline the path to each obstacle. Select movements that do not require the child's feet to leave the floor, for example, crawl through a tunnel, push a large therapy ball, or roll across a floor mat.

 Take a photograph of each activity in the obstacle course. Place the photos in order on a clipboard. The child can carry the clipboard through the obstacle course to remind her of the steps.

Select simple movements that may be completed by a child who uses assistive mobility such as a wheelchair or a walker. For example, the child can walk through Hula Hoops placed on the floor, rather than jumping through them, or the child can maneuver a wheelchair around Hula Hoops or cones placed on the floor.

The Essential Literacy Connection

Books

Carle, Eric. 1999. **From Head to Toe**. New York: Harper Collins. *This book will keep children active by imitating the moves of the animals.* *

Gray, Libba M. 1995. **My Mama Had a Dancing Heart**. New York: Orchard Books. *A ballet dancer recounts the days when she was young and danced with her mother.*

Kalan, Robert. 1989. **Jump Frog Jump**. New York: Harper Trophy. *As the frog tries to catch a fly, other animals try to catch him. Each time he is close to being captured, the text, "Jump, frog, jump," is repeated.* *

Martin, Bill, & Archambault, John. 1998. **Here Are My Hands**. New York: Henry Holt. *Children learn self-awareness of their various body parts, while viewing illustrations of children from various backgrounds.* *

Schaefer, Carole Lexa. 1996. **The Squiggle**. New York: Crown Publishers. *On a walk with her class, a girl finds a string, which takes the form of many different things.*

Walton, Rick. 2000. **My Two Hands, My Two Feet**. New York: Putnam. *This book shows children what hands do. Flip the book over and it shows children what feet do.*

Walton, Rick. 2001. **How Can You Dance?** New York: Putnam. *Children are encouraged to dance in unique situations.*

(*Available as a board book)

Other Literacy Materials

- pictures and names of animals
- sign with directions for obstacle course

Adding Spark to the Gross Motor Center

Place a skateboard or scooter in the *Gross Motor Center*. Allow the children to explore this new piece of equipment. The children may ride the skateboard in unusual ways such as on their stomach or sitting on it and scooting around with their legs.

Safety Note: Supervise closely and follow all necessary safety precautions.

Evaluation of the Individual Child

Is the child:

1. Moving her body to experience the environment?
2. Demonstrating a new gross (large) motor skill?
3. Playing alongside or with another child in the *Gross Motor Center*?
4. Able to identify simple body parts?

Fine Motor Center

Overview

The *Fine Motor Center* will provide playful experiences to help the young child expand her small motor skills. These abilities are helpful as preschoolers begin to draw and make scribbles that resemble letters or shapes. Other fine motor skills—grasping and releasing objects, in-hand manipulation, and bilateral hand use—also develop during these early years. It is important that the young child with special needs not be overwhelmed by writing and cutting activities, which may be especially challenging. In the *Fine Motor Center*, children's motivation to develop their skills is encouraged through playful activities with unique materials. These fine motor skills provide important foundations for later handwriting development.

Learning Objectives

The child with special needs will:

1. Develop pre-writing skills.
2. Participate in pre-cutting or cutting activities.
3. Improve grasp-and-release skills.
4. Expand bilateral hand use (using two hands together).

Time Frame

The *Fine Motor Center* should be available for the entire year. Carefully observe children's interest level in the materials; as the children become less motivated to participate in fine motor activities, add new materials.

Letter to Parents or Guardians

Dear Parent or Guardian,

When most people think about preschool activities, they think about learning to draw and to cut with scissors. These are very important skills for young children. In our classroom, we have a *Fine Motor Center* available for all the children. In this center, the children can explore drawing, cutting, and other hand skills. We use both common and unusual materials to keep the children interested in learning these skills.

We are looking for donations of the following items: new or used greeting cards, kitchen tongs, tweezers, cotton balls, sandpaper, clothespins, new or used cookie sheets, sidewalk chalk, and sponges. All of these items will be used to stimulate interest in using small motor skills. We will appreciate any materials you can donate.

Layout of the Fine Motor Center

A stable work surface is important in the *Fine Motor Center*. It should include a table and chairs, with a table of appropriate height to allow the children's elbows to rest comfortably on top. Children should be seated or standing with their feet firmly resting on the floor. An easel is valuable for developing drawing and pre-writing skills. Because the children will be working with messy materials, this center works best if it is placed on a floor that is easy to clean. Items for the center may be stored in small, clear containers with both picture and word labels so children can identify the objects they want to use.

Vocabulary Enrichment

button

clay

cut

describe

find

fingers

marker

paint

playdough

scissors

stylus (a wooden utensil used to make marks in clay)

write

Teacher- and Parent-Collected Props

- child-safe scissors
- clay (see page 311 in Chapter 5 for directions to make play clay and playdough)
- cotton balls
- dressing boards or dolls with buttons, snaps, zippers, and laces
- easel
- glue
- old shirts or smocks
- pegboards and pegs
- puzzles
- tongs
- tools for painting, such as paintbrushes, sponges, feathers, turkey baster, cotton balls, and paint rollers
- variety of items to glue, such as paper scraps, tissue paper, craft sticks, and fabric scraps
- variety of materials to paint, draw, or write on, such as sandpaper, bubble wrap, foil, newspaper, and wrapping paper
- writing utensils, such as washable markers, crayons, pencils, chalk

Web of Integrated Learning

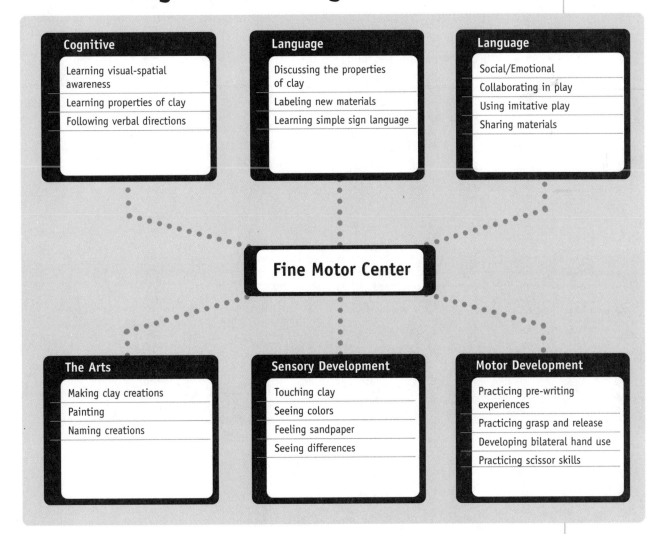

Cognitive
- Learning visual-spatial awareness
- Learning properties of clay
- Following verbal directions

Language
- Discussing the properties of clay
- Labeling new materials
- Learning simple sign language

Language
- Social/Emotional
- Collaborating in play
- Using imitative play
- Sharing materials

Fine Motor Center

The Arts
- Making clay creations
- Painting
- Naming creations

Sensory Development
- Touching clay
- Seeing colors
- Feeling sandpaper
- Seeing differences

Motor Development
- Practicing pre-writing experiences
- Practicing grasp and release
- Developing bilateral hand use
- Practicing scissor skills

Activities

Clay Boards

Materials

- modeling clay (see page 311 in Chapter 5 for directions)
- cookie sheets or pizza pans (pans with a small lip)
- stylus (a wooden utensil used for making marks in clay, can be purchased at a craft store), or use pens after the ink has run out
- plastic bags or plastic wrap
- laminated sheets of white paper with a single, simple design drawn on them, such as straight line, wavy line, or circle

Procedure

1. Create clay boards by smoothing modeling clay over the entire surface of cookie sheets so clay is approximately ¼" to ½" thick.
2. Give each child a clay board and stylus.
3. Demonstrate how to use the stylus to write or draw; show the children how to use their fingers to "erase" the drawing.
4. You may draw for the child and then ask her to erase the drawing with her fingers.
5. These clay boards may be kept for a long time if stored in plastic bags or wrapped in plastic.
6. Give the children extra pieces of clay and the laminated patterns to follow. The children can roll the clay into long pieces and then place the clay on top of the patterns.

"It is important that the young child with special needs not be overwhelmed by writing and cutting activities, which may be especially challenging. In the Fine Motor Center, children's motivation to develop their skills is encouraged through playful activities with unique materials."

Adapt "Clay Boards"

  Increase the size of the drawing utensil by wrapping it with tape or placing foam around it.

 Cover the pan with black contact paper. Use red or yellow clay and paint the stylus black for children who need more visual contrast.

  Discuss how the clay responds to the child's use of the drawing utensil. "Nate, look how the clay moves."

 If the child does not have enough hand strength to mark in the clay, cover the cookie sheet in soap foam and let the child use her fingers to draw.

 Pre-roll the clay for the children to use on laminated pattern sheets.

 First ask the child to feel the shape that you have drawn in the clay. Then, assist the child in tracing the letter.

 Some children may not like the texture of the clay. Do not force them to touch the clay with their hands, but encourage them to use the writing utensil to draw. They can use spoons to erase their drawings.

Tong Pick Up

Materials

- large and small empty aluminum cans with edges covered in tape
- plastic kitchen tongs, tweezers, or clothespins
- items to pick up, such as large coins, cotton balls, large buttons, and small balls

Procedure

1. Give each child one aluminum can, a pair of tongs, tweezers or clothespins, and items to pick up.
2. Ask children to fill up their cans with the materials by using their tools.
3. Listen for the sounds that the items make as they drop into the can.
4. See if the children can take the items out of the can.

Activities

Adapt "Tong Pick Up"

  Glue a craft stick to the end of the wooden clothespin so the child can place more fingers on the clothespin.

 Place cotton balls or light colored, large buttons on black paper for greater visual contrast.

 Help the child label the specific item she is picking up with tongs. "I like the way you are picking up those cotton balls."

 Tweezers will encourage more refined finger movements than tongs.

   Place items on a cookie sheet or plastic drawer liner to help focus attention and visual awareness to the task.

Hide and Seek

 (sidebar) **Activities**

Materials
- playdough, putty, or clay (see page 311 in Chapter 5 for directions)
- small items, such as marbles, coins, and small pegs
- small containers or bowls

Procedure
1. Give each child a lump of playdough, putty, or clay with small items hidden inside.
2. Ask the children to find the items and place them into a small container. They may count the items as they go.
3. Ask the children to hide the items inside the putty; they can also switch putty with another child to search for the hidden items.

Note: This activity is not recommended for children who mouth objects.

Adapt "Hide and Seek"

  If the child is unable to grasp or see small items, hide larger materials such as plastic animals.

 Hide items in sand or dry rice, if the child does not have the strength needed to pull items out of putty.

  If this activity is too easy for the child or if the child does not like to touch the putty, let her use tweezers to pull items out of putty.

  Let a peer hide one item at a time inside the putty.

Rainbow Sign Language and Other Fingerplays

Activities

Materials

- sign language book, such as *Signing for Kids* by Mickey Flodin
- drawing or picture of a rainbow
- fingerplay book
- CD or tape player and recording of songs that children can accompany by signing or making animals with their hands

Procedure

1. To introduce this center activity, talk about rainbows during Circle Time. On the same day or the next day, discuss sign language and show the sign language book that will be placed in the center.
2. Show a picture of a rainbow. Ask children to identify a color.
3. Demonstrate the sign for that color.
4. Create a melody or chant the words to Rainbow Song: "Blue is the color of the rainbow. Blue is the color of the rainbow. Blue is the color of the rainbow. Blue is the color I know."
5. Each day, add a new color to the rainbow and sing the song.
6. Leave the sign language book and fingerplay book in the center so the children can practice new signs or fingerplays.

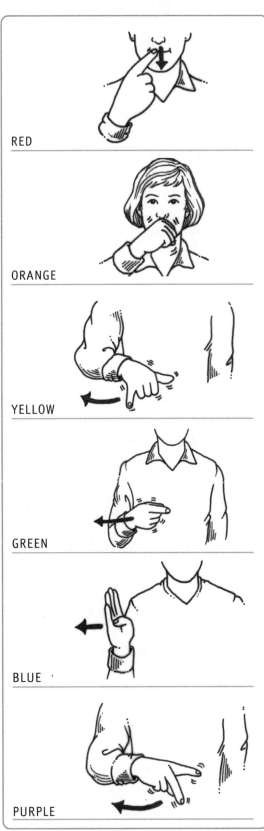

RED

ORANGE

YELLOW

GREEN

BLUE

PURPLE

Adapt "Rainbow Sign Language and Other Fingerplays"

 Point to a color of the rainbow and ask the child to identify it before signing the color and singing the song.

 Ask child to verbalize the color selected.

  Physically assist the child with forming the sign.

 Show the child a picture of the sign in the book.

   Encourage all children to learn simple signs such as "thank you," "yes," "no," "eat," "drink," and "music." This will allow all children to communicate with their peers.

 Use the sign language for colors during your daily activities.

The Essential Literacy Connection

Books

Cauley, Lorinda Bryon. 2001. **Clap Your Hands**. New York: Putnam. *This book encourages children to get up and move, just like the kids and animal characters in the book.* *

Flodin, Mickey. 1991. **Signing for Kids**. New York: The Berkley Publishing Group. *This signing manual, written for children, is organized by subject area. It is an invaluable learning guide.*

Hood, Susan. 2002. **Look! I Can Tie My Shoes!** New York: Grosset & Dunlap. *A little girl who loves shoes gets a lesson on tying them.*

Perkins, Al. 1969. **Hand, Hand, Fingers, Thumb**. New York: Random House. *A group of dancing monkeys explains hands and fingers in this simple rhyming text.* *

Rankin, Laura. 1991. **The Handmade Alphabet**. New York: Dial Books. *Beautifully illustrated hands are shown making all the letters of the alphabet.*

Reid, Margarette. 1990. **The Button Box**. New York: Dutton Children's Books. *A little boy sorts buttons that he finds in his grandmother's box by size and shape, as he imagines where the buttons came from.*

(*Available as a board book)

Other Literacy Materials

- letter-lacing boards
- writing journal
- writing tools, such as markers, pencils, brushes, and chalk

Adding Spark to the Fine Motor Center

Textured Drawing

Materials

- sandpaper or bubble wrap
- chalk or nontoxic paint and paintbrushes
- sponges cut into 1" squares

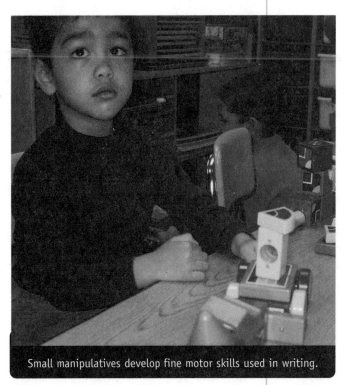

Small manipulatives develop fine motor skills used in writing.

Procedure

1. Provide children with sheets of sandpaper or bubble wrap.
2. Give the children large or small chalk to draw on the sandpaper, or paint and paintbrushes to paint the bubble wrap.
3. The children may erase the sandpaper drawings with their fingertips or by using a very small (1" to 2") sponge that has been dipped in water.
4. Children may fingerpaint on the bubble wrap, if preferred.

Evaluation of the Individual Child:

Is the child:

1. Demonstrating finger isolation to point or make animals with her hands?
2. Participating in pre-cutting or cutting activities?
3. Improving her grasp/release of tools?
4. Developing bilateral hand skills (using two hands together)?

Pre-Writing Center

Overview

Writing is among the most important life skills. Communication in written form includes a variety of components such as organization, sequencing, memory, eye-hand coordination, posture, and hand function. Many students with learning disabilities, developmental delays, or neurological problems struggle to write legibly. Even though we live in a world of computers, handwriting is still a necessary component of daily living. The *Pre-Writing Center* will use interesting activities to encourage each child to develop the essential skills for handwriting and will prepare young children for written communication through developmentally appropriate methods.

Some children with special needs will require alternative methods of written communication or adaptations to make their workspaces accessible. In those instances, you may consult an occupational therapist to assist you in making appropriate recommendations for the individual child.

Learning Objectives

The child with special needs will:
1. Improve posture needed for pre-writing skills.
2. Imitate simple shapes or letters using a finger or writing utensil.
3. Use a functional grasp of the writing utensil.
4. Trace simple shapes or letters using a finger or writing utensil.

Time Frame

The *Pre-Writing Center* is appropriate for use throughout the year. It may be organized alongside the *Fine Motor Center*. The *Pre-Writing Center* may be alternated with the *Fine Motor Center* to maintain the children's interest levels.

Letter to Parents or Guardians	Dear Parent or Guardian,

Dear Parent or Guardian,
Writing is an essential life skill. Yet, pre-writing can be one of the most challenging tasks for preschoolers. Legible handwriting takes many years to develop; preschool is the time to begin this process. In our *Pre-Writing Center*, we will work on many of the skills that are needed for preschoolers to begin learning how to write. For example, we will offer fun activities that will encourage the children's grasp, posture, and shape formation.

Wall painting is a fun outdoor activity that will encourage pre-writing skills. Grab a bucket of water and a large paintbrush (the size you would use to paint walls). On an outside wall, ask your child to paint simple shapes like a circle or triangle. You can even begin by painting one area of the wall. You can write a letter in chalk and then let your child erase the letter with water. When you are finished, there is no cleanup. The water will just dry!

Layout of the Pre-Writing Center

The *Pre-Writing Center* will work well in an area of the room with few distractions. Table and chairs and a standing easel are necessary, while a blank wall or wall with a dry-erase board is useful. Try to keep clutter to a minimum. Children need to be able to focus on the activity, rather than be distracted by outside stimuli.

Vocabulary Enrichment

Using markers develops pre-writing skills.

chalk	letter
color	marker
copy	paper
draw	pencil
easel	shape
hand	write

Teacher- and Parent-Collected Props

- big (fat) and small chalk
- carpet squares
- chalk board (individual size or wall size)
- dry-erase board (individual size or wall size)
- felt-tip pens
- foam soap
- laminated paper for writing

- large and small paintbrushes
- paper
- sandpaper
- small crayons
- standard adult-style pencils
- standing easel
- washable dry-erase markers
- washable markers
- washable paint

Web of Integrated Learning

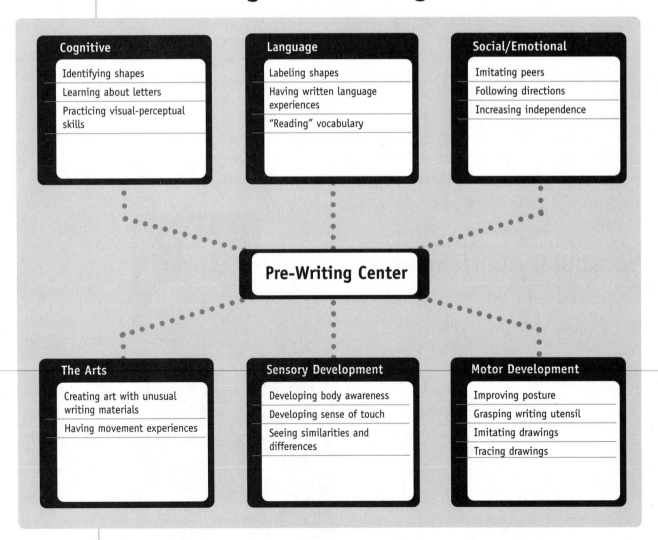

Cognitive
- Identifying shapes
- Learning about letters
- Practicing visual-perceptual skills

Language
- Labeling shapes
- Having written language experiences
- "Reading" vocabulary

Social/Emotional
- Imitating peers
- Following directions
- Increasing independence

Pre-Writing Center

The Arts
- Creating art with unusual writing materials
- Having movement experiences

Sensory Development
- Developing body awareness
- Developing sense of touch
- Seeing similarities and differences

Motor Development
- Improving posture
- Grasping writing utensil
- Imitating drawings
- Tracing drawings

Vertical Writing

Activities

Materials

- vertical writing surfaces, such as
  - blank walls covered with paper
  - wall dry-erase board
  - wall chalkboard
  - standing easels
  - tabletop easels
  - tabletop incline boards (see pages 306–307 in Chapter 5 for directions)
- writing utensils, such as crayons, markers, chalk, pencils, and pens

Procedure

1. Drawing on an upright surface may decrease directional confusion for letter formation. On a vertical surface, *up* means *up* and *down* means *down*. This helps children understand where to begin their letters.
2. Drawing on a vertical surface also promotes a functional grasp of the writing utensil and an appropriate wrist placement.
3. You may have the child trace your shapes or letters on a board using "Rainbow Writing." You make the letter in one color, and then allow the child to trace your letter in as many different colors as possible, to make a rainbow letter.
4. Make sure the child's feet are placed firmly on the floor while she is writing.
5. If the child is writing on a tabletop incline board, make sure that the table height is even with the child's elbow.

> *"Writing is among the most important life skills. The Pre-Writing Center uses interesting activities to encourage each child to develop the essential skills for handwriting and will prepare young children for written communication through developmentally appropriate methods."*

Adapt "Vertical Writing"

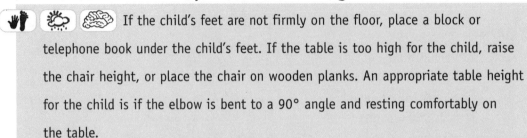 If the child's feet are not firmly on the floor, place a block or telephone book under the child's feet. If the table is too high for the child, raise the chair height, or place the chair on wooden planks. An appropriate table height for the child is if the elbow is bent to a 90° angle and resting comfortably on the table.

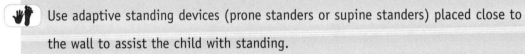 Use adaptive standing devices (prone standers or supine standers) placed close to the wall to assist the child with standing.

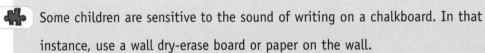 Some children are sensitive to the sound of writing on a chalkboard. In that instance, use a wall dry-erase board or paper on the wall.

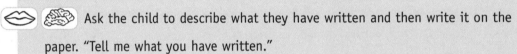 Ask the child to describe what they have written and then write it on the paper. "Tell me what you have written."

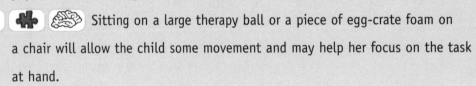 Sitting on a large therapy ball or a piece of egg-crate foam on a chair will allow the child some movement and may help her focus on the task at hand.

Floor Writing

Materials

- floor mats, blankets, or towels and/or wedges (see page 316 in Chapter 5 for directions)
- materials on which to draw or write, such as paper or carpet samples

Note: Place drawing paper on materials with unique textures, such as carpet samples. The children's drawings will make interesting marks.

- writing utensils, such as markers, crayons, or chalk

Procedure

1. Lying on the stomach while drawing or writing may increase back, shoulder, and elbow strength. Good posture and stability in these parts of the body makes for legible handwriting. This position also encourages small movement of the hand.
2. Writing while on the stomach is more physically demanding than writing while sitting or standing. Some children may only manage this position for several minutes at a time. Invite the child to take breaks by rolling onto her side or sitting on the floor in between.

3. Place mat, blankets, or wedges on the floor. Help the child position the writing materials on the floor in front of her. You may place the child with a small wedge or towel roll under her armpits to increase comfort.

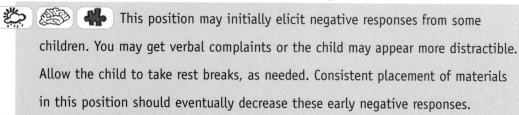

Adapt "Floor Writing"

This position may initially elicit negative responses from some children. You may get verbal complaints or the child may appear more distractible. Allow the child to take rest breaks, as needed. Consistent placement of materials in this position should eventually decrease these early negative responses.

Lying on the stomach will place the child closer to the writing materials; this may be of great benefit to children with visual impairments.

This position may not be appropriate for children with significant physical impairments and children with stomach feeding tubes. You may place the child in a side-lying position by using pillows or wedges for support. If you have specific questions about this position, ask an occupational therapist or physical therapist.

A child with mild motor delays may need a larger wedge or towel roll placed under her armpits. This will provide more support for the shoulders and back.

Provide the child with sandpaper and chalk for added texture.

Name the tools that are being used during painting. "Caroline is using a paintbrush."

Itty Bitty Writing Tools

Materials
- pieces of chalk, crayons, small pencils measuring between 1 ½" to 3" long
- paper and other writing surfaces

Procedure
1. Pencil grasp is a very important part of writing. Most people throw away broken crayons, chalk, or pencils. However, small utensils can encourage more efficient grasps in preschoolers.
2. Save these small pieces and encourage the children to utilize them in pre-writing or drawing.

Adapt "Itty Bitty Writing Tools"

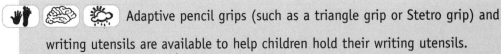 Adaptive pencil grips (such as a triangle grip or Stetro grip) and writing utensils are available to help children hold their writing utensils.

Children can straddle a chair that is turned backwards. This may provide more support for the pre-writing task.

Children can stand at a tall table or kneel at a child-size table to complete the task.

Offer the child two choices to decrease the chance of non-compliant behavior. "Would you like to draw with chalk or with a pencil?"

Body Writing

Materials
- blackboard and chalk or whiteboard and marker

Procedure
1. Begin by drawing a simple shape on the board or showing the children a picture of a shape, such as a circle, vertical line, horizontal line, or triangle.
2. Ask the children to make their bodies into that shape. You may need to assist them.
3. Next, ask the children to make a simple shape out of their bodies without showing them the shape. For example, "Can you be a circle?"
4. After children can imitate simple shapes, begin with easy-to-form letters, such as "I," "O," "T," "C," "L," and "P." Follow the same steps.

Adapt "Body Writing"

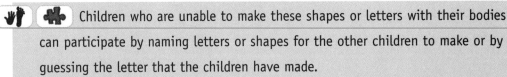 Children who are unable to make these shapes or letters with their bodies can participate by naming letters or shapes for the other children to make or by guessing the letter that the children have made.

Children can "air write" shapes or letters, using a finger or arm to form them in the air, rather than using their entire body.

Children can make the phonetic sounds that correspond with the letter.

Give the child specific, positive reinforcement for her participation, "Carla, I really like your letter O."

Activities

The Essential Literacy Connection

Books

Campbell, Rod. 1999. **Dear Zoo**. New York: Little Simon. *A child writes to the zoo and asks the zoo to send him a pet. The zoo sends him one animal at a time, but each one is either too heavy, too tall, too fierce, and so on. They finally send him a dog, which is the perfect pet for him.* *

Caseley, Judith. 1994. **Dear Annie**. New York: HarperCollins. *A grandfather begins writing letters to his granddaughter, Annie, when she is born. The mother answers the letters, until Annie is old enough to read and write the letters herself. Annie is excited to tell her class about her penpal and show the letters to her classmates.*

Hoban, Tana. 1987. **26 Letters and 99 Cents**. New York: Greenwillow Books. *Brightly illustrated pictures begin with the letter that is highlighted on each page. Turn the book over, and children learn how to count various coins.*

James, Simon. 1996. **Dear Mr. Blueberry**. New York: Aladdin Library. *While Emily is on vacation, she writes letters to her teacher about the whale that she has seen in the backyard pond. Mr. Blueberry writes Emily back describing whales' habitats and why it could not be a whale in the pond. Emily learns all about whales, while Mr. Blueberry learns all about imagination.*

Girls writing intensely in their journals

Rau, Dana Meachen. 1998. **The Secret Code**. New York: Children's Press. *Oscar, who is blind, shows the other children in his class how to read the Braille alphabet.*

(*Available as a board book)

Other Literacy Materials

- dry-erase board
- chalkboard
- writing utensils

Adding Spark to the Pre-Writing Center

Feely Shapes or Letters

Materials
- poster board
- pencil or markers
- clear-drying glue or neon-color glue
- yarn or string

Procedure
1. Cut poster board into squares.
2. Copy shapes or letters onto the poster squares with a pencil or marker.
3. Trace shapes or letters with neon-color glue or glue string or yarn onto the board. Children with good fine motor skills may be able to help you with this task.
4. Allow glue to dry thoroughly.
5. Children can trace the "feely shape" or "feely letter" with their fingers before they attempt to copy it on paper.

Evaluation of the Individual Child

Is the child:
1. Able to maintain appropriate posture (with or without adaptations) for pre-writing activities?
2. Able to imitate simple shapes or letters?
3. Able to trace simple shapes or letters?
4. Demonstrating an efficient grasp of the writing utensil?

Sociodramatic Centers 2

Centers that focus around a specific theme and encourage role playing are often referred to as Sociodramatic Centers. In these centers, young children's play is stimulated by props and materials that encourage them to try out new roles and expand their language.

Centers included in this chapter:

Doctor's Office Center
Grocery Store Center
Beach Center
Transportation Center
Farm Center
Family Center
Bakery Center
Gardening Center
Nighttime Center
Restaurant Center

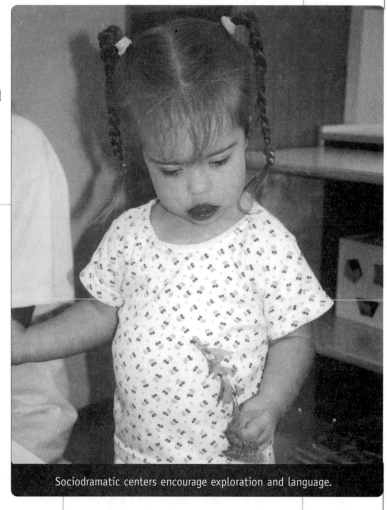
Sociodramatic centers encourage exploration and language.

Doctor's Office Center

Overview

By the time children are preschoolers, most have been to a doctor's office. Some have also been in the hospital or visited someone there. The doctor's office and the hospital can be scary places for young children. The *Doctor's Office Center* is useful for helping children understand the role of health professionals. Through playful experiences, the *Doctor's Office Center* may encourage children to be more comfortable with common medical procedures.

Before opening this center, talk with the children about the experience of going to the doctor's office or hospital. It is important to place the focus on health professionals as helpers. Honesty and candor in discussions of and reasoning behind painful medical procedures such as vaccinations will help young children process these experiences and use the information in their play.

Learning Objectives

The child with special needs will:

1. Participate in social play experiences to decrease fears.
2. Learn self-care skills.
3. Use vocabulary related to doctor's offices and hospitals.
4. Expand understanding of his own emotions and feelings.

Time Frame

The *Doctor's Office Center* should remain set up for at least two weeks so the children have time to explore the props and begin sociodramatic play experiences. This center may remain open for a longer time if children remain interested.

Letter to Parents or Guardians

Dear Parent or Guardian,

Going to the doctor's office is part of life for almost everyone. Also, accidents or illnesses occur that require immediate medical attention in the emergency room or hospital. For most young children, visiting the doctor or hospital can be a scary and confusing experience. Children have difficulty understanding what is happening and why they must go.

We have just opened the *Doctor's Office Center* in our room. In this center, the children can explore medical equipment such as a stethoscope, thermometer, and blood pressure cuff. They can also use medical supplies as props in social play experiences with other children. We hope these experiences will educate children about the roles of medical professionals and help decrease their fears of these experiences.

Layout of the Doctor's Office Center

Place the medical supplies and equipment within easy reach of the children.
Accessible shelves or clear plastic containers work well to store materials. Be sure to
label all pieces of equipment. A floor mat or pillow is useful for children who want to
lie down for their checkup.

Vocabulary Enrichment

appointment

blood pressure

chart

checkup

doctor

emergency

germs

height/weight

hospital

medicine

nurse

prescription

stethoscope

thermometer/temperature

treatment

Teacher- and Parent-Collected Props

- bandages
- Band-Aids
- blood pressure cuff
- brochures from doctor's offices, Health Department, hospitals, or clinics
- clothes for dress up, such as a white lab coat, scrubs, or uniforms
- cotton balls
- doctor's bag
- dolls
- eye chart
- flashlight
- pads of paper for prescriptions
- plastic play thermometers
- play plastic syringes
- rubber gloves (**Note:** Be cautious of latex allergies, particularly in children with Spina Bifida.)
- scales
- stethoscope
- surgical masks
- tongue depressors
- writing utensils

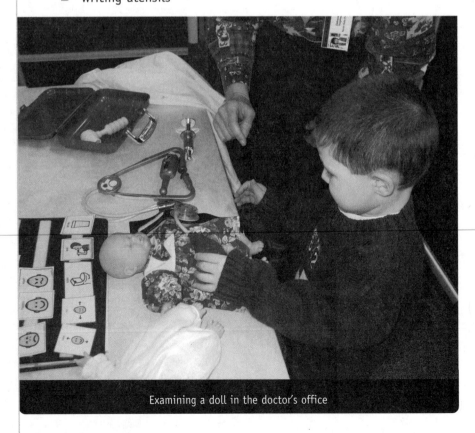

Examining a doll in the doctor's office

Web of Integrated Learning

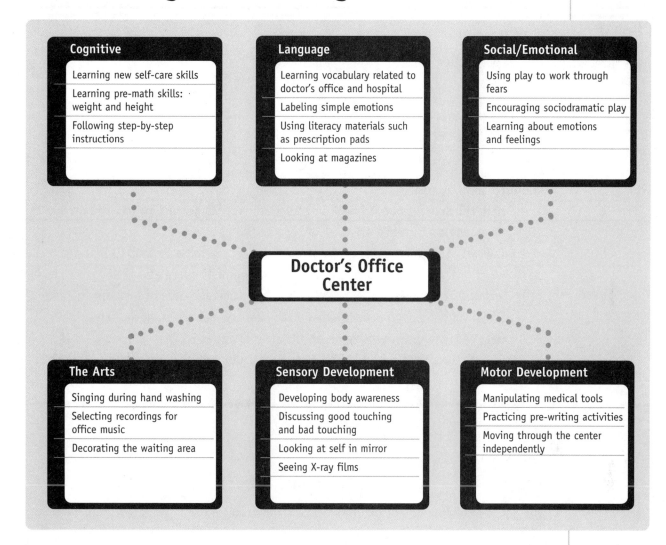

Cognitive
- Learning new self-care skills
- Learning pre-math skills: weight and height
- Following step-by-step instructions

Language
- Learning vocabulary related to doctor's office and hospital
- Labeling simple emotions
- Using literacy materials such as prescription pads
- Looking at magazines

Social/Emotional
- Using play to work through fears
- Encouraging sociodramatic play
- Learning about emotions and feelings

Doctor's Office Center

The Arts
- Singing during hand washing
- Selecting recordings for office music
- Decorating the waiting area

Sensory Development
- Developing body awareness
- Discussing good touching and bad touching
- Looking at self in mirror
- Seeing X-ray films

Motor Development
- Manipulating medical tools
- Practicing pre-writing activities
- Moving through the center independently

"In the beginning level of sociodramatic play, real objects assist children in developing symbolic representations. Some children begin simple role playing at this stage. This type of play can be encouraged with centers such as...Doctor's Office. Children will pretend to be...the doctor giving a shot."

Activities

Patient ID Bracelets

Materials

- construction paper
- scissors
- markers
- stickers
- tape or stapler

Procedure

1. Help children cut out strips of construction paper large enough to write on and to fit around each child's wrist.
2. Talk with the children about the importance of wearing a Patient ID Bracelet when one goes to the hospital. Explain the use of ID bracelets. "Everyone at the hospital has to wear an ID bracelet with his name and date of birth on it," and "This helps the doctors and nurses make sure you get the right medicine."
3. Help each child write his name on the strip of paper.
4. Discuss the child's date of birth. Help each child write his birth date on the strip of paper.
5. Allow the child to decorate the Patient ID Bracelet with stickers.
6. Use a stapler or tape to close the bracelet.

Adapt "Patient ID Bracelets"

 If the children do not like the feel of the bracelet on their arms, use nametags to stick on the children's clothing.

 Ask each child to talk about his date of birth and to mark his birthday on the calendar.

  Pre-cut the strips of construction paper for the bracelet or let the children tear strips of paper.

Hand Washing

Materials

- chart with drawings or pictures and labels of hand-washing steps
- sink
- liquid soap
- paper towels
- trash can

Procedure

1. Post a chart in the *Doctor's Office Center* and at the sink to demonstrate the appropriate steps of hand washing:

    1. Wet hands.
    2. Add soap.
    3. Lather well.
    4. Rinse thoroughly.
    5. Dry hands with a paper towel.

2. Briefly explain the vocabulary word "germs." Tell the children how important hand washing is to decrease germs.
3. Demonstrate and discuss the appropriate steps of hand washing to the children.

Adapt "Hand Washing"

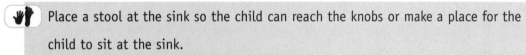 Place a stool at the sink so the child can reach the knobs or make a place for the child to sit at the sink.

Some children do not like the sound of running water. Placing ear plugs in the child's ears or allowing the child to control the water may help.

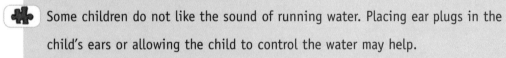 Sing, "This is the way we wash our hands, wash our hands, wash our hands..." to the tune of "Here We Go 'Round the Mulberry Bush."

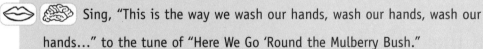 Place liquid soap in a squirt bottle for easy dispensing.

Assist the child with all the steps of hand washing, except drying with a paper towel. Allow the child to make this final step of the process independently to help him feel successful.

Activities

How Big Are You?

Materials

- poster-size graph paper
- tape
- markers
- measuring tape or ruler
- scales

Procedure

1. Place two pieces of poster-size graph paper on a wall or board in the center.
2. Make a chart labeled "Height" and a chart labeled "Weight." Place each child's name in columns across the bottom of the charts.
3. When introducing the *Doctor's Office Center*, talk about the different things that doctors and nurses measure, such as height, weight, blood pressure, and temperature. Be sure to add that taking these measurements do not usually hurt!
4. Measure each child's height and chart it on the graph paper. Discuss who is the tallest and who is the shortest in the class.
5. Measure each child's weight and chart it on the graph paper. Discuss who is the heaviest and who is the lightest in the class.

Adapt "How Big Are You?"

 Give the child his own graph paper and chart each child's height or weight on the paper in a different color, or allow the child to chart his own measurements.

 Use plain white paper with black and red markers to chart measurements.

 Use words to describe the process of measuring. "I am using a ruler to measure your height."

"That Hurts Me!"

Materials

- pieces of medical equipment, such as
  - play plastic syringes
  - blood pressure cuff
  - thermometer
  - scales

- otoscope (for checking ears and nose)
- tongue depressor
- reflex hammer
■ pictures of people exhibiting different emotions, such as
  - pain
  - fear
  - happiness
  - sadness

A stethoscope doesn't hurt.

Procedure

1. Talk with the children about common experiences at a doctor's office. Discuss why these procedures are necessary, for example, "To find out why you don't feel good," or, "To make sure you don't get sick."

2. Ask the children to tell you what scares them or makes them afraid at the doctor's office.

3. Show each piece of medical equipment (one by one) and let the children touch each piece. Label the piece of equipment; for example, "This is a blood pressure cuff for measuring your blood pressure."

4. Ask the children, "Does this hurt you?" If the equipment causes pain—for example, a syringe—ask the children to pick out which face looks like "hurt." Be honest and explain why sometimes a shot is necessary. If it does not cause pain, be sure to help the children pick out a happy face.

Adapt "That Hurts Me!"

 Give the child an unbreakable mirror and ask him to make a face that goes along with the piece of equipment.

 If this activity has too many steps for the child, talk about only one piece of medical equipment each day. For example, on Monday talk about the stethoscope. On Tuesday, discuss the syringe and shots.

 Help the child hold and manipulate the piece of medical equipment as you talk about it.

The Essential Literacy Connection

Books

Berenstain, Stan & Berenstain, Jan. 1981. **The Berenstain Bears Go to the Doctor.** New York: Random House. *It is time for a routine doctor's visit, so the Berenstain Bears go to see Dr. Grizzly.*

Bridwell, Norman. 2000. **Clifford Visits the Hospital.** New York: Scholastic. *Clifford gets into mischief at the hospital, as he is learning about what happens there.*

Oxenbury, Helen. 1994. **The Checkup.** New York: Penguin Putnam. *While at the doctor's office, a little boy causes a commotion.*

Rey, Margaret & Rey, H.A. 1966. **Curious George Goes to the Hospital.** Boston, MA: Houghton Mifflin. *Readers learn that the hospital is not so bad after all, when they see Curious George have an operation to remove a puzzle piece he has swallowed.*

Rockwell, Harlow. 1973. **My Doctor.** New York: Macmillan. *A young boy goes for a routine checkup at the doctor's office.*

Rogers, Fred. 1997. **Going to the Hospital.** New York: Puffin. *Explanations of what happens during a hospital stay.*

(*Available as a board book)

Other Literacy Materials

- chart for hand washing
- chart of height and weight
- ID bracelet
- magazines and brochures for the waiting area
- pads of paper or prescription pads for writing prescriptions
- rack or shelf where health-related brochures can be displayed

Adding Spark to the Doctor's Office Center

Add clipboards with copies of growth charts or graph paper attached. Encourage the children to take notes or write prescriptions on their charts.

Evaluation of the Individual Child

Is the child:

1. Interacting socially in the center?
2. Able to wash his hands independently or with assistance?
3. Using new vocabulary in the center? What are the words?
4. Participating in activities that stimulate awareness of feelings and emotions?

Grocery Store Center

Overview

Most young children have been to a grocery store. The *Grocery Store Center* provides a place where the children can connect a real experience to their play. Here, they can select the groceries they want, push the cart, and pay for their purchases. It is a place filled with environmental print and numbers. In the *Grocery Store Center*, children can take on roles and pretend to be a cashier, customer, baker, shelf stocker, or deli cook. During this play, the children will increase their understanding of the grocery store and its operation.

Learning Objectives

The child with special needs will:
1. Use real experiences as content of play in the *Grocery Store Center*.
2. Chose grocery items by using symbols or environmental print.
3. Role play while participating in the center.
4. Cooperate with others to make the *Grocery Store Center* function effectively.

Time Frame

This changing center will rotate into the classroom for two to three weeks at a time. Because it is a high interest center, it can be set up several times during the year. Each time it appears, provide new food items or props to expand the children's play.

Letter to Parents or Guardians

Dear Parent or Guardian,

When we plan our classroom, we try to include centers that focus on things young children have experienced. Connecting classroom centers with children's experiences will help them move to a higher level of thinking, and assist them as they try to understand how things work and how they can participate in their world.

The *Grocery Store Center* is set up to allow a small group of children to work together in the center. The children can discuss what they like and want to buy. They can collect the items in a cart and roll it around. They can go through the checkout line and pay with cash or a credit card. In this environment, they will recognize symbols of their favorite foods—a literacy activity. They will also learn math as they begin to think about cost and money.

If you have empty packages, bags, or plastic bottles of your child's favorite foods, please send them to us. We want to stock the shelves with items they have seen and enjoy eating. We will also need plastic or paper bags for shopping. At home, talk about items you buy at the grocery store and the food label that helps you know what it is. Our *Grocery Store Center* will be open for business next week.

Layout of the Grocery Store Center

This can be a freestanding center designed to resemble a grocery store. It will include shelves or bookshelves for popular food items, cereal, crackers, pastas, breads, and snacks.

Be sure to include items that the children in your classroom eat. Have an area where plastic fruit and vegetables are displayed. Use a table or low shelf for pricing and checking out.

Toy shopping carts or baskets should be available for collecting foods. If there is limited space in the classroom, this center can be set up in the *Home Living Center* for the two- to three-week period.

Vocabulary Enrichment

bags

basket

cash register

check out

favorite

food

fruit

groceries

grocery cart

label

price

vegetable

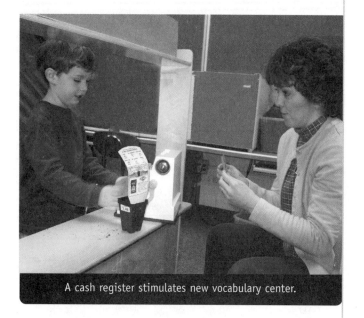

A cash register stimulates new vocabulary center.

Teacher- and Parent-Collected Props

- balance scales
- boxed items, such as cereals, pasta, and crackers
- cart or basket
- cash register
- grocery bags
- plastic fruits and vegetables
- pocketbooks, purses, and wallets
- stick-on labels

Paying for groceries at the checkout

Web of Integrated Learning

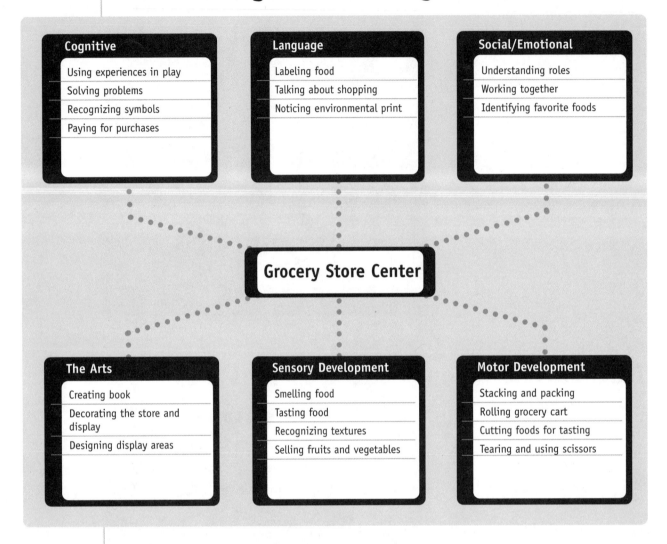

Cognitive
- Using experiences in play
- Solving problems
- Recognizing symbols
- Paying for purchases

Language
- Labeling food
- Talking about shopping
- Noticing environmental print

Social/Emotional
- Understanding roles
- Working together
- Identifying favorite foods

Grocery Store Center

The Arts
- Creating book
- Decorating the store and display
- Designing display areas

Sensory Development
- Smelling food
- Tasting food
- Recognizing textures
- Selling fruits and vegetables

Motor Development
- Stacking and packing
- Rolling grocery cart
- Cutting foods for tasting
- Tearing and using scissors

"Young children learn through manipulation of objects. As with all young children, children with special needs work best with objects that are real and concrete."

Stocking the Shelves

Materials

- collection of empty food containers, including boxes and bags (make sure there are duplicates of some of the items)
- carts or boxes
- shelves or bookcases
- paper and pencil
- labels with words and pictures, such as cereal, pasta, bread, crackers, and cookies

Sorting vegetables for the produce area

Procedure

1. Fill carts or boxes with food containers.
2. Children can sort items and place them on shelves.
3. Items can be grouped, and the same items placed together.
4. Make a list of items that are needed.

Adapt "Stocking the Shelves"

👁 🧩 Line shelves with light-colored paper or black paper to provide a good background for groceries.

👁 🧩 🌤 Place only a few items on shelves with space between them, so there is less clutter and confusion.

🧩 👄 With the children, sing, "This is the way we stock the shelves so early in the morning..." to the tune of "Here We Go 'Round the Mulberry Bush."

🧩 ✋ Place cans of food in the shopping cart to weigh it down. This will make the cart more stable for walking behind.

Activities

Activities

Book of Favorite Foods

Materials

- old magazines, fruit and vegetable catalogs, pictures of foods from magazines
- scissors
- scrapbook with adhesive pages or plastic pockets
- markers
- labels from containers

Procedure

1. Children can select and cut out pictures of their favorite foods from magazines or fruit and vegetable catalogs.
2. Let the children place the pictures on a page in the scrapbook.
3. Add each child's name and the written name of his favorite food.
4. This book can stay in the *Grocery Store Center* while it is open. Later, it can be moved to the *Home Living Center*.

Adapt "Book of Favorite Foods"

   The child can tear (instead of cut) paper with scissors.

   Place the magazine on a clipboard to stabilize it for cutting; this will decrease the child's frustration.

  Pre-cut pictures of foods and let the child choose pictures of his favorite foods.

Tasting Area

Materials

- fruit
- knife (adult only)
- tray
- napkins
- plastic tablecloth
- "free" sign
- pictures of fruit glued to note cards

Procedure

1. Cut up pieces of fruit including some fruit that is familiar to children and some that is less familiar.
2. Let children taste and compare.
3. Provide pictures for children to match with the fruit they taste.

Adapt "Tasting Area"

 Say the name of the fruit the child tastes. Show him a picture of the fruit he tastes.

 Tell the child the name of the fruit he will taste and let him smell it beforehand.

 If the child does not want to taste the fruit, let him touch or smell it. Discuss the feel and smell of the fruit.

 Pair the child with a peer who is willing to try new foods. Let him observe the other child eating the food.

The Essential Literacy Connection

Books

Baggette, Susan. 1998. **Jonathan Goes to the Grocery Store**. Sterling, VA: Brookfield Reader, Inc. *Jonathan's grandparents take him to the grocery store where interactions with employees provide positive experiences for young readers.* *

Cousins, Lucy. 2001. **Maisy Goes Shopping**. Cambridge, MA: Candlewick Press. *When Charley comes to visit Maisy the mouse at lunchtime, they realize that there is no food in the refrigerator. They head to the grocery store on their bicycles where they buy healthy foods such as cheese, juice, and yogurt.*

Hautzig, Deborah. 1994. **At the Supermarket**. New York: Orchard Books. *A trip to the grocery store can be fun, especially when you know about the activity that takes place to keep the shelves stocked.*

MacCarone, Grace. 1998. **I Shop With My Daddy**. New York: Scholastic. *Going up and down the aisles at the grocery store, a little girl and her father buy items from their list. Her father will not let her buy sweets, and surprises her with a frozen yogurt after shopping.*

Mayer, Mercer. 1989. **Just Shopping With Mom**. Racine, WI: Western Publishing. *When Mom takes her three children to the grocery store and dress shop, little sister pulls groceries off the shelves, gets lost, and cries for candy. Mom brightens up the day when she takes the children to the ice cream shop.*

(*Available as a board book)

Other Literacy Materials

- advertisements and posters
- book of favorite food
- labels and prices on food and shelves
- magazines with food products
- "Open" and "Closed" signs with hours of operation

Adding Spark to the Grocery Store Center

Add a deli, where pizza is being made and tasted. Children can add ingredients to frozen pizza or an English muffin. They can prepare and taste food in the new area of the grocery store.

Evaluation of the Individual Child

Is the child:

1. Relating play to real experiences? In what way?
2. Using labels/symbols to identify the products? Which ones?
3. Taking on a role in play? What role?
4. Working with others? How?

Beach Center

Overview

The beach offers many opportunities for young children to play and learn. Some children visit the beach once a year for vacation, while others may never have the opportunity to explore a beach. At the *Beach Center*, young children can learn about important aspects of our world such as the sand, the ocean, and marine life. Children can develop new motor skills by building sandcastles. There are many different sensory experiences at the beach, including sand, seashells, and seaweed. The *Beach Center* will provide children with interesting activities to expand their cognitive skills, motor skills, and social skills.

Learning Objectives

The child with special needs will:

1. Participate in cognitive activities, such as ones that explore cause and effect.
2. Use tools in sand and water play.
3. Develop peer interactions through play activities.
4. Improve fine motor skills such as eye-hand coordination.

Time Frame

The *Beach Center* will work well for approximately two weeks. If the children in the classroom maintain their interest in the center, keep it set up longer.

Letter to Parents or Guardians

Dear Parent or Guardian,

We have recently opened a *Beach Center* in our classroom. In this center, the children will be learning more about their world and the environment. We will provide playful experiences with sand and water in activities like building sandcastles and catching fish. The children will learn about marine life, seashells, and boats. We will read stories about the ocean. We plan to go on a beach picnic next week, and would love it if you would bring a lunch and join us at the beach!

Layout of the Beach Center

The *Beach Center* should be located in an area of the room where sand and water play is possible. The sand/water table will need to be accessible with a variety of toys for play. A beach umbrella placed securely in the center can add visual interest and boundaries to the space.

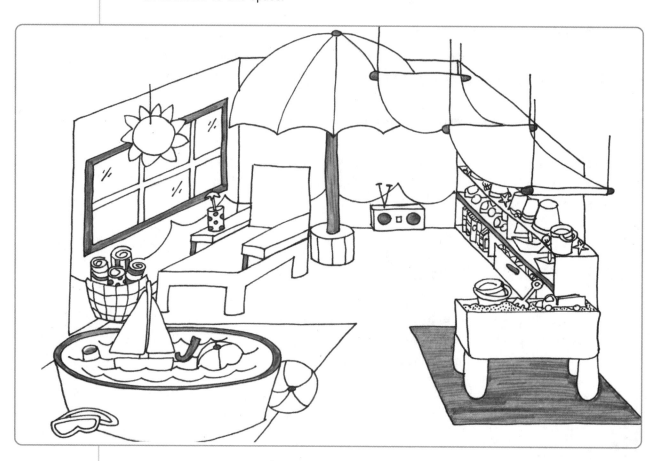

Vocabulary Enrichment

beach	sand
crab	sandcastle
fish	shell
float	shovel
marine	sunburn
ocean	sunscreen
pail	umbrella
sailboat	waves

Teacher- and Parent-Collected Props

- beach chair and beach umbrella
- beach toys, such as beach balls, swim rings, sand pails, shovels, scoops, and rakes
- CD player or tape player with beach music or ocean sounds
- dress-up clothes, such as swimsuits, hats, sunglasses, goggles, and flip-flops
- empty sunscreen containers and towels
- magazines or travel brochures with pictures of the beach
- sand/water table
- seashells
- small push toys, such as cars, trucks, and construction equipment
- small sticks, straws, or small wooden dowels for writing in the sand

Web of Integrated Learning

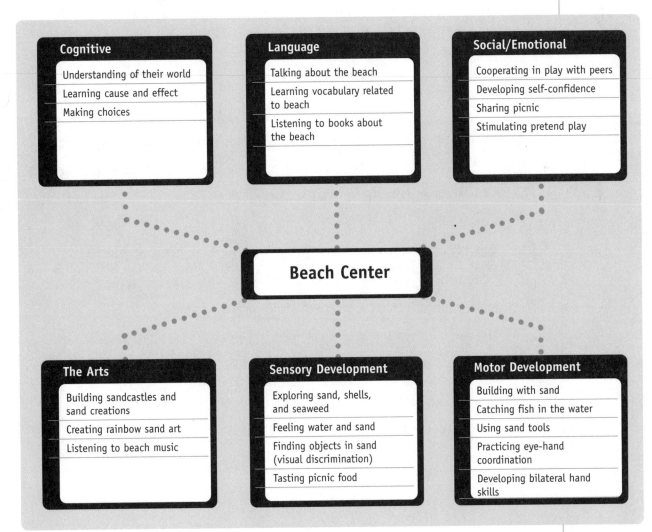

Cognitive
- Understanding of their world
- Learning cause and effect
- Making choices

Language
- Talking about the beach
- Learning vocabulary related to beach
- Listening to books about the beach

Social/Emotional
- Cooperating in play with peers
- Developing self-confidence
- Sharing picnic
- Stimulating pretend play

Beach Center

The Arts
- Building sandcastles and sand creations
- Creating rainbow sand art
- Listening to beach music

Sensory Development
- Exploring sand, shells, and seaweed
- Feeling water and sand
- Finding objects in sand (visual discrimination)
- Tasting picnic food

Motor Development
- Building with sand
- Catching fish in the water
- Using sand tools
- Practicing eye-hand coordination
- Developing bilateral hand skills

Activities

Beach Picnic

Materials

- picnic basket(s) or baskets with handles for carrying
- blanket
- plastic plates and utensils
- napkins
- picnic food such as sandwiches, fruit, and juice boxes

Procedure

1. This activity may be used indoors or outdoors.
2. Allow children to pack their picnic basket with utensils, food, and drinks.
3. Children may help make sandwiches.
4. Children can take turns carrying their picnic basket to the picnic site.
5. Ask children to help you place a blanket on the floor or ground.
6. Let the children help arrange plates, utensils, napkins, and food for the picnic.
7. Enjoy the picnic!

Adapt "Beach Picnic"

 Use adaptive seating devices if the child cannot sit independently on the floor.

 If a child cannot carry the picnic basket, he can put his picnic food in a backpack.

 Children can take turns being the leader as the rest of the children follow to the picnic.

 To encourage appropriate participation in the activity, give children a choice between two foods that they would like to take on the picnic. "Rafael, would you like to make a cheese sandwich or a ham sandwich?"

 Talk with the children about which foods they would like to take on a picnic. "Dominique, what do you like to eat at a picnic?"

Sandcastle Creations

Materials

- sandbox or baby pool partially filled with moist sand (add water as needed)
- sand tools, such as scoops, shovels, spoons, funnels, and sifters
- sandcastle molds, cookie cutters, pots, gelatin molds, and plastic cups
- shells, sand dollars, coral, or starfish, to use as decoration
- paper
- markers
- camera (optional)

Use a camera to take pictures of sandcastles.

Procedure

1. This activity may be completed outdoors or indoors using a baby pool placed on top of a shower curtain or large plastic mat.
2. Assist children into or to the edge of the sandbox and encourage them to create a sandcastle.
3. Demonstrate how to make imprints with shells to decorate the castle.
4. After each child has completed his sandcastle, ask him to draw a picture of his castle using paper and markers.
5. You may want to document each child's creation by taking a picture.
6. Display the photos of their creations in the *Beach Center*.

Adapt "Sandcastle Creations"

   Children may wear garden gloves or use tools rather than touching the sand.

 Use words to describe the wet sand.

 You may place sand in a large plastic container on a tabletop for children who need to use adaptive seating devices or sit in chairs.

 Use large handled tools or wrap tape around handles of tools to make them easier to grasp.

  Allow each child to initiate sand play at his own pace. Place the child's favorite plastic toy in the sand to encourage him.

Wading in the Ocean

Materials

- shower curtain or large plastic mat
- baby pool
- boats and other floating objects, such as toy fish and crabs, sponge toys
- large spoons
- nets
- scoops
- funnels
- buckets to catch fish
- swimsuits for the children (optional)

Procedure

1. This activity may take place outdoors or indoors. If outdoors, please remember to apply sunscreen to the children before beginning.
2. Partially fill the pool with warm water.
3. Help children change into swimsuits or clothes that can get wet.
4. Encourage children to catch the toy fish swimming in the "ocean."

Adapt "Wading in the Ocean"

 Children may use a swim ring or flotation device to assist with their sitting balance while in the pool.

 Children may use their hands to catch the fish if holding a tool is difficult.

 Children may prefer to kneel or sit outside the pool for play.

 Peers can help count fish as another child catches them.

Rainbow Sand Art

Materials

- dry tempera paint (several colors)
- sand
- small plastic bowls or containers
- spoons
- newspaper or plastic
- clean baby food jars with lids or clear plastic bottles with large openings and lids
- small funnels

Activities

Procedure

1. Mix dry tempera paint with sand to make several colors of sand.
2. Place colored sand in small plastic bowls or containers with spoons.
3. Cover table with newspaper or plastic for easy cleanup.
4. Give each child a clean baby food jar.
5. Demonstrate how to layer colors of sand using a spoon and funnel.
6. Allow each child to make his own rainbow sand art.
7. Secure lid on baby food jar or bottle.

Adapt "Rainbow Sand Art"

 Use larger jars with wider mouths and plastic pouring cups for ease in filling.

 Use large-handled spoons or wrap spoon handles with tape for children who have difficulty grasping.

 Label each sand container by color and name the color as the child adds it to the jar.

  Repeat the words "dip" and "pour" as the children fill the jars.

The Essential Literacy Connection

Books

Florian, Douglas. 1990. **A Beach Day**. New York: Greenwillow. *Great illustrations and simple text take readers for a day at the beach.*

Mayer, Mercer. 2001. **Beach Day**. New York: McGraw-Hill. *Little Critter and Dad spend the day at the beach.*

Pfister, Marcus. 1995. **Rainbow Fish**. New York: North-South Books. *Rainbow Fish learns a lesson about sharing and friendship when he shares his beautiful scales with the other fish.* *

Robbins, Ken. 1987. **Beach Days**. New York: Viking. *Real pictures portray what people do during a day at the beach.*

Rockwell, Anne, & Rockwell, Harlow. 1987. **At the Beach**. New York: Simon & Schuster. *Experience all there is to do with a toddler and her mother during their day at the beach.*

(*Available as a board book)

Other Literacy Materials

- beach postcards and brochures
- food items with labels for picnic
- photos of creations with names

Adding Spark to the Beach Center

Add a rocking boat or large appliance box decorated as a boat for the children to sit inside. Sing "Row, Row, Row Your Boat" with the children as they ride the boat in the ocean.

Evaluation of the Individual Child

Is the child:

1. Demonstrating an understanding of cause and effect?
2. Using new tools in the sand/water activities?
3. Interacting with adults and peers in the *Beach Center*?
4. Improving in fine motor activities such as eye-hand coordination?

A collection of shells encourages exploration and language.

Transportation Center

Overview

Cars, trucks, trains, planes, and boats are all ways to move from place to place. The *Transportation Center* provides opportunities to learn about these modes of transportation and to play with related props. Young children will enjoy experimenting with different ways of travel, planning trips, and purchasing tickets. This active area will encourage motor development as young children move and watch the vehicle's responses.

Learning Objectives

The child with special needs will:

1. Learn about modes of transportation that relate to his environment.
2. Expand vocabulary and language related to transportation.
3. Collaborate with others while playing with cars, trucks, trains, and/or boats.
4. Develop motor skills as they manipulate the toys in this center.
5. Build an understanding of cause and effect through experimentation.

Time Frame

This center can focus on the general topic of transportation or on a specific mode that is important to the children in this classroom. For example, a *Train Center* might be appropriate for a classroom that is close to a railroad track where children see trains each day. Another way to organize the *Transportation Center* is to begin with the general topic and then move to specific modes of transportation. The *Transportation Center* can be set up for several weeks or up to one month.

Letter to Parents or Guardians

Dear Parent or Guardian,

Americans enjoy their cars and trucks! Many people like to drive and travel to interesting places. Our new *Transportation Center* builds on this interest and provides a place for our children to learn about transportation. We are going to include miniature cars, trucks, buses, and planes in the center. We will even have a repair shop where children can take their broken vehicles.

In this center, your child will learn how things move. He or she will plan trips, look at maps, buy tickets, and enjoy the process. In the *Transportation Center*, your child will work with others and talk about his or her experiences. If you have been on a trip or are planning to take one, please come share your travel plans or experiences with us.

Layout of the Transportation Center

This center includes props related to moving and transportation. The *Transportation Center* will need ample room to encourage this type of activity. It will work well placed next to the *Block Center*, so materials can be interchanged for expanded play. A low table or riser (see page 313 in Chapter 5 for directions) can provide a surface for moving cars, trucks, buses, or trains at the children's eye level. Slanted boards or inclines can encourage experimentation with movement and speed. A station can provide a place for buying tickets, getting maps, and checking schedules.

Vocabulary Enrichment

boat	road
bus	ticket
car	train
delivery	transportation
map	travel
move	truck
plane	

Teacher- and Parent-Collected Props

- cardboard boxes, including large and shoe-size
- cardboard tubing in different sizes
- dowel rods (½" thickness)
- gravel
- large plastic storage container with low sides
- piece of vinyl
- PVC pipe pieces of varying widths and lengths
- sand
- scraps of wood/lumber
- variety of cars, trucks, trains, planes, or boats (include different materials and varying sizes)

Web of Integrated Learning

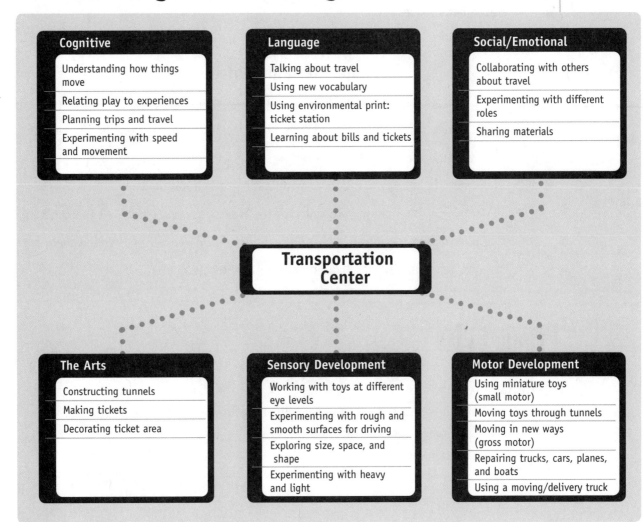

Cognitive
- Understanding how things move
- Relating play to experiences
- Planning trips and travel
- Experimenting with speed and movement

Language
- Talking about travel
- Using new vocabulary
- Using environmental print: ticket station
- Learning about bills and tickets

Social/Emotional
- Collaborating with others about travel
- Experimenting with different roles
- Sharing materials

Transportation Center

The Arts
- Constructing tunnels
- Making tickets
- Decorating ticket area

Sensory Development
- Working with toys at different eye levels
- Experimenting with rough and smooth surfaces for driving
- Exploring size, space, and shape
- Experimenting with heavy and light

Motor Development
- Using miniature toys (small motor)
- Moving toys through tunnels
- Moving in new ways (gross motor)
- Repairing trucks, cars, planes, and boats
- Using a moving/delivery truck

Terrain Vehicles

Materials

- 2 or 3 large plastic storage containers with low sides
- pieces of plastic
- shower curtain or large plastic bag
- small amount of sand, gravel, or rocks

Procedure

1. Prepare containers by lining them with plastic.
2. Place shower curtain or plastic bags on the floor of the *Transportation Center*.
3. Pour a layer of sand in one container, rocks or gravel in another container, and water in another.
4. Place a collection of small cars, trucks, and boats in each terrain.
5. Children can experiment with driving and moving the cars and trucks on the different surfaces.

Adapt "Terrain Vehicles"

 Put plastic containers on the tabletop where children can stand or kneel at play.

 Have child-size gloves available for children to wear if they do not want to touch sand or other terrain.

Make sure the area is well-lighted with lamps and natural light.

  Have one or two rules for the *Transportation Center*. Tell the children the rules during the introduction to the *Transportation Center* and remind them as needed, for example, "Sand and rocks stay in the containers."

Tunnel Play

Materials

- collection of tubes, such as paper rolls, toilet rolls, carpet, and plastic
- masking tape, electrical tape, or glue
- construction paper

Procedure

1. Children can connect the tubes with tape or glue to create tunnels for their cars, trucks, and trains.
2. Use clamps to hold tunnels together until dry, if glue is used.
3. As children move the toys through the tunnels, they experiment with size, space, and shape.

Adapt "Tunnel Play"

   Use duct tape to secure the regular tape dispenser to the tabletop so that it will not slide.

 Encourage children to use the words "in" and "out," as they move vehicles through the tunnels.

  Pre-cut small pieces of tape and stick them to the edge of a table for child to pull off and use.

 Connect the tunnels and give them to the child to use in his play if the child will not touch glue or tape.

 Adults or peers can paint the outside of tubes with red or yellow paint.

Tickets for Travel

Materials

- children's chairs
- collection of travel brochures or travel books
- chart paper
- markers or crayons
- materials to make tickets, including construction paper or poster board
- hole punch
- maps
- ink pad
- stamps that have symbols of different modes of transportation, such as a car, bus, plane, or boat

Procedure

1. Set up a ticket station with chairs for waiting.
2. Include a chart with different ways to travel, such as by bus, car, train, plane, or boat. Have words and pictures to represent the mode of transportation.
3. Include materials to create tickets.
4. Children can decide where they want to go and make tickets or purchase tickets to use for travel.
5. Tickets can be stamped or punched before the children leave for their trip.

Adapt "Tickets for Travel"

  Markers are easier to grasp and mark with than crayons or pencils.

 Write the words "Tickets for Sale" on the ticket station. Encourage children to use the words "Tickets" and "Sale," when working in the ticket station.

 Put an incline board (see pages 306–307 in Chapter 5 for directions) on a tabletop for placing tickets to stamp or write on.

  Pair a child with a peer who participates in sociodramatic play in the *Transportation Center*.

 Glue craft stick to the top of stamp to make it easier to grasp.

Delivery Truck

Children take turns using bulldozers and trucks.

Materials

- paper and markers to make signs
- small wagon or cardboard box
- rope or nylon string
- collection of boxes and food packages

Procedure

1. Place delivery signs around the *Transportation Center*. Deliveries can be made to the station, garage, airplane, or boat.
2. Put a sign on the "Delivery Truck" wagon or box.
3. Provide boxes and food packages for delivery.
4. Children can use the truck to deliver items to appropriate areas.

Adapt "Delivery Truck"

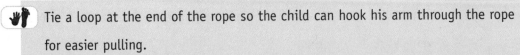 Tie a loop at the end of the rope so the child can hook his arm through the rope for easier pulling.

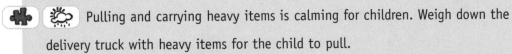 Pulling and carrying heavy items is calming for children. Weigh down the delivery truck with heavy items for the child to pull.

Use red or black tape on the floor to map out the road the delivery truck should follow.

Tell the child when you see him interacting appropriately in the *Transportation Center*. "I like the way you and Damon take turns making deliveries."

Garage/Fix-It Shop

Activities (sidebar)

Materials

- raised area created with blocks
- oil can (empty and clean)
- gas tank (made from cardboard box with hose)
- receipt book with pencil
- collection of tools, such as a wrench, screwdriver, hammer, and funnel
- work gloves

Procedure

1. Set up a garage where cars, trucks, and buses can come for repair and gas.
2. Children can determine which cars, trucks, and buses need repair.
3. The children can use tools and supplies as they repair the vehicles.

Children drive small cars and trucks on a narrow road.

Adapt "Garage/Fix-It Shop"

  Discuss with the children what type of work occurs in a garage and what types of vehicles need repairing.

   Place work tools on a table or on a tray with space between each item, providing a more organized environment for making choices.

 Vehicles may be repaired on a table if the child is unable to get down on the floor for play.

 Sing "Johnny Works With One Hammer" and insert the child's name into the song as he works.

The Essential Literacy Connection

Books

Burleigh, Robert. 1999. **It's Funny Where Ben's Train Takes Him**. New York: Orchard Books. *Ben draws a train with his crayon one night and hops on for a magical journey.*

Lewis, Kevin. 2002. **My Truck Is Stuck!** New York: Hyperion Press. *Two dogs driving a truckload of bones are stuck in a pothole. Smaller to larger vehicles try to pull them out with no success, until the tow truck finally gets the truck unstuck.*

Mayo, Margaret. 2002. **Dig Dig Digging**. New York: Henry Holt. *Different types of work trucks, from diggers to fire engines, are shown in action.*

O'Garden, Irene. 2003. **The Scrubbly Bubbly Car Wash**. New York: HarperCollins. *As the children and their father take their dirty car through the car wash, they describe, in rhyme, everything that happens inside.*

Powell, Alma. 2003. **My Little Wagon**. New York: HarperCollins. *A young bear uses her wagon to carry items for recycling, to take flowers into the garden, and to carry trash to the neighborhood cleanup. The message being sent is the importance of pulling your own weight to help the community.* *

Steen, Sandra, & Steen, Susan. 2003. **Car Wash**. New York: Puffin. *When they hit a mud puddle on the way to lunch, a father, daughter, and son go to the car wash and imagine they are going deep into the ocean in a submarine.*

Willems, Mo. 2003. **Don't Let the Pigeon Drive the Bus**. New York: Hyperion Press. *The bus driver asks that you watch the bus while he is taking a break, and he explains to never let the pigeon drive the bus. Sounds easy, except that the pigeon has always dreamed of driving a bus.*

(*Available as a board book)

Other Literacy Materials

- advertisements for cars and trucks
- signs created for the station
- tickets made by the class
- price list for the "fix-it" shop
- schedule books

Adding Spark to the Transportation Center

Place a suitcase and a variety of clothing in the *Transportation Center* for children to pack, unpack, and carry to other places in the center.

Evaluation of the Individual Child

Is the child:

1. Using new vocabulary related to transportation?
2. Using toys to represent actual modes of transportation? How?
3. Working out issues with others during play?
4. Developing fine or gross motor skills while moving transportation toys?

Farm Center

Overview

The *Farm Center* is popular with young children. They are very interested in the animals and activities that occur on a farm. In this center, they can wear farm clothes, plant seeds, prepare food, and pretend they are farmers. Playing in the *Farm Center* will help young children understand how farms work and how food is grown. This center provides a place to make connections to their heritage and learn to value the work of those who live on farms.

Learning Objectives

The child with special needs will:

1. Learn about farm animals.
2. Develop coordination through the use of farm tools.
3. Use names of farm equipment and tools in his play.
4. Work with other children on farm-related projects.

Time Frame

The *Farm Center* works well in the spring and/or fall of the year. Observe the interest of the children to determine how long the center will remain in the classroom. In most preschool classrooms, young children remain interested in the activity for three to four weeks. Adding the spark when participation is declining can expand this time.

Letter to Parents or Guardians	Dear Parent or Guardian,

Dear Parent or Guardian,

This spring, we will add a *Farm Center* to our classroom. In this center, the children will pretend to live on a farm and help with the farmer's work. They will feed pretend farm animals, plant seeds, and eat vegetables. All of these activities will lead to a better understanding of the workings of a farm. During this play, the children will enrich their language, develop motor skills, and learn to work together.

To get ready for our *Farm Center*, we will go on a field trip to a local farm. If you would like to go with us to see the cows, horses, chickens, and farm equipment, we would be happy to have you join us. Seeing a real working farm will help your child understand how farms operate and how important they are for each of us. They will use what they learn in their new *Farm Center*.

Layout of the Farm Center

This center can work indoors or outdoors. A cardboard box barn, a bale of hay, and large cardboard horse, cow, and chickens will add to the farm look. A clothesline for displaying and drying work clothes will add interest. A set of garden tools, gloves, and hand tools can also be included for farm play.

Vocabulary Enrichment

chicken	pick-up truck
cow	plant
eggs	rooster
farm	seeds
feed	tractor
horse	vegetables

Teacher- and Parent-Collected Props

- cake pans
- catalogs of farm equipment and supplies
- farm tools, such as a plastic hoe, shovel, bucket, and set of hand-held tools
- large cardboard boxes
- plastic eggs
- plastic or metal wash tub
- potting soil
- seed catalogs
- small farm toys
- wagon
- work clothes, such as overalls, farm hats, gloves, aprons, boots, plaid shirts, and bandanas

Web of Integrated Learning

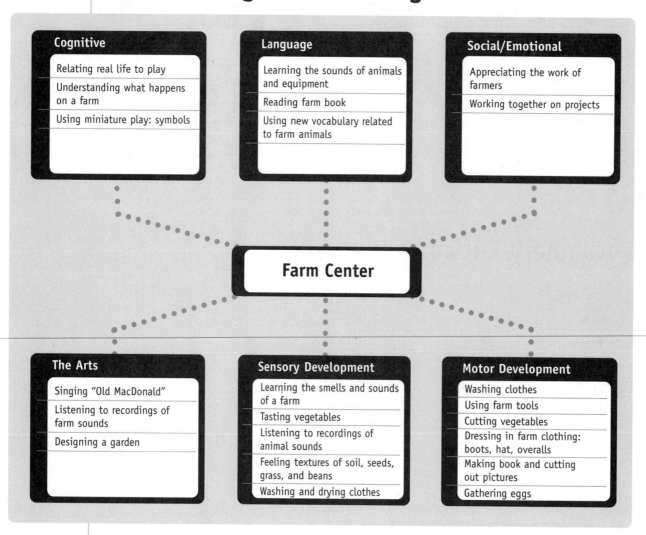

Cognitive
| Relating real life to play |
| Understanding what happens on a farm |
| Using miniature play: symbols |

Language
| Learning the sounds of animals and equipment |
| Reading farm book |
| Using new vocabulary related to farm animals |

Social/Emotional
| Appreciating the work of farmers |
| Working together on projects |

Farm Center

The Arts
| Singing "Old MacDonald" |
| Listening to recordings of farm sounds |
| Designing a garden |

Sensory Development
| Learning the smells and sounds of a farm |
| Tasting vegetables |
| Listening to recordings of animal sounds |
| Feeling textures of soil, seeds, grass, and beans |
| Washing and drying clothes |

Motor Development
| Washing clothes |
| Using farm tools |
| Cutting vegetables |
| Dressing in farm clothing: boots, hat, overalls |
| Making book and cutting out pictures |
| Gathering eggs |

Fresh Vegetables

Materials

- fresh green beans, potatoes, carrots, or other in-season vegetables
- plastic tablecloth
- plastic knives
- plate or plastic tray
- small paper or plastic cups
- salad dressing dip

What vegetable is growing here?

Procedure

1. Collect and wash the fresh vegetables.
2. Cover the table with a plastic tablecloth.
3. Let children cut and taste the fresh vegetables.
4. Provide an individual cup of dip to encourage children to eat the veggies.

Adapt "Fresh Vegetables"

Note: Raw vegetables can be difficult to chew and swallow. Make sure children do not have any feeding or swallowing problems, or consult with a speech pathologist.

 Select and consistently label a vegetable or two that will be familiar to the child.

 Let the child touch and smell the vegetables. Do not force them to taste vegetables.

 Talk about the color and shape of the vegetables.

 If the child is unable to cut with a plastic knife, he may be able to pull vegetables apart by using his fingers or bite into a whole vegetable.

"Social and emotional development expands during the preschool years. Young children learn how to interact with others."

Activities

Farm Animal Book

Materials

- farm magazines or pictures of farm animals
- zipper-closure plastic bags (quart size)
- markers
- colored construction paper
- stapler
- masking or electrical tape

Procedure

1. Provide pictures of farm animals for children in the *Farm Center*.
2. Place one picture inside a zipper-closure plastic bag to demonstrate how this can work.
3. Let the children select and cut out farm animal pictures they want to include in their book.
4. When children have completed their selections, add the name of the animal to the bag.
5. Staple the zipper-closure plastic bags together on the zipper side.
6. Cover the staples with masking or electrical tape.
7. During Circle Time, let children share the animal books they have created in the *Farm Center*.

Adapt "Farm Animal Book"

 Glue pictures to poster board or card stock and staple the pages together for a book that is easier to turn.

 Encourage the child to make the sounds of the farm animals he has selected for the book.

 If the child is unable to turn the pages of a book or cannot see the book, try placing individual pictures on an incline board (see page xxx in Chapter 5 for directions).

 Enlarge pictures of the animals.

 Most children who have Autism Spectrum Disorder like to look at books and pictures, so this activity is naturally appropriate for them.

Miniature Farm

What vegetable is growing here?

Materials

- large roasting tray (3" to 5" deep) or sturdy cardboard box
- plastic sheeting
- potting soil
- grass seed, beans, or corn seeds
- collection of small toy farm equipment, farm animals, and people

Procedure

1. Line the tray or box with plastic.
2. Place the potting soil inside the tray or box.
3. Plant and water the seeds.
4. Place miniature tractor, truck, car, and plastic people in the tray.
5. Set the miniature farm on a table or floor.
6. Children can use the props to play in the miniature farm.

Adapt "Miniature Farm"

   Provide plastic shovels or scoops with large handles to scoop the soil if child does not want to touch the dirt, or has difficulty using hands.

 Inform the children of one or two rules for this activity before beginning. For example, "Keep the dirt in the box."

 Sing "Old MacDonald Had a Farm" or play a recording of the song. Encourage children to sing along or to make animal sounds at appropriate times.

 Place tray or box on a table for easy access. The child may stand, kneel, or sit at the table.

Activities

Gathering Eggs

Materials

- hay or small twigs
- white glue
- 3 small cardboard boxes or 1 large box
- plastic white or tan eggs
- 2 small baskets or plastic strawberry containers

Procedure

1. Mix hay and twigs with glue to create a hen's nest.
2. Place two or three nests inside a cardboard box.
3. Set the box of nests inside the barn or in a corner of the *Farm Center*.
4. After the children leave, place eggs in the nests.
5. When they return, encourage the children to gather the eggs.
6. They can count, sort, and place eggs in the nests.

Adapt "Gathering Eggs"

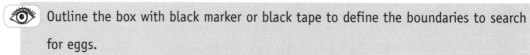 Outline the box with black marker or black tape to define the boundaries to search for eggs.

Use fabric instead of hay or leave the box empty if the child does not want to touch hay.

Add a plastic or cardboard hen to the nest. Talk about the hen and egg. Encourage the child to make the sound of a clucking hen.

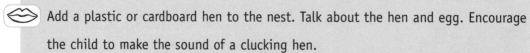 Peers can gather the eggs and then give them to another child to count.

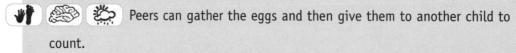 Label the box with the word "nest."

The Essential Literacy Connection

Books

Brown, Margaret Wise. 1995. **Big Red Barn**. New York: HarperCollins. *Rhyming text explains the daily routine for different animals on the farm.* *

Downey, Lynn. 2000. **The Flea's Sneeze**. New York: Henry Holt. *Flea needs a tissue, but all of the other animals in the barn are asleep, until...ah-choo, the flea sneezes. Can the animals all go back to sleep?*

Ehlert, Lois. 1993. **Growing Vegetable Soup**. New York: Harcourt. *After a father and son have planted, watered, and harvested their garden, they make delicious vegetable soup.*

Florain, Douglas. 1992. **Vegetable Garden**. San Diego, CA: Harcourt. *A family (father, mother, daughter, son, and dog) works together to grow a wonderful vegetable garden.*

Gunson, Christopher. 1996. **Over on the Farm**. New York: Random House. *This rhyming book counts the baby animals on the farm.*

Johnson, Paul Brett. 1997. **Farmer's Market**. New York: Orchard Books. *Take a journey with the family as they sell vegetables at the farmer's market.*

Lenski, Lois. 2001. **Cowboy Small**. New York: Random House. *Cowboy Small takes good care of his horse, Cactus, who helps him work on the farm.*

Meeker, Clare Hodgson. 1996. **Who Wakes Rooster?** New York: Simon & Schuster. *Rooster has the job of waking everyone on the farm, but who wakes rooster? The rising sun awakens rooster.* *

(*Available as a board book)

Other Literacy Materials

- farm and seed catalogs
- labels for miniature farm
- Farm Animal Books with labels of animals

Adding Spark to the Farm Center

Purchase or create a recording of animal and farm sounds. Play it in the *Farm Center*.

Evaluation of the Individual Child

Is the child:

1. Playing in the *Farm Center*?
2. Making animal sounds? Naming the animals? Which ones?
3. Able to use farm tools? What skills are developing?
4. Working with another child or in a group on an activity?

Family Center

Overview

A young child's family is the most important element in his life. The family unit provides the base for the developing child. This *Family Center* will focus on families of the children in the classroom. Today's families are composed of many combinations of people. In this center, all families are respected and included. Many young children have new babies in their families or know a family with a new addition. This center provides an opportunity to value babies as well as to recognize that the preschool child is older and more skilled.

Learning Objectives

The child with special needs will:

1. Recognize the importance of his family.
2. Learn the responsibilities of being a family member.
3. Use language as he talks about family.
4. Build confidence by making toys for babies.

Time Frame

This center works well when set up at the beginning of the year. It connects the classroom to the home and helps with the transition to a new place. It will usually be in the classroom for two to three weeks.

| **Letter to Parents or Guardians** | Dear Parent or Guardian, |

Dear Parent or Guardian,
Your family is very important to your child and to our program. Next week, we will focus on the families of our children. We would like to have pictures of your family and important people in your child's life for display in the *Family Center* in our classroom. Include the names of the people in the picture and the names your child uses for them.

We value your family and all the special people that are a part of your young child's life. If you do not have any photos available, we will have several days when we will take pictures in the *Family Center*. We are happy to make a picture of family members if you come by our classroom. During this week, we will also have several activities that involve the family, including a family picnic. Please join us in celebrating the family and the importance of these people in the lives of our young children.

Layout of the Family Center

This center can be located in any part of the classroom. It will need a wall space for display and family items. On this wall, display the words "Our Family" in large letters and display pictures of children and families. Remember to include pictures of different types of families and those from diverse cultures. If you have children from a specific race, culture, or heritage, be sure to include pictures of these families in the grouping. If there is limited space in the classroom, this center can be set up in the *Home Living Center* for the duration.

Vocabulary Enrichment

baby

brother

celebrations

family

grandparents

home/house

love

meals

parents (name used by child)

play

sister

Teacher- and Parent-Collected Props

- family pictures
- family treasures
- recipes

A display shares information with parents.

Web of Integrated Learning

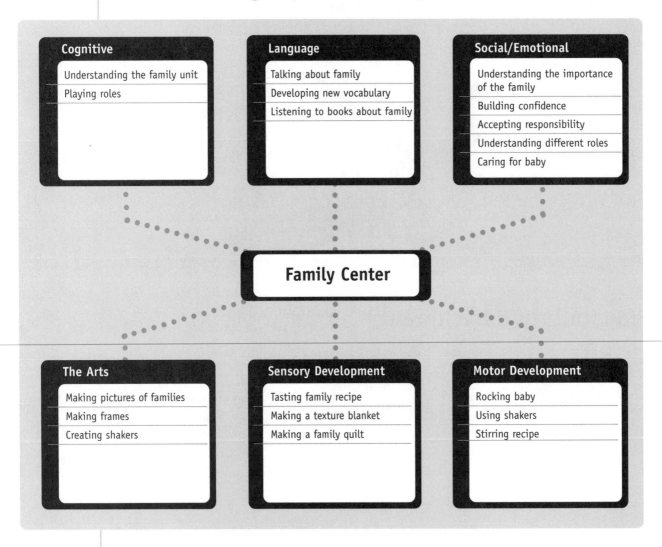

Cognitive
- Understanding the family unit
- Playing roles

Language
- Talking about family
- Developing new vocabulary
- Listening to books about family

Social/Emotional
- Understanding the importance of the family
- Building confidence
- Accepting responsibility
- Understanding different roles
- Caring for baby

Family Center

The Arts
- Making pictures of families
- Making frames
- Creating shakers

Sensory Development
- Tasting family recipe
- Making a texture blanket
- Making a family quilt

Motor Development
- Rocking baby
- Using shakers
- Stirring recipe

Family Gallery

Activities

Materials

- collection of pictures of children and their family members
- cardboard or poster board
- scissors
- glue
- foil

A child and her family are featured in the gallery.

Procedure

1. Ask families to send pictures of their family. (Be sure the pictures are labeled so they can be returned.)
2. Include pictures of your family or relatives. (Children will enjoy these, too.)
3. Create frames for pictures. Cut frames from poster board or cardboard, apply glue, and cover with foil.
4. On a wall in the *Family Center*, display the collection of family pictures.
5. For two to three days while the center is up, take additional pictures of family members.
6. Label each picture with names of the people in the photo.

Adapt "Family Gallery"

Talk with the child about the picture. Let him tell you the names of the people in the picture using his own personal identifier. Repeat the name and let him point to the person in the picture.

If foil is too flimsy to hold or manipulate, try construction paper for decorating the frames.

One child can apply the glue and another child can cover the frame with foil to stimulate cooperative play.

Pre-cut the frame from white or black poster board. Give the child pre-glued foil to stick to the frame.

Use glue sticks or glue pens so the child does not have to touch the glue.

Activities

New Family Members

Materials

- collection of diverse baby dolls
- baby equipment, such as baby clothing, bottles, eating equipment, baby bathtub, blankets, baby toys, rocking chair, diapers, high chair, and baby bed
- lullaby music

Procedure

1. Set up an area for celebration of new babies in the family.
2. Children can care for "new" babies by feeding them, bathing them, rocking them, singing to them, and playing with them.

Adapt "New Family Members"

  Sing "Rock-a-Bye Baby," as the child rocks a baby to sleep.

 Make sure there is enough space in the center for the child to maneuver mobility devices, such as a wheelchair, walker, or cane.

   Demonstrate how to hold, rock, and feed the baby to stimulate appropriate sociodramatic play.

  Put a baby, blanket, toy, and piece of clothing on the tabletop with space between each item for easy access and viewing.

Shaker

Materials

- small plastic bottles
- small or bright color items to float in liquid
- oil
- water
- funnel
- glue gun (adult only) to secure the lid after items are added

Activities

Procedure

1. Children create a toy for a baby with materials provided on a tray in the *Family Center*.
2. Children will select items they want to add to the bottle.
3. They can also pour the oil and water mixture into the bottle with a funnel.
4. Glue top securely.
5. Children can experiment with how they will teach the baby to use the shaker.
6. The baby toy may be given to a baby brother or sister or a baby friend.

Adapt "Shaker"

   Place the bottle and items for filling on a tray or in a shallow cardboard box to provide a boundary for the activity.

   Complete all steps for the child except filling with bright-color items to decrease the number of steps in the process.

  Give the child a choice between two items to place in the bottle.

  Use short sentences when talking with the child about the shaker. "Show the baby how to shake it."

 Sort materials and label the containers with words or pictures.

Texture Blanket

Materials

- square pieces of fabric with different textures and designs
- plastic tablecloth or piece of vinyl cut into an appropriate size for baby blanket
- quick-drying glue
- small paintbrush
- pie tray (for glue)

Procedure

1. Children can select the fabric pieces they will use.
2. Using a paintbrush, they can put glue on the base and add their piece of fabric.
3. Add to these pieces for several days. Allow to dry completely.
5. Add this texture blanket to the baby area and later move it to the *Home Living Center*.

Adapt "Texture Blanket"

 Look at baby pictures. Ask, "Who this is? What sounds did you make?" Suggest crying, or saying, "goo-goo," "Mama," and "Papa."

 Place pie tray on non-skid mat close to the child for easier access and less dripping.

  If too many choices overwhelm the child, try offering only two pieces of fabric.

  Give the child tongs or tweezers to pick up and dip fabric into the glue.

Family Recipe/Cookbook

Materials
- families' favorite recipes
- poster board
- markers
- lamination or clear plastic contact paper
- ingredients for the recipe
- cooking equipment needed for the recipe

Procedure
1. Create a cookbook of families' favorite recipes (keep the recipes simple).
2. Write recipe with pictures to help with directions. Laminate or cover with clear contact paper.
3. Keep the recipe charts in the center, so children can pretend to prepare the food with props.
4. Ask family members to come to the center to demonstrate a simple recipe their family enjoys.
5. It might be helpful to begin with a recipe you enjoy with your family.

Activities

MUFFIN RECIPE

muffin mix | ½ cup milk | cooking spray | mixing bowl | spoon / muffin tray

Set oven to 450°F.

Spray muffin tin with nonstick cooking spray.

Pour muffin mix into bowl.

Pour milk into bowl.

Mix together.

Fill muffin tin about ⅔ full.

Bake at 450°F for 10-14 minutes. Enjoy.

Adapt "Family Recipe/Cookbook"

If the child cannot attend to every step in the process, ask him to help you with the final step. He can feel proud that he finished the recipe.

Choose recipes with only two or three steps; for example, a grilled cheese sandwich.

To encourage taking turns and cooperation, pass the bowl around the table and let everyone have a turn stirring the food or let one child hold the bowl while the other stirs.

Use a recipe chart with pictures for the steps and ask the child to help you read the recipe. Encourage the child to identify the pictures.

Enlarge the handles of cooking utensils with foam or tape so they are easier to grasp.

The Essential Literacy Connection

Books

Cairo, Shelley. 1985. **Our Brother Has Down's Syndrome**. Toronto, Canada: Annick Press. *Two sisters tell about a typical day with their little brother, Jai, who has Down's Syndrome.*

Carle, Eric. 1994. **My Apron**. New York: Philomel Books. *Carle writes this story, based on his childhood visit to his uncle and aunt's house. While there, the boy's aunt makes him an apron so he can work with his uncle.*

Murphy, Mary. 1997. **I Like it When...** Orlando, FL: Harcourt. *The young penguin tells his mother all the things that he likes about their time together.* *

Root, Phyllis. 2001. **Rattletrap Car**. Cambridge, MA: Candlewick Press. *Each time the family's car breaks down on the way to the lake, the family works together to find a solution to get back on the road.*

Rylant, Cynthia. 2001. **The Relatives Came**. New York: Simon & Schuster. *When the relatives come, the house fills with people and hugs. There are so many people that meals have to be eaten in rotation, and arms and legs get tangled at bedtime! When summer ends and the relatives leave, beds feel "too big and too quiet," yet we know that the relatives will return next summer.*

Skutch, Robert. 1995. **Who's in a Family?** Berkeley, CA: Tricycle Press. *The illustrations show how different people make up a family.*

Williams, Vera B. 1997. **Lucky Song**. New York: Greenwillow Books. *Evie has a lucky day when she finds a new outfit hanging in her closet, her grandma cooks something that she likes, and her grandpa helps her make a new kite. At bedtime, her mother and father sing about her wonderful day.*

(*Available as a board book)

Other Literacy Materials

- family recipe book
- phone book
- photographs with names and labels

A quilt of squares decorated by families

Adding Spark to the Family Center

In the *Family Center*, plan a family picnic or family social for the children and their families. Let them help decide the menu, the activities, and the music. Try out the plans in the center. Prepare invitation cards with essential information, such as time, place, and other details. Children can decorate the invitations and place them in classroom mailboxes for parents or guardians.

Evaluation of the Individual Child

Is the child:

1. Talking about family and important people in his life? What language is he using?
2. Identifying and naming the people in the pictures on the Family Board?
3. Preparing a gift for a baby?
4. Confident working with others? How?

Bakery Center

Overview

Young children enjoy cooking activities. They are proud of the delicious food they have helped prepare. In the *Bakery Center*, preschoolers will learn cognitive sequencing, as they follow instructions in a step-by-step manner. Measuring items for a recipe allows the child to participate in pre-math activities. Children will manipulate new tools such as a hand-held mixer or measuring spoon. Children in the *Bakery Center* will be provided with opportunities to collaborate with others to make a final product. This center allows for playful, creative explorations that encourage cognitive, language, social, and motor development.

Learning Objectives

The child with special needs will:

1. Gain experience with pre-math skills in a meaningful way.
2. Cooperate with adults and peers to make a product.
3. Improve fine motor skills by using cooking tools.
4. Participate in activities related to daily living.

Time Frame

The *Bakery Center* is designed to remain open in a classroom for a period of two or three weeks. You might choose to open the *Bakery Center* to correspond with a special holiday or celebration. Observe children's participation in the center. If interest declines, it is time to change the *Bakery Center* or close it.

| **Letter to Parents or Guardians** | Dear Parent or Guardian,
Cooking with your child provides wonderful learning experiences. Children can learn simple pre-math and pre-reading skills while you help them look at the pictures on the back of a box, follow directions, and measure ingredients. Cooking allows children to practice important motor skills, such as pouring and stirring. Most importantly, when you finish cooking together, your child has made something that he or she can be proud of and can eat!

We have opened a *Bakery Center* in our classroom. We intend to compile a class cookbook to put in the center. Please help by sending in one of your child's favorite recipes to include in the cookbook. Simple recipes with a few simple steps and basic ingredients will work best! |

Layout of the Bakery Center

The *Bakery Center* is best suited for an area of the room with easy-to-clean floors and a table as a workstation. An accessible sink also assists with cleanup. You may choose to combine the *Bakery Center* with the *Home Living Center* for a short time so the sink, oven, and stove may be utilized in their play.

Vocabulary Enrichment

bake	oven
cook	recipe
cookbook	roll
cool	sift
hot	stir
ingredients	taste
measure	
mix	

Teacher- and Parent-Collected Props

- cash register
- clothes for dress up, such as aprons, oven mitts, chef's hat, and plastic or latex gloves
- cook books and magazines with recipes
- cooking utensils, including rolling pin, plastic or aluminum mixing bowl, hand-turned mixer or electric mixer, large spoons, cookie sheets, muffin tins, pie pans, measuring cups, and measuring spoons
- grocery items, such as empty boxes of cookie mix, oatmeal, disinfected egg cartons, milk containers, and other appropriate items
- plastic shower curtain for covering the work area table

Web of Integrated Learning

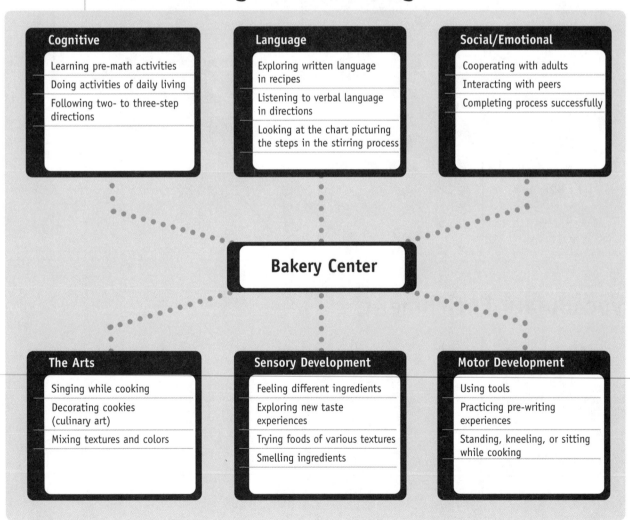

Cognitive
- Learning pre-math activities
- Doing activities of daily living
- Following two- to three-step directions

Language
- Exploring written language in recipes
- Listening to verbal language in directions
- Looking at the chart picturing the steps in the stirring process

Social/Emotional
- Cooperating with adults
- Interacting with peers
- Completing process successfully

Bakery Center

The Arts
- Singing while cooking
- Decorating cookies (culinary art)
- Mixing textures and colors

Sensory Development
- Feeling different ingredients
- Exploring new taste experiences
- Trying foods of various textures
- Smelling ingredients

Motor Development
- Using tools
- Practicing pre-writing experiences
- Standing, kneeling, or sitting while cooking

Chef's Hat

Materials

- white poster board
- scissors
- white paper bags
- stapler
- unbreakable mirror

Procedure

1. Cut out strips of poster board to make the headband of the hats.
2. Help the children fold down the top edge of each paper bag.
3. Assist the children in stapling the folded portion of the paper bag to the headband.
4. Children can decorate or write their names on their hats with markers.
5. Show the children what they look like in their hats using an unbreakable mirror.

Adapt "Chef's Hat"

  Sing, "This is the way we make chef's hats, make chef's hats, make chef's hats...so early in the morning" to the tune of "Here We Go 'Round the Mulberry Bush."

  Pre-make chef's hats and allow children to decorate them.

  A child who is sensitive to touch may not want to wear the chef's hat. Don't force the child to wear the hat, but praise the effort of making the hat. "Austin, you worked really hard on your hat."

Homemade Applesauce

Materials

- apples
- sharp knife (adult only)
- table knives
- cutting board(s)
- sugar (sweet apples may not need sugar added)
- measuring cup
- saucepan

Activities

- stove or hot plate (adult only)
- oven mitt or pot holder
- potato masher
- spoons
- bowls

Procedure

1. Peel apples for children. (Leave one apple unpeeled to show to children as a "before" model.)
2. Assist children in chopping apples using table knives. Please use close supervision for this task!
3. Children can add chopped apples, pour the sugar (as needed), and pour water into the saucepan.
4. Cook apples on the stove or hot plate, mashing them as they soften. Use words to describe the process and how the apples are changing.

Note: Closely supervise the use of a stove or hot plate.

5. Allow the cooked apples to cool, and then serve.
6. Discuss the taste, texture, feel, and smell of the applesauce as the children try it. "Were the apples hard or soft before we cooked them?" "Are the apples hard or soft now?"

Spreading applesauce on a biscuit

Adapt "Homemade Applesauce"

 Pre-chop apples for the children. Be sure to show the children a pre-peeled apple and a pre-chopped apple so they can understand the steps.

 Children can taste the raw apples and the applesauce to help them learn to discriminate between items.

  If the child is sensitive to the textures of foods, encourage him to touch and smell the applesauce, rather than eat it.

 If the child is having difficulty attending to the task, ask him to help you pour, throw away, and clean up the mess as you go.

Making Cookies

Materials

- simple sugar cookie recipe and ingredients
- measuring spoons and cups
- spoons
- spatula
- mixing bowl
- mixer
- rolling pins
- wax paper
- flour
- cookie cutters
- cookie sheet
- sprinkles or other decoration
- oven mitt
- oven (adult only)

Procedure for Mixing Cookies

1. Read the recipe to the children.
2. Present each ingredient to the children.
3. Invite children to take turns measuring and pouring ingredients into the mixing bowl.
4. Assist children in mixing the cookie dough.

Procedure for Baking Cookies

1. Give each child the prepared cookie dough on floured wax paper.
2. Demonstrate flattening out dough with fingers and then rolling out dough with a rolling pin. Assist children with this process, if necessary.
3. Allow children to select their cookie cutter(s).
4. Cut out cookies, decorate them, and place them on a cookie sheet, helping as needed.
5. If possible, let children watch you place cookies in the oven and set the timer. If not, explain to the children the next step in the process.
6. Be sure to discuss the entire process with the children as you go, using words such as "measure," "stir," "roll," and "bake."
7. Allow cookies to cool and then serve!

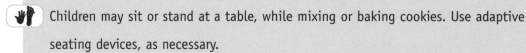

Adapt "Making Cookies"

 Break this activity up into two different days, mixing cookies one day and baking cookies the next.

Children may sit or stand at a table, while mixing or baking cookies. Use adaptive seating devices, as necessary.

Let children feel each ingredient before it is placed in the bowl. Help them identify cookie cutters by touch.

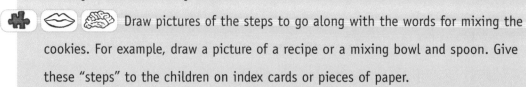 Draw pictures of the steps to go along with the words for mixing the cookies. For example, draw a picture of a recipe or a mixing bowl and spoon. Give these "steps" to the children on index cards or pieces of paper.

Cleaning Up Our Mess

Materials
- accessible sink or sand/water table slightly filled with warm water
- liquid soap
- washcloths, sponges, scrub brushes
- pots, pans, cooking utensils (dirty or clean)

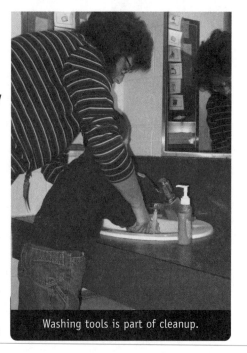

Washing tools is part of cleanup.

Procedure
1. Cleaning up is a necessary part of cooking and can be just as much fun when bubbles and water are involved!
2. Place warm water and liquid soap in a sink or water table. Mix well to make many bubbles.
3. Assist children in placing pots, pans, and cooking utensils into the sink.
4. Make sponges, washcloths, and scrub brushes available.
5. Children can sing "The Cleanup Song" ("This is the way we wash our dishes...") to the tune of "Here We Go 'Round the Mulberry Bush."
6. Children can also use cleaning materials to wash the table or preparation area.

Activities

Adapt "Cleaning Up Our Mess"

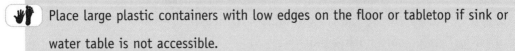 Place large plastic containers with low edges on the floor or tabletop if sink or water table is not accessible.

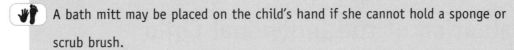 A bath mitt may be placed on the child's hand if she cannot hold a sponge or scrub brush.

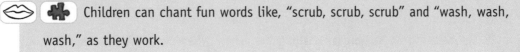 Children can chant fun words like, "scrub, scrub, scrub" and "wash, wash, wash," as they work.

The Essential Literacy Connection

Books

Carle, Eric. 1995. **Walter the Baker**. New York: Simon & Schuster. *Walter the baker discovers pretzels when he is challenged to make a roll that the rising sun can shine through three times.*

Hayward, Linda. 1998. **Baker, Baker, Cookie Maker**. New York: CTW Publishing. *Cookie Monster wants a cookie, so he bakes batch after batch of cookies, but sells them faster than he can eat them.*

Hutchins, Pat. 1989. **The Doorbell Rang**. New York: HarperCollins. *Ma bakes a dozen cookies for her two children, but when the doorbell rings and rings and rings, they have to figure how to divide the cookies, so they share them equally.*

Morris, Ann. 1993. **Bread Bread Bread**. New York: William Morrow. *This book shows a variety of breads that are eaten all over the world.*

Numeroff, Laura. 1996. **If You Give a Mouse a Cookie**. New York: HarperCollins. *When a young child gives a mouse a cookie, he finds that the mouse will ask for many other things, which in turn teaches a lesson in cause and effect.*

Numeroff, Laura. 1999. **The Best Mouse Cookie**. New York: HarperCollins. *Mouse works in the kitchen mixing and baking cookies to share with his friend.*

(*Available as a board book)

Other Literacy Materials

- advertisements for bakeries
- photographs of ingredients with names and prices
- recipe cards and charts

Adding Spark to the Bakery Center

Take a visit to a kitchen in your school, or to a local bakery or restaurant. Talk about the large stoves, ovens, and cooking tools. Ask questions such as, "What is the oven used for?" to guide children's thoughts.

Evaluation of the Individual Child

Is the child:

1. Participating in the simple measuring of ingredients?
2. Cooperating or participating alongside others when making products?
3. Using new tools in the *Baking Center*?
4. Participating in simple activities of daily living such as cleaning up?

Gardening Center

Overview

Growing plants provides concrete experiences for young children. In the *Gardening Center*, they are able to see and care for plants while observing the changes that occur. Here, children can actively participate in planting, watering, and arranging. These opportunities help young children learn about their world and how they can influence the environment. They will develop confidence in their abilities as they work in new areas and take responsibility for an important task.

Learning Objectives

The child with special needs will:

1. Experience growing plants and observe changes.
2. Develop a consistent pattern for caring for plants.
3. Learn the names of plants and tools used in gardening.
4. Share in work and tasks that relate to gardening.
5. Appreciate the plants in their environment.

Time Frame

Spring is the best time for this center. It will be in operation for a month or more, so the children will have the opportunity to observe changes. If this amount of time is not possible, the plants can be moved outdoors to continue their growth. This will expand the environment and area where plants can grow and be cared for.

Letter to Parents or Guardians

Dear Parent or Guardian,

Spring is here and we are setting up our *Gardening Center*. This area provides a place to plant, water, and enjoy growing things. During this process, your child will experience the care and growth of real plants.

If you are a gardener or enjoy working with plants, we invite you to participate in our *Gardening Center*. We will also plant flowers and vegetables on our playground. This extension of our *Gardening Center* will provide another place to observe and enjoy the changes in plants during this season.

Layout of the Gardening Center

Create a covered area over a portion of the *Gardening Center*. This can be built with plastic and dowel rods or plastic hung from fishing line attached to the ceiling. This area will be the greenhouse where plants are grown. The water table can be used for the potting area. Another section can have a table with displays of pots, baskets, and garden tools.

Vocabulary Enrichment

dig

flowers

grow

plants

roots

seeds

shovel

soil

transplant

vegetables

water

Washing tools is part of cleanup.

Teacher- and Parent-Collected Props

■ clear plastic cups and measuring cups

■ collection of pots of varying sizes

■ garden gloves

■ hand gardening tools, such as a shovel, rake, and hoe

■ magnifying glasses

■ plant trays

■ plastic

■ plastic tray

■ potting soil

■ spray bottle and watering can

■ tongue depressors or craft sticks

Web of Integrated Learning

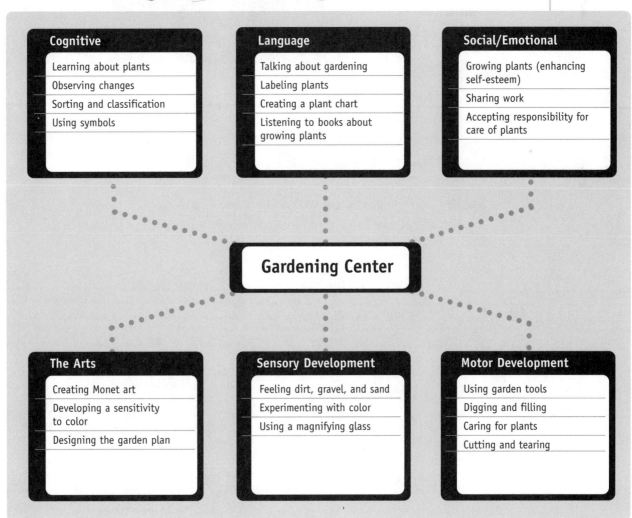

Cognitive

| Learning about plants |
| Observing changes |
| Sorting and classification |
| Using symbols |

Language

| Talking about gardening |
| Labeling plants |
| Creating a plant chart |
| Listening to books about growing plants |

Social/Emotional

| Growing plants (enhancing self-esteem) |
| Sharing work |
| Accepting responsibility for care of plants |

Gardening Center

The Arts

| Creating Monet art |
| Developing a sensitivity to color |
| Designing the garden plan |

Sensory Development

| Feeling dirt, gravel, and sand |
| Experimenting with color |
| Using a magnifying glass |

Motor Development

| Using garden tools |
| Digging and filling |
| Caring for plants |
| Cutting and tearing |

Activities

Baby Plants From Parent Plant

Materials

- cuttings from plants (those that root well include airplane plant, cane, coleus, piggyback plant, and ivy)
- potting soil and small pots or trays
- watering can
- books about plants
- chart paper, markers, and paper for journal writing
- magnifying glasses

A tent becomes a greenhouse.

Procedure

1. Include plants in this center.
2. Children can start new plants by making cuttings and rooting them in water.
3. Provide informational books about plants to stimulate ideas.
4. Draw a simple chart with plant parts including roots.
5. Observe the growth of the roots. Have magnifying glasses available.
6. Transfer the rooting to a pot with soil.
7. A plant journal can be used to record plantings and growth over time.

Adapt "Baby Plants From Parent Plant"

  If the child does not want to touch dirt, provide child-size gloves.

  Place word labels on the plants, such as "ivy" or "airplane plant." Talk about the colors, shapes, and textures of the plants as the children plant them.

 Place all materials on the tabletop within easy reach of the child.

  Organize materials onto trays or pans so the environment is less cluttered.

Experimenting With Color

Materials

- 5 identical white cut flowers, such as a carnation, daisy, marigold, or any other white flower
- 5 clear plastic bottles or vases
- food coloring (to make 4 different colors)
- magnifying glasses
- large calendar

Procedure

1. Set up an experiment.
2. Follow these steps in the process:

   1. Place water in each bottle.
   2. Put one flower in each of the five bottles.
   3. Let them sit in the center for several days.
   4. Go to the *Gardening Center* and add one food coloring to each of the four bottles.
   5. After three to five days, observe changes.

3. Discuss with the children the changes and why they occurred. How are the flowers different and how are they the same?

Adapt "Experimenting With Color"

 Name the color of the flowers before and after the experiment.

  Give the child a choice between two colors to add. "Would you like red or blue?"

  Pair the child with a friend to share in the experiment with one flower.

 Set bottles on top of a light colored tray or paper. Add extra drops of food coloring to the water.

Activities

Flowers or Vegetables?

Materials

- pictures of flowers and vegetables
- scissors
- index cards
- markers
- plastic vegetables and flowers
- 2 small baskets
- catalogs of fruits and vegetables

Procedure

1. Children can cut out pictures of flowers and vegetables.
2. Glue each picture to an index card.
3. Label two baskets: "flowers" and "vegetables."
4. Children can sort the pictures into the appropriate basket.

Adapt "Flowers or Vegetables"

  Use the word "flower" or "vegetable," rather than specific names of the plants. Discuss how they differ.

  A child who has difficulty with picture symbols can use the plastic and artificial flowers to sort into the baskets.

 Place baskets on a non-skid mat so they will be more stable for filling.

 Demonstrate how to sort the pictures.

Monet Garden Mural

Materials

- print or picture of one of Monet's garden watercolors (See *Linnea in Monet's Garden* by Cristina Bjork)
- large piece of paper
- tape
- blue and green tempera paint
- paintbrushes of various sizes

Activities

Procedure

1. During Circle Time talk about the *Gardening Center*. Include information about how many artists liked to paint pictures of beautiful gardens. Identify Monet as one of those artists and include a children's book about his garden paintings in the center.

2. Tape a large piece of paper on the wall of the *Gardening Center*. Place plastic behind the paper and on the floor to minimize cleanup.

3. Provide containers of two colors of paint, one blue and one green

4. Children can paint flowers and forms they see in flower gardens.

5. The mural can be developed over several days.

6. When it is complete, talk about the mural in blues and greens in discussion after Center Time.

Adapt "Monet Garden Mural"

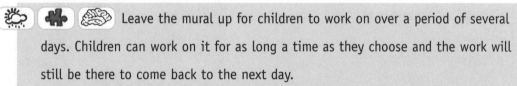 Leave the mural up for children to work on over a period of several days. Children can work on it for as long a time as they choose and the work will still be there to come back to the next day.

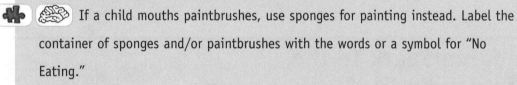 If a child mouths paintbrushes, use sponges for painting instead. Label the container of sponges and/or paintbrushes with the words or a symbol for "No Eating."

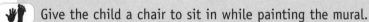 Give the child a chair to sit in while painting the mural.

Tape netting under the paper. Then, tape paper to the wall with black or red tape. This will provide a child tactile and visual cues as to where to paint.

The Essential Literacy Connection

Books

Bunting, Eve. 1994. **Flower Garden**. San Diego, CA: Harcourt Brace. *As a birthday surprise for her mother, a young girl and her father make a window box flower garden for their apartment in the city.*

Carle, Eric. 2001. **The Tiny Seed**. New York: Aladdin Library. *This story teaches children about the life cycle of a plant by showing the stages of growth from seedling to beautiful flower.* *

Ehlert, Lois. 1998. **Planting a Rainbow**. San Diego, CA: Harcourt Brace. *In simple steps, Ehlert takes her young readers through the steps of planting a garden, from planning the garden and choosing seeds to planting them and enjoying the flowers.*

Gliori, Debi. 2002. **Flora's Surprise!** New York: Orchard Books. *Flora's family loves to plant gardens, but they all laugh when she plants a brick and says she is growing a house. They are all surprised in the spring when a bird makes her home in the brick.*

Parkinson, Kathy. 1986. **The Enormous Turnip**. Morton Grove, IL: Albert Whitman & Company. *Join the family as they try to pull an enormous turnip from the garden.*

Rockwell, Anne. 1998. **One Bean**. New York: Walker and Company. *A young narrator describes the process of planting a bean, how it sprouts, and what it grows into.*

Schaefer, Lola. 2000. **This Is the Sunflower**. New York: Greenwillow. *This book explains how nature helps continue the life cycle of the plant by spreading the seeds of the sunflower.*

(*Available as a board book)

Other Literacy Materials

- advertisements and sales tags created by children
- Monet posters or prints of garden with bridge
- plant catalogs
- plant journal

A child looking at plants in a catalog

Adding Spark to the Gardening Center

Have a plant sale. Create advertisements for the sale, decorate pots, and set up the sales area with a cash register, wagons, and shopping baskets.

Evaluation of the Individual Child

Is the child:

1. Participating in rooting and planting?
2. Following a planned sequence in caring for plants or the experiment?
3. Focused on an activity in the *Gardening Center*? For how long?
4. Using vocabulary and language related to plants?

Nighttime Center

Overview

Young children are interested in what happens at night. This center will provide a non-frightening night environment and allow children to play through fears they might have. It will also include experiences that will build their understanding of the activities that occur during the night.

Learning Objectives

The child with special needs will:

1. Explore materials that relate to night.
2. Deal with feelings about nighttime.
3. Develop language that is inspired by nighttime.
4. Share props while working with others.

Time Frame

This center will be set up in the classroom for a short time. It will maintain the children's interest for approximately two to three weeks. It works especially well during the winter, when nights are longer and more time is spent in the dark.

Letter to Parents or Guardians

Dear Parent or Guardian,

We will set up a *Nighttime Center* next week. Many young children are concerned about night and things that might happen during the night. In this center, they can pretend that it is nighttime and play without fear.

When your child is at home, talk to him or her about the *Nighttime Center*. Ask your child questions about the shadow screen and night box. Talk to your child about what he or she does at nighttime at home, talk about the bedtime routine, and share stories he or she likes to hear at this special time. This area will assist your child in adjusting and accepting the nighttime period.

Layout of the Nighttime Center

Placing a canopy over a large corner section of the *Nighttime Center* will create a semi-dark area (see pages 304–305 in Chapter 5 for directions). Stars may be hung from the fabric to create a nighttime atmosphere. A clamp lamp or small floor lamp can provide low light for the area. Nighttime clothing may be displayed with flashlights and lanterns. A blanket could be placed on the floor at the edge of the dark area.

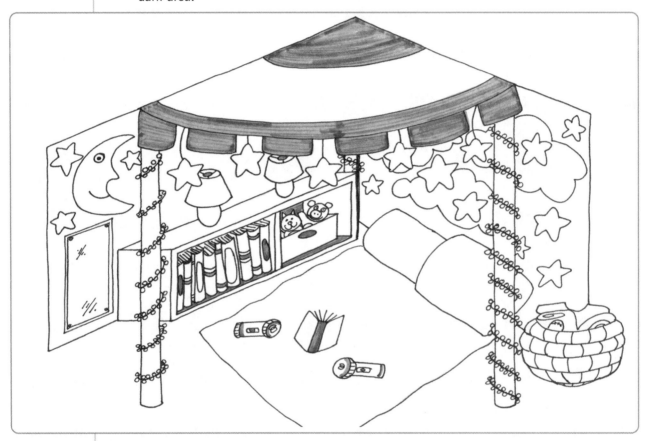

Vocabulary Enrichment

afraid	pajamas
baby	shadow
dark	sleep
flashlight	stars
night	twinkle

Teacher- and Parent-Collected Props

- blankets and sheets
- clamp light or floor lamp
- dark colored sheet
- flashlights
- foil
- pajamas or slippers
- soft toys

Flashlights add intrigue to the center.

Web of Integrated Learning

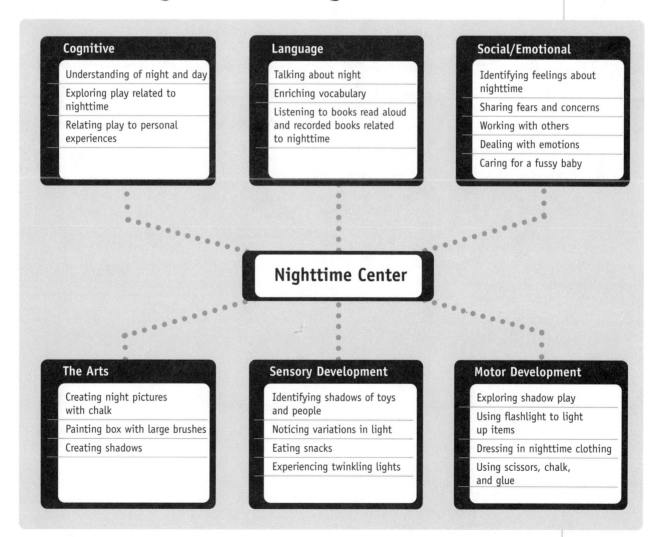

Cognitive
- Understanding of night and day
- Exploring play related to nighttime
- Relating play to personal experiences

Language
- Talking about night
- Enriching vocabulary
- Listening to books read aloud and recorded books related to nighttime

Social/Emotional
- Identifying feelings about nighttime
- Sharing fears and concerns
- Working with others
- Dealing with emotions
- Caring for a fussy baby

Nighttime Center

The Arts
- Creating night pictures with chalk
- Painting box with large brushes
- Creating shadows

Sensory Development
- Identifying shadows of toys and people
- Noticing variations in light
- Eating snacks
- Experiencing twinkling lights

Motor Development
- Exploring shadow play
- Using flashlight to light up items
- Dressing in nighttime clothing
- Using scissors, chalk, and glue

Activities

Night Pictures

Materials

- black construction paper
- colored chalk
- foil
- scissors
- glue
- clothesline

Procedure

1. Provide black construction paper.
2. Children use chalk to draw pictures of night.
3. Night features can be cut or torn from foil and added to the picture.
4. Creations can be hung on a line in the *Nighttime Center*.
5. Children can add to the pictures during the operation of the center.

Adapt "Night Pictures"

  Secure black paper with tape, a clipboard, or non-skid backing.

  Have a peer demonstrate how to cut or tear foil pieces and adhere them to the picture.

 Label pictures with the child's name and let the child return to work on the picture later if he chooses.

 Tape black paper to the table. Make borders with white paper. Provide foil and white chalk for high contrast.

  Use pictures with labels to show the child the order in which the activity should be completed.

Night Box

Materials

- large cardboard boxes
- black paint and paintbrushes
- scissors
- glow-in-the-dark paper
- glue
- collection of flashlights

Procedure

1. Children will help create a night box.
2. They can use black paint on the inside and outside of the cardboard box.
3. Cut holes in the sides of the box to provide some light.
4. Glue pieces and stars that glow-in-the-dark on the inside of the box.
5. Provide flashlights to use inside the box.
6. Children can light stars and glowing pieces in the box using flashlights.

Adapt "Night Box"

 Wrap foam or tape around handles of paintbrushes so they are easier to hold.

   Provide glow-in-the-dark stickers to decorate the box.

 Set a flashlight inside the box if the child cannot hold or manipulate the light independently.

 This activity should be visually stimulating for children.

  Use words to describe things seen at night ("stars," "moon," or "dark").

Pajama Party

Materials

- collection of unusual pajamas
- snack food
- paper plates
- books or recordings
- soft toys
- blanket

Procedure

1. Children can select and wear pajamas.
2. They can prepare a midnight snack.
3. Snack possibilities might include crackers, pretzels, or fruit.
4. After eating their snack, the children can read or listen to stories.
5. If they feel sleepy, they can lounge on a blanket in the *Nighttime Center*.

Activities

Adapt "Pajama Party"

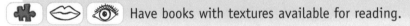 Provide large-size pajamas or nightgowns with short sleeves and/or short pants for easier dress up.

Provide a chair for child to sit on while trying on pajamas or slippers.

Decrease the number of materials available in the *Nighttime Center* if child is having difficulty making choices.

Have books with textures available for reading.

Midnight Baby Feeding

Materials

- recording of babies crying and CD or tape player
- collection of baby dolls
- baby equipment, such as bottles, blankets, diapers, cribs, and rocking chair
- books or soft music

Procedure

1. Play the recording of crying babies in the *Nighttime Center*.
2. Children can feed and rock babies.
3. Others may choose to read to the babies or to listen to music.

Adapt "Midnight Baby Feeding"

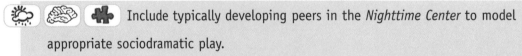 Include typically developing peers in the *Nighttime Center* to model appropriate sociodramatic play.

When introducing the *Nighttime Center*, inform the children of one or two simple rules. For example, "Keep your feet on the floor when you rock the baby."

Children with Autism typically enjoy the movement of a rocking chair.

Sing simple lullabies with children as they rock their babies and put them to bed.

Make sure there is plenty of floor space in the center for moving around.

Shadows on the Wall

Shadows respond to children's moves.

Materials

- shadow screen (see pages 314–315 in Chapter 5 for directions)
- light source
- collection of items that might cast a unique shadow, such as a tree branch, puppet, stuffed animals, toy mop, or broom

Procedure

1. Build a shadow screen.
2. Place a light behind the screen to produce shadows.
3. Provide a collection of props that children can use to create shadows.
4. Talk with the children about the shadows they are making in the *Nighttime Center*.

Adapt "Shadows on the Wall"

  Some children are afraid of stuffed animals. Replace them with plastic animals for making shadows.

  Have a seat available for children in case they get tired of standing.

 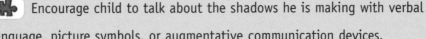 Encourage child to talk about the shadows he is making with verbal language, picture symbols, or augmentative communication devices.

 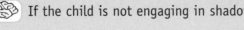 If the child is not engaging in shadow play, ask him to make a specific shadow. "Julio, show me how you make a shadow with that tree branch."

The Essential Literacy Connection

Books

Boynton, Sandra. 1982. **The Going to Bed Book**. New York: Little Simon. *All of the animals on the boat watch the sun go down and get ready for bed.* *

Boynton, Sandra. 2000. **Pajama Time!** New York: Workman. *Join the lovable animals as they prepare for bedtime.*

Johnson, Ryerson. 1989. **Why Is Baby Crying?** Niles, IL: Albert Whitman. *Mommy and Daddy try to soothe the crying baby by feeding, diapering, offering a pacifier, and so on. However, nothing calms the baby. Finally, Mommy realizes the baby only wants to be held and loved.*

Keller, Holly. 1988. **Geraldine's Blanket**. New York: HarperCollins. *Geraldine's parents want her to part with her blanket, but what will Geraldine decide?*

Rathmann, Peggy. 2002. **Goodnight, Gorilla**. New York: Putnam. *In this picture book, follow the zookeeper through his nightly routine, and watch as the animals follow him home.*

Schaefer, Carole Lexa. 2003. **Full Moon Barnyard Dance**. Cambridge, MA: Candlewick Press. *When the barnyard animals cannot sleep, they dance by the pond and learn to be friends.*

(*Available as a board book)

Other Literacy Materials

- label night pictures
- listen to recordings: books, sounds, or music
- read bedtime books to baby

Adding Spark to the Nighttime Center

Add a string of twinkle holiday lights to the edge of the canopy (see pages 304–305 in Chapter 5 for directions) or inside the night box, to make the area more visually interesting and less dark.

Evaluation of the Individual Child

Is the child:

1. Talking about his feelings about night?
2. Using vocabulary related to the night? What words are used?
3. Using motor skills in manipulating props? Which ones?
4. Working with others? In what ways?

Restaurant Center*

Overview

Many children have experienced eating in restaurants. These individual experiences can range from eating fast food to dining in elegant settings. In this center, children can use their experiences in their play. They can buy, sell, cook, decorate, create menus, and talk with their customers. During these activities, they will try out new roles and learn about working with people.

Learning Objectives

The child with special needs will:

1. Use personal experiences in his play.
2. Create items that relate to the restaurant.
3. Talk with co-workers and customers.
4. Work with others to operate the restaurant.

Time Frame

Select a type of restaurant that many of the children in the classroom have experienced. It can be a fast food restaurant, an ethnic restaurant, or any popular restaurant in their area. Their experiences will help the *Restaurant Center* sustain the children's interest for three to four weeks.

Letter to Parents or Guardians

Dear Parent or Guardian,

In today's busy times, many families eat some of their meals in restaurants or use carryout. Our new *Restaurant Center* will help the children understand how these businesses work. In this center, they will plan and prepare food, create menus, and take orders. They will also serve food and play the part of customers, allowing them to experience different roles in a restaurant operation.

Our restaurant will be "open to the public" for lunch during the third week of operation. We will let you know when it will be open so you can join us for a light lunch in the *Restaurant Center*.

---

*In this book, a Mexican restaurant is used to demonstrate how the center can work. The same format can be used with other types of restaurants by changing the decoration and props.

Layout of the Restaurant Center

This center will need several different areas. It should include a food preparation area, drive-by pickup area, and tables and chairs for serving food. Provide charts of the food and cost, so customers can see what is being served. Decorate the eating area with the theme of the restaurant. Tables should have tablecloths and eating utensils. There should be a place to pay the bill with a cash register and other relevant props.

Vocabulary Enrichment

bill	manager
charge	menus
cleanup	money
cook	prepare
customer	purchase
food	serve
food for specific restaurant, such as tacos, burritos, nacho chips, salsa, and other related food	waiter

Teacher- and Parent-Collected Props

- advertisements
- cleaning cloths and spray bottles
- cooking utensils
- decorations for restaurant theme (in this case, Mexican)
- dishes and eating utensils
- highchair
- large containers for cooking and serving
- paper for bills
- plastic play food
- sample menus
- serving trays
- stove or oven
- tablecloths

Pancakes with syrup at a restaurant

Web of Integrated Learning

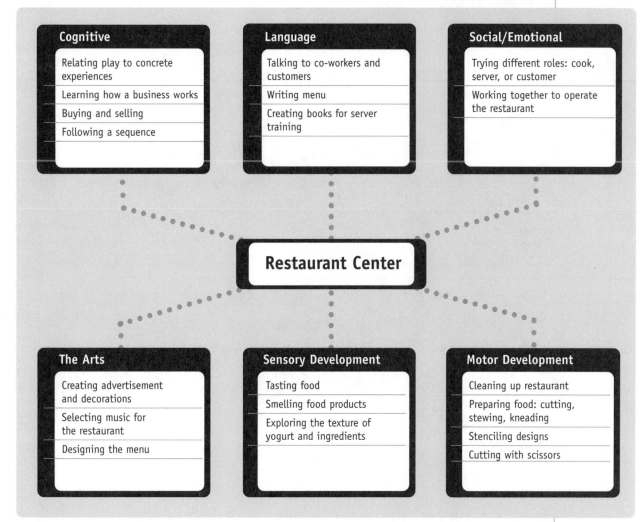

Cognitive

Relating play to concrete experiences
Learning how a business works
Buying and selling
Following a sequence

Language

Talking to co-workers and customers
Writing menu
Creating books for server training

Social/Emotional

Trying different roles: cook, server, or customer
Working together to operate the restaurant

Restaurant Center

The Arts

Creating advertisement and decorations
Selecting music for the restaurant
Designing the menu

Sensory Development

Tasting food
Smelling food products
Exploring the texture of yogurt and ingredients

Motor Development

Cleaning up restaurant
Preparing food: cutting, stewing, kneading
Stenciling designs
Cutting with scissors

Activities

Creating Advertisements

Materials

- large sheets of paper
- markers
- Styrofoam meat or vegetable trays
- craft knife (adult only)
- old magazines
- newspaper advertisements
- glue
- scissors

Procedure

1. In Circle Time, talk about the opening of the new restaurant and the need to advertise.
2. Provide paper and tools for use in creating a large advertisement for the restaurant.
3. Include Styrofoam trays with shapes cut in them (done with a craft knife).
4. Children can stencil shapes on the chart, if they choose.
5. Use magazines and newspapers to add other decoration.
6. Include the names of the children who developed the advertisement.

Adapt "Creating Advertisements"

 Discuss what the advertisements should say. Write the children's words on the advertisement.

 Partially complete steps of the process so that each child can complete the task independently.

 Allow the child to stand and work at an easel or sit on a chair turned around with the back facing the table.

 Pre-cut pictures and identify them for the child. This allows the child to choose which pictures he would like to use.

Food Preparation

Activities

Materials

- simple recipe that matches theme of restaurant
- large index cards
- markers
- ingredients needed for the recipe
- large serving trays
- rubber gloves

Procedure

1. Create a recipe card for the food preparation.
2. Use drawings to make the steps easy to follow.
3. Children can follow directions and create the food.
4. Provide the utensils and tools needed in food preparation.
5. Food can be displayed on the counter and sold.

Adapt "Food Preparation"

Note: Children with Spina Bifida and other diagnoses may have a latex allergy, which can be life-threatening. Be sure to check for latex allergies before using latex gloves with any child.

  Make a large recipe poster with simple steps and enlarged pictures.

  Set up the food preparation like an assembly line with each child taking one step in the process.

  If the child does not like to be touched by other children, place him at the end of the table where he has more room.

"[Young children's] thinking is concrete, focusing on the real things they can see, touch, and manipulate."

Activities

Book for Server Training

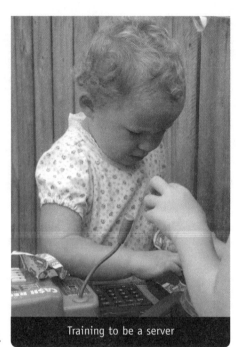

Training to be a server

Materials

- paper
- marker or pencil
- plastic picture covers
- folder
- receipt/bill pad
- play money
- credit card
- clothing or costume for waiter (apron, shirt, etc.)

Procedure

1. Create a book that lists the job of a waiter.
2. Provide steps that are to be completed:

   1. Take menu to the customer.
   2. Take customer's order.
   3. Serve food.
   4. Present the bill.
   5. Collect the money.

3. Provide all the props that are needed for each of the steps.
4. If necessary, visit the *Restaurant Center*, go over the training, and then leave the center.

Adapt "Book for Server Trainig"

   Decrease the number of jobs for the waiter.

 Practice saying, "May I take your order?" with the children.

  Make the book out of poster board or use cardboard on the back of pages so they are easier to turn. Make print larger.

Music for the Restaurant

Materials

- collection of a variety of types of recordings, such as jazz, soft rock, classical, and children's songs
- CD or tape player

Procedure

1. Children can listen to music.
2. Select the music that will be played in the restaurant.
3. Make sure the music is playing while the restaurant is open.

Adapt "Music for the Restaurant"

   Team the child with at least one peer who can work the CD or tape player.

 Glue or tape a craft stick to the on/off switch for easier access.

  Talk with the children about the types of music available.

Room for Dessert

Materials

- pint of vanilla yogurt
- bowl
- large mixing spoon
- small clear plastic cups
- ingredients to add to the yogurt, such as cereal, fruit, sprinkles, nuts, raisins

Procedure

1. Children can create small cups of yogurt to sell.
2. They can choose things to add, such as cereal, fruit, nuts, and sprinkles.
3. Mix the ingredients.
4. Price and display the desserts.
5. Customers can choose and pay for the dessert they want.

Adapt "Room for Dessert"

  Use a nonskid mat on the table so materials will not slide.

   Illustrate the steps of cooking by using cards with pictures and labels.

 Use large print when labeling desserts.

 Label food items with words. Identify each food for the child.

  Limit the child to two topping choices.

The Essential Literacy Connection

Books

Calmenson, Stephanie. 1995. **Dinner at the Panda Palace**. New York: HarperCollins. *In this counting book, Mr. Panda greets his customers as they arrive at his restaurant.*

Lin, Grace. 2001. **Dim Sum for Everyone**. New York: Knopf. *A family with three daughters visits a Chinese restaurant where they share and learn about dim sum.*

London, Jonathan. 2003. **Froggy Eats Out**. New York: Puffin Books. *When the Froggy family goes to a fancy restaurant, there are only a few simple rules, but it is very difficult for such a young frog to follow the rules.*

Mayer, Mercer. 1974. **Frog Goes to Dinner**. New York: Dial Books. *When the family goes to dinner, chaos ensues.*

Valvassori, Maureen. 1998. **Barney and Baby Bop Go to the Restaurant**. New York: Scholastic. *Baby Bop learns the importance of using good manners when she and Barney go to a Pizzeria.*

Weeks, Sarah. 2003. **Two Eggs, Please**. New York: Atheneum. *The fox waitress has her work cut out for her when all of the animals eating at the diner ask for their eggs to be cooked in a different way.*

Other Literacy Materials

- "Open" and "Closed" signs for restaurant
- blank pads for writing bills
- book for server training
- charts of advertisement and prices
- menus
- play money

Adding Spark to the Restaurant Center

Close the restaurant and reopen it with a new theme or type of restaurant. Maintain the same layout, but change the type of food served or the way it is served. Add new props that relate to the new restaurant.

Evaluation of the Individual Child

Is the child:

1. Participating in role playing? In what way?
2. Using vocabulary that relates to the restaurant?
3. Showing cooperation in his play?
4. Demonstrating understanding of the operation of a restaurant?

Unique
Centers

Unique Centers provide interesting additions to early childhood classrooms. Their design encourages creative thinking and playing with unusual materials. Here, children are challenged to think about new ideas and possibilities.

Centers included in this chapter:

Private Place Center
Music Center
Nature Center
Giggle Center
Hat Center
I See: Vision Center
I Hear: Hearing Center
I Touch: Tactile Center
In and Out Center
Ball Center
Big and Little Center
Pet Shop Center

Two friends share a picnic lunch.

Private Place Center

Overview

Preschoolers are learning to deal with emotions. Young children need to learn how to identify their own emotions and the emotions of those around them. They are beginning to understand and follow established rules of behavior. These skills help young children interact appropriately with adults and peers and learn self-control. The *Private Place Center* provides an environment that will give preschoolers a place to become calm and collected. Activities in this center will lead to self-awareness and a greater understanding of how feelings and behaviors can be managed appropriately.

Learning Objectives

The child with special needs will:

1. Identify her emotions.
2. Identify the behaviors and emotions of others.
3. Demonstrate an appropriate coping technique for feelings.
4. Follow established rules related to center use.

Time Frame

This center is a must for all preschool classrooms. It should remain available to young children throughout the year. It may take several weeks before the preschoolers learn to use the center appropriately.

Letter to Parents or Guardians	Dear Parent or Guardian,

Dear Parent or Guardian,

Learning to deal with emotions is a difficult task for preschoolers. However, it is a very important life skill for young children to develop. Sometimes the environment is overly noisy or busy and can easily overwhelm young children. You may have experienced your child's temper tantrum or outburst during a long shopping trip to the grocery store at the end of a long day. We all need a little time and a place to unwind when we are feeling upset or overwhelmed.

Young children can learn to identify their emotions, such as anger, fear, happiness, or sadness, and to respond appropriately. As children mature, they can begin to understand some of the feelings and behaviors of others. This is a long process. We believe our *Private Place Center* will help preschoolers develop these important skills. The center is a quiet comforting spot where a child can choose to visit to calm down and prepare to learn. Please come by and visit our *Private Place Center*.

Layout of the Private Place Center

The *Private Place Center* does not need a large space, but it does help if it can be located in a low traffic area. A large appliance box is very effective for this center. Turn the box on its side so there is only one entrance and exit. You may cover the entrance with sheer fabric or strings of beads. Fill the box with pillows, a crib mattress, blankets, a CD player with headphones, stuffed animals or comfort items, and several books. Do not put toys and objects that make noise in the *Private Place Center*.

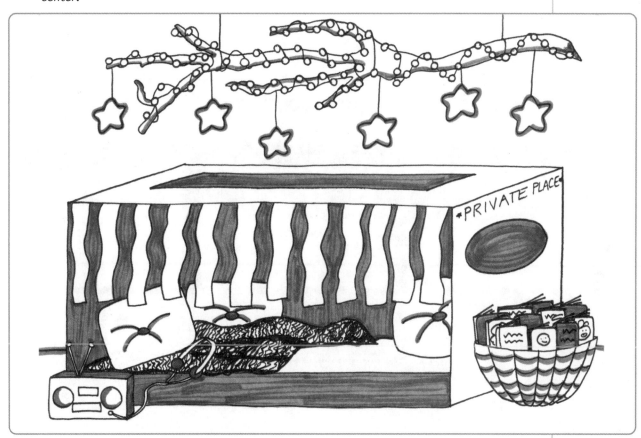

Vocabulary Enrichment

afraid	frustrated
angry	happy
calm	private
emotions	quiet
feelings	sad

Teacher- and Parent-Collected Props

- blanket
- books about feelings
- crib mattress or soft bedding
- flashlight or string lights
- large appliance box
- pillows or beanbag chair
- rhythmic and soft music (classical, environmental, easy listening)
- stuffed animals
- tape or CD player with headphones

Web of Integrated Learning

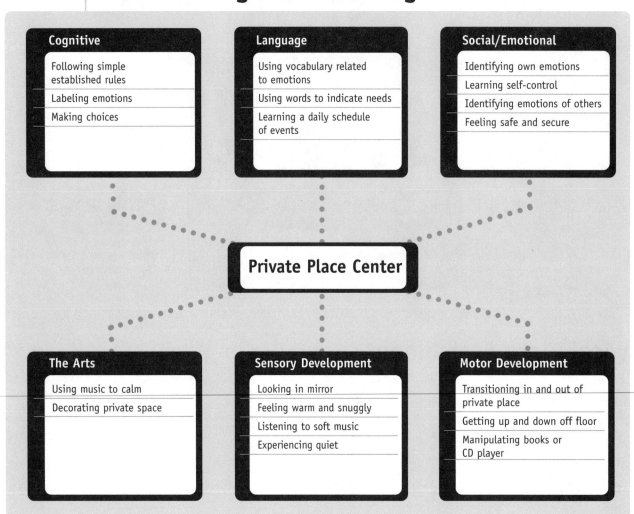

Cognitive
- Following simple established rules
- Labeling emotions
- Making choices

Language
- Using vocabulary related to emotions
- Using words to indicate needs
- Learning a daily schedule of events

Social/Emotional
- Identifying own emotions
- Learning self-control
- Identifying emotions of others
- Feeling safe and secure

Private Place Center

The Arts
- Using music to calm
- Decorating private space

Sensory Development
- Looking in mirror
- Feeling warm and snuggly
- Listening to soft music
- Experiencing quiet

Motor Development
- Transitioning in and out of private place
- Getting up and down off floor
- Manipulating books or CD player

Rules to Follow

Once the *Private Place Center* is available for the children, you must introduce the center and its rules. Rules should be kept simple, with a maximum of four rules in place. Keep the rules positive in nature. For example, instead of "Do not go in the center with another child," say, "Only one child can go into the Private Place Center." Write the rules and post them at the *Private Place Center* for the children to see. At first, you may have to review these rules frequently. Examples of rules include the following:

1. Only one child at a time is allowed in the *Private Place Center.*
2. You must tell a teacher before entering the *Private Place Center.*
3. You may use the *Private Place Center* when you are feeling _____ (sad, angry, afraid, tired, etc.).

It will take several weeks for children to learn how to use this center. Until the individual child learns to go into the center and return independently, an adult will need to guide the process. With consistency and time, this center will become a very beneficial learning tool for your classroom. Children with autism and behavioral disabilities can use the center effectively after practice. Some suggestions for using this center are as follows:

- Respect each child's right to feel angry, sad, or afraid and allow the child to use the center when he or she needs it.
- Never use this center as a punishment for inappropriate behavior! It must remain a safe place if it is to work effectively.
- Help the child identify the emotion she is feeling and label it for her. "Audrey, it looks like you are feeling angry."
- Suggest that the child go to the *Private Place Center* for a few moments. "Audrey, I will help you go to the *Private Place Center* where you can calm down."
- Observe the child inside the *Private Place Center* and when she is noticeably calmer, help her return to the classroom. "Audrey, I see that you are calm. Let's go back to the classroom now."
- Allow the child to take as much time in the *Private Place Center* as she appears to need. Each child has her own pace. One child may need two minutes to get organized and another child may need 10 minutes.
- Do not allow children to hide or escape from classroom activities by entering the center.

Adapt "Rules to Follow"

  Use pictures to identify rules of the center and post them outside.

   Place a timer in the center and set it for several minutes if the child consistently remains in the center longer than it appears necessary.

 A child with physical disabilities may need assistance to enter the *Private Place Center*. You may also need to remove some of the pillows and blankets so that the child can lie comfortably on her back or side.

If the child is nonverbal, she may be able to use sign language, an augmentative communication device, or point to a picture to indicate her desire to go to the *Private Place Center*.

A covered mattress is on the floor for easy access.

Making Faces

Materials

- pictures of children demonstrating different emotions, such as anger, frustration, happiness, sadness, fear, and hurt, with word labels on each picture
- wall mirror or hand mirrors for each child

Procedure

1. Hand each child a picture of an emotion.
2. Ask each child to identify the emotion shown in the picture.
3. Ask the child to imitate that emotion.
4. Allow the child to look in the mirror at her face as she imitates the emotion.
5. Ask all the children to copy that emotion.
6. You may ask the children questions about the emotion to stimulate conversation, such as, "When have you felt sad?" or "What do you do when you are frustrated?"
7. To transfer this skill to real-life situations, ask children in the classroom to look at their peers' faces as they demonstrate emotions. Then, suggest an appropriate response. Use words to describe what you see. "Look at Chloe's face. Her face is saying, I'm angry, so stop doing that."

Adapt "Making Faces"

 Use a magnifying make-up mirror and added light for children to see themselves better.

 Use one-word labels to describe feelings, such as "mad" or "happy."

 Children who are unable to identify emotions in pictures may be able to identify an emotion on your face as you demonstrate it.

   When trying to label an emotion, give the child two choices. "Does Ms. Lynn look happy or sad?"

My Daily Schedule

Materials

- camera
- poster board
- labels
- sticky-back Velcro or glue and magnets
- envelopes

Activities

Procedure

1. Transitions sometimes lead to emotional outbursts in preschoolers. This activity is useful in preparing young children to transition smoothly.
2. Take pictures of activities that occur on a regular basis in the classroom. Activities might include Circle Time, Center Time, lunch, bathroom, and Nap Time.
3. Attach each picture to poster board, and label each picture appropriately.
4. Place sticky-back Velcro to the back of each picture and to the poster board, or glue magnets to the back of each picture and to the poster board.
5. Place an envelope on the poster board.
6. Make a daily schedule for each child. Place the child's name and a picture of the child at the top of the poster. Use only pictures of activities that the particular child participates in on a regular basis. For example, if the child does not usually go outdoors, then do not place a picture of outdoors on her schedule.
7. Place the daily schedule in a place that is convenient and accessible for each child, for example, on her cubby or locker.
8. Help the child visit the daily schedule each morning and throughout the day.
9. Pictures of unusual activities, such as a field trip, may be placed in the "pocket" for use as needed.

Adapt "My Daily Schedule"

Note: Announce the upcoming transition several minutes before you begin transitioning, "In two minutes, we will clean up."

 For children who have a particularly difficult time transitioning, assist them in visiting their daily schedule before each change. You may help them remove the picture of the corresponding activity and place it in the pocket so they realize that the particular activity will no longer be available.

 Children who are unable to touch a hanging daily schedule or remove pictures can have a smaller version for their lap or wheelchair tray.

  Children who are nonverbal can use the pictures to indicate their wants.

The Essential Literacy Connection

Books

Cain, Janan. 2000. **The Way I Feel**. Seattle, WA: Parenting Press. *The range of emotions expressed in this simple wordbook reassures young children that it is okay to have different feelings.*

Carle, Eric. 1987. **Do You Want to Be My Friend?** New York: HarperCollins. *Mouse is trying to find a friend and finally meets another mouse that wants to be friends.**

Carle, Eric. 1998. **The Mixed Up Chameleon**. New York: HarperCollins. *When the chameleon visits the zoo, he wishes to become everything except himself, so parts of him change into other animals. He learns he was happier before he changed.**

Carlson, Nancy. 2002. **Smile a Lot!** Minneapolis, MN: Carolrhoda Books. *This book reassures children that when life has its ups and downs, it is great to keep smiling.*

Parr, Todd. 2001. **It's Okay to Be Different**. Boston, MA: Little & Brown. *The message of self-acceptance and appreciating diversity is portrayed in this brightly colored book.**

Seuss, Dr. 1998. **My Many Colored Days**. New York: Knopf. *Colors are paired with emotions to illustrate feelings.**

(*Available as a board book)

Other Literacy Materials

- daily schedule
- word labels on pictures
- written rules displayed

Adding Spark to the Private Place Center

Place a ticking clock inside the *Private Place Center*. The rhythm of the clock can be calming for some children.

A soft chair and fabric create a private place.

Evaluation of the Individual Child

Is the child:

1. Aware of her own basic emotions?
2. Beginning to notice the behavior of others?
3. Demonstrating simple coping techniques?
4. Able to follow the basic rules of the *Private Place Center*?

Music Center

Overview

Brain research indicates that young children are sensitive to music during their early years. Music stimulates connections in the brain that children will benefit from now and for years to come. The *Music Center* is a wonderful place for children to enjoy sounds and rhythms. In this space, they can play instruments, sing songs, and listen to beautiful music. Here, they can create music and select ways to accompany their compositions. The activities and materials in the center will challenge them to think creatively and inspire them to use their growing musical abilities.

Learning Objectives

The child with special needs will:

1. Listen to a variety of types of music.
2. Determine how to create music with instruments.
3. Move to music and clap rhythms.
4. Participate in singing songs and echoing words.

Time Frame

This center can remain in the classroom for a long time. Some teachers may chose to have the *Music Center* available for three weeks at a time, while others may find that this will be an essential part of the classroom for the entire year. In either case, this center makes an important connection between the child and music that is essential for the development of the whole child.

Letter to Parents or Guardians

Dear Parent or Guardian,

In our classroom, we have a very popular area called the *Music Center*. In this area, the children listen to music, play rhythm instruments, and move to the beat. Music is very important for young children. Not only does music make for an enjoyable activity, but it also builds important connections in your child's brain.

We would like to include music in our center that your child or family enjoys at home. If you have a tape or CD that can be used by the children, we would like to add that special choice to our *Music Center*. If you play an instrument or sing, we would like you to share that talent with our children. Young children enjoy live music; they are a very appreciative audience.

Layout of the Music Center

The effectively designed *Music Center* is filled with activity and sounds. Therefore, it should be located in an area of the classroom where there are other loud activities. For example, it might be placed near the *Block Center* but not near the *Books/Library Center*. Contain the sound in this center by using carpet or rugs and sound boards to absorb the noise (see page 315 in Chapter 5 for directions for building the sound boards).

Vocabulary Enrichment

beat

clap

fast/slow

instruments

listen

loud/soft

move

music

musician

rhythm

sing

tape/CD

Teacher- and Parent-Collected Props

- bells
- CD and tape player
- collection of recordings, such as marching bands, jazz, classical, choral, symphony, Native American flute, guitar, drums, singers, children's recordings
- community drum (see pages 309–310 Chapter 5 for directions)
- microphone
- old guitar or ukulele
- rhythm sticks (see page 310 in Chapter 5 for directions)
- sand blocks
- triangles
- variety of shakers (see page 310 in Chapter 5 for directions) or maracas
- water drum (see page 311 in Chapter 5 for directions)
- wind chimes

Web of Integrated Learning

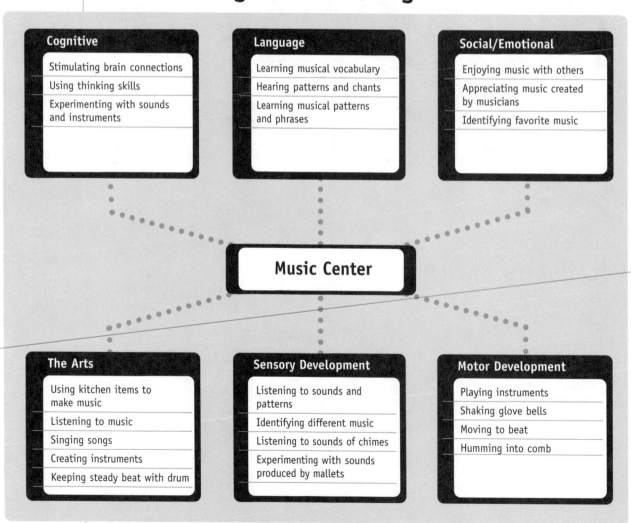

Cognitive
- Stimulating brain connections
- Using thinking skills
- Experimenting with sounds and instruments

Language
- Learning musical vocabulary
- Hearing patterns and chants
- Learning musical patterns and phrases

Social/Emotional
- Enjoying music with others
- Appreciating music created by musicians
- Identifying favorite music

Music Center

The Arts
- Using kitchen items to make music
- Listening to music
- Singing songs
- Creating instruments
- Keeping steady beat with drum

Sensory Development
- Listening to sounds and patterns
- Identifying different music
- Listening to sounds of chimes
- Experimenting with sounds produced by mallets

Motor Development
- Playing instruments
- Shaking glove bells
- Moving to beat
- Humming into comb

Shake, Rattle, and Roll

Materials

- PVC pipe in 3", 6", and 8" pieces (consider different diameters: 1" and 2" work well; bigger and longer pipes produce lower sounds)

Note: Check with local plumbers for scraps of pipe.

- heavy fabric, such as canvas, glazed cotton, or plastic tablecloth
- thick rubber bands or end caps for pipes
- sound makers, such as dried beans, bells, coins, birdseed, small stones, coins, nails, and gravel
- recording and tape or CD player

Procedure

1. Select five or six pieces of PVC pipe in different lengths.
2. Cover one end with heavy fabric. Attach cloth to pipe using a heavy-duty rubber band or use a pipe end cap.
3. Children can select the sound-making item they want to pour into a pipe. They may also determine the amount included.
4. Cover the other end with heavy fabric, using a heavy-duty rubber band or a pipe end cap.
6. Children experiment with shaking the different pipes.
7. Talk about the sounds that are produced by the different sizes and sound items.
8. Select a recording that children can accompany with their shakers.

Adapt "Shake, Rattle, and Roll"

  Use funnels, scoops, or spoons to assist with filling the pipe.

  Use the words "shake" or "rattle," as the children are making music.

  Provide close supervision or fill the pipes for children who mouth objects.

 Give the child a choice between two materials to put in the pipes.

Activities

Activities

Hummer

Materials

- 5 small plastic combs
- container
- pieces of cellophane paper cut into sizes to cover one side of the comb

Note: Closely supervise the use of cellophane if children are still mouthing objects.

- recording of familiar songs (possibilities include "The Wheels on the Bus," "If You're Happy and You Know It," and "Twinkle, Twinkle, Little Star")

Procedure

1. Place five small plastic combs in a container.
2. Provide appropriate-size pieces of cellophane paper.
3. Children can combine the two items.
4. Experiment producing sounds using the comb and paper (this works best if the child hums on the side without the paper).
5. Demonstrate humming into the comb and paper. Practice making music.
6. Play a recording of a familiar song and invite children to hum along.

Adapt "Hummer"

 Help the child understand how to make the humming sound without the comb.

   For easier holding, use larger combs, or place clothespins on the side of comb to hold paper easier.

Give the child sheet music or a songbook to play along to. This provides a new literacy experience for the child.

Hanging Chimes

Materials

- pieces of metal pipe (various lengths)
- electric drill (adult only)
- fishing line (at least 10- to 20-pound test) or heavy string
- dowel rod
- mallets, such as sticks and rubber mallets
- hacksaw

Procedure

1. Using an electric drill, place small holes in two sides of metal pipes.
2. Place fishing line through the holes.
3. Attach to a 3' to 4' dowel rod.
4. Suspend the dowel rod so pipes can vibrate.
5. Hang in the corner of the *Music Center*.
6. Provide a variety of mallets, such as rubber, cotton, sticks, large railroad nail, metal spoon, and wooden spoon.
7. Children can experiment with making sounds by tapping on the pipes with various items.

Children can explore a musical wall.

Adapt "Hanging Chimes"

Each time the child taps on the pipe say "bong." This draws attention to their action and the sound produced.

Have chimes low to the ground or on the edge of a table so the child can play while sitting.

Children can use their hands to run across the chimes and make sounds.

Encourage children to take turns by getting one child to play while another dances.

Use a piece of masking tape to label each chime with the sound it makes, for example, "low," "high," "higher," or "highest."

For easier viewing, place a piece of black or yellow electrical tape around the bottom edges of the metal pipes and hang the pipes near a white wall.

Activities

Glove Bells

Materials

- 2 pairs of cotton work gloves
- small bells
- nylon thread
- sewing needle with a large eye
- recording with bell sounds and tape or CD player

Procedure

1. Sew a bell on each finger of the work gloves.
2. Place the bell gloves in the *Music Center*.
3. Children can discover how to make sounds.
4. Play a recording that has bell sounds and invite children to play along.

Adapt "Glove Bells"

 Chant "Ring, ring, ring the bells."

  Child can hold the glove and shake it if unable or uninterested in wearing the glove.

  Some children may not want to put a glove on their hands. If so, attach bells to a ribbon or piece of fabric they can hold in their hands.

   Demonstrate how to play the glove bells and talk about the beat of the music.

 Choose a bright yellow, red, or solid black glove to attach the bells.

Kitchen Music

Materials

- collect kitchen items that produce interesting sounds, such as
  - 2 pie pans
  - muffin pan
  - egg beater
  - lids of various sizes
  - spoons
  - washboard
  - metal bucket
- large plastic container
- cassette tape and tape recorder

Procedure

1. Place a collection of kitchen items in a large plastic container.
2. Let children explore the items and find ways of combining them to produce interesting sounds.
3. After experimenting, children can select the sound they like.
4. Record the kitchen music the children make.
5. Put the tape with player in the *Music Center* for them to hear.
6. The listening will inspire more musical creations.

Adapt "Kitchen Music"

 Label the kitchen items as they are examined.

 Use words to describe the kitchen items as they are examined.

  Make music with two large wooden spoons.

 Use masking tape or white tape to label the kitchen items.

 Have a peer physically assist the child in playing the kitchen music.

 Verbally praise the child for attending to the activity. "I like the way you make music with your pie pans."

Water Jug Drums

Materials

- 2 or 3 plastic water jugs (used in water coolers)
- food coloring
- lids for water jugs
- glue gun and/or strong glue (adult only)

Procedure

1. Pour water into empty jugs.
2. Fill each jug with a different amount of water. Add a different food color to each jug of water.
3. Glue lid on each water jug.
4. Children can experiment with the sounds produced when they tap the jug with their hand.
5. Use other mallets to hear differences.
6. Use jug drums to accompany singing and recordings.

Adapt "Water Jug Drums"

 Name the color of the drum as it is tapped.

  Place jug in a stand or on the floor so it can be played more easily.

 Add music that has a steady beat.

 Use one drum with the child.

Tap Shoes

Materials

- metal lids from concentrated juice cans (**Note**: Make sure there are no rough edges.)
- elastic pieces ½" to ¾" wide
- scissors
- thread and needle (adult only)
- stage or raised piece of plywood
- recording of dance music and CD or tape player

Procedure

1. Let children create tap shoes by putting metal lids on the bottom of their shoes.
2. Cut elastic pieces into lengths that will go over children's shoes (measure and check the size).
3. Securely sew the elastic piece together so it will slip over the shoe and hold the lid.
4. Children can choose to place a lid on one or both feet.
5. They can dance and tap to the music on the stage.

Adapt "Tap Shoes"

 Say, "Tap, tap, tap," as the children make noise with their tap shoes.

   Demonstrate how to "dance" with the tap shoes.

 If the child is unable to move her feet, place taps on her hands and let her tap on a tabletop or lap tray.

The Essential Literacy Connection

Books

Andreae, Giles. 2001. **Giraffes Can't Dance**. New York: Orchard Books. *All of the other animals at the jungle dance tease Giraffe because he can't dance. When he learns to feel the natural rhythm of the jungle, he learns that he can be a great dancer.*

Boynton, Sandra. 1993. **Barnyard Dance**. New York: Workman. *Join the animals on the farm as they dance in their own unique way.*

Carle, Eric. 1996. **I See a Song**. New York: Scholastic. *In this picture book, bright colors and shapes come to life when the man plays his violin.*

Carle, Eric. 1997. **Today Is Monday**. New York: Philomel Books. *Animals eat their way through each day of the week until Sunday when all the world's children come together for a meal.*

Fleming, Denise. 2001. **Barnyard Banter**. New York: Henry Holt. *All of the animals on the farm are busy with their normal, noisy day except for goose. Follow goose all around the farm as he quietly chases a butterfly.*

Loomis, Christine. 1995. **The Hippo Hop**. Boston, MA: Houghton Mifflin. *At the Hippo Hop, animals come together to make music and dance the night away.*

MacDonald, Margaret Read. 1998. **Pickin' Peas**. New York: HarperCollins. *As a little girl walks through the garden singing and picking peas, she discovers that rabbit is behind her eating the peas that she has left in the garden to grow. After she catches rabbit and takes him home, he tricks her into letting him go.*

Ziefert, Harriet. 1999. **Animal Music**. Boston, MA: Houghton Mifflin. *All of the animals on the farm come together to play music in the marching band.*

Other Literacy Materials

- CDs and recordings
- charts with words to songs
- music books

Adding Spark to the Music Center

Invite someone to play or sing in the *Music Center*. Potential musicians could be a middle school band member, high school string players, a teacher, parent, primary-age child, or grandparent. Make the performer the "star" of the day in the *Music Center*.

A microphone and "real" guitar encourage musical performances.

Evaluation of Individual Child

Is the child:

1. Participating in making music?
2. Manipulating musical instruments?
3. Able to recognize familiar songs or recordings?
4. Clapping or tapping a steady beat?

Nature Center

Overview

Young children are curious about the world in which they live. As young scientists, they investigate natural materials through manipulating, touching, looking, and comparing them to things they already know. The *Nature Center* provides items and tools to assist them in this ongoing process. As the center changes with the seasons, young children learn about the environment of the natural world. During this discovery process, they will develop their thinking and increase their understanding of the environment.

Learning Objectives

The child with special needs will:

1. Identify ways to learn about natural materials.
2. Expand language and vocabulary related to nature.
3. Use creative problem solving to investigate nature.
4. Enhance motor development by participating in the *Nature Center*.
5. Develop an interest and appreciation of the environment.

Time Frame

This center can be introduced each season. Each time, the natural items may be different, while the tools used for investigation will remain constant. Interest usually lasts three to four weeks, if the new materials invite manipulation and exploration.

Letter to Parents or Guardians

Dear Parent or Guardian,

There are so many wonderful things to enjoy during this season. Take your child on a walk and collect interesting nature items you see along the way. Brings some to the *Nature Center* that is being set up in our classroom.

Our *Nature Center* provides a place where children can investigate interesting items that can be found in nature at this time of year. Things we have already collected include leaves, bark, pinecones, rocks, stones, worms, bugs, and moss. In this center, the children will have magnifying glasses to help in their study of natural materials. Here, they will be able to touch, manipulate, and compare the items. This creative problem solving will help them learn about the world in which they live.

Layout of the Nature Center

This center invites exploration and manipulation. It works well if it is in a central location that allows children to move in and out of the area for short periods. The *Nature Center* should include a low table and display area where children can stand and investigate the materials. They also need tools for exploration in the area. Because this examination may sometimes be messy, it is helpful if the area is covered with a sheet of plastic or washable rugs. Include growing plants in this center, such as corn plants, hanging baskets, and wild flowers.

Vocabulary Enrichment

compare

environment

explore

feel

look

names of seasonal items in center

nature

scientist

season of center: fall, winter, spring, summer

Teacher- and Parent-Collected Props

- flashlights
- informational books/brochures about nature or seasons
- magnifying glasses
- measuring tape, yardstick, balance scale, cups, and spoons
- paper, pencils, markers, and journals
- prism or color paddles
- tweezers or tongs

Web of Integrated Learning

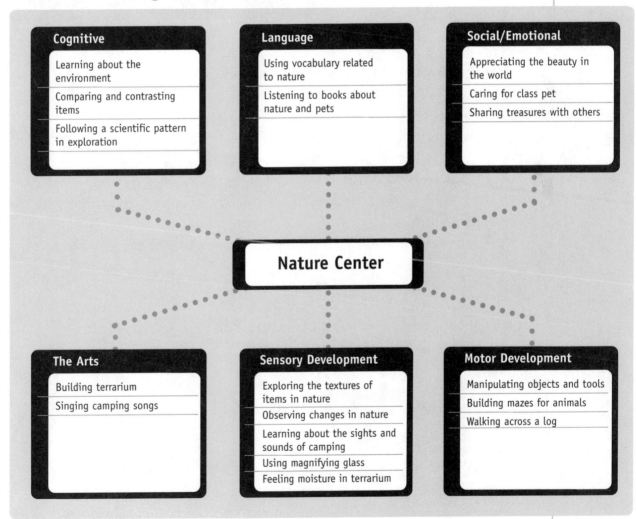

Cognitive
- Learning about the environment
- Comparing and contrasting items
- Following a scientific pattern in exploration

Language
- Using vocabulary related to nature
- Listening to books about nature and pets

Social/Emotional
- Appreciating the beauty in the world
- Caring for class pet
- Sharing treasures with others

Nature Center

The Arts
- Building terrarium
- Singing camping songs

Sensory Development
- Exploring the textures of items in nature
- Observing changes in nature
- Learning about the sights and sounds of camping
- Using magnifying glass
- Feeling moisture in terrarium

Motor Development
- Manipulating objects and tools
- Building mazes for animals
- Walking across a log

Activities

Class Pet

A guinea pig makes a good class pet.

Materials

- pet possibilities, such as a guinea pig, gerbil, or rabbit
- cage and nesting materials
- food, water, and containers
- book or brochure about the care of the pet
- chart paper
- markers
- cardboard tubes

Procedure

1. Keep the pet in a special place in the *Nature Center*.
2. For one week, let one child feed and care for the pet. This teaches them about caring for an animal.
3. Make a chart showing the amount of food, water, and frequency of cleaning for the pet. Each child can mark the chart when pet care is completed.
4. Lead an occasional health examination of the pet, focusing on weighing the pet, listening to its heart, checking its eyes, looking at its feet, and examining its eating pattern.
5. Create mazes for the animal with cardboard tubes. Children can build the maze and watch the pet use it.

Adapt "Class Pet"

   Use hand-over-hand assistance to help the child gently pet the animal.

 Let the children name the pet. Refer to the pet by that name. Encourage the child to call the pet by name.

 Let children help develop the rules for playing with the pet and caring for it.

 Some children may not want to touch the pet. Do not force them to hold the animal. However, let them observe their peers playing with or nurturing the animal.

Across the Creek or Stream

Activities

Materials

- blue paper
- scissors
- masking tape
- pieces of plastic or foil
- colored construction paper
- stones or pebbles
- balance beam or landscaping timber
- paper and markers

Procedure

1. Create a stream through the *Nature Center* by cutting out a curvy pattern from blue paper, taping it to the floor, and placing plastic or foil over it.
2. Cut out fish or tadpoles from construction paper and place them in the "water."
3. Place some stones and pebbles around the edge or in the water.
4. Place a log (beam or timber) across the creek.
5. Add a sign that says "No Swimming" or "Do Not Go in the Water."
6. Children can walk on the log from one side to the other.

Adapt "Across the Creek or Stream"

 Make a bridge out of light-colored paper and tape it down across the stream. Mobility devices can easily roll across the bridge.

 Ask children to identify the colors of the fish in the water.

 Use reflective or bright colored tape along the edges of the balance beam.

  A peer can demonstrate how to walk across the log to get to the other side of the creek.

Activities

Camping in Nature

Materials

- small or dome tent
- tree branches
- bucket or large clay pots
- plaster of Paris
- books and stories about camping
- camping props, such as sleeping bags and blankets; campfire props; packages of food items for camping; raincoat or poncho; hats; appropriate clothing for the season; backpacks; walking cane; emergency first aid kit; and camping tools, such as canteen, flashlight, cooking utensils, shovels, and lantern
- brochures about camping safety

Procedure

1. Set up a tent at the edge of the *Nature Center* or create a camping site that can be set up outdoors.
2. Create a forest of trees by placing large branches of trees in buckets of plaster of Paris. Allow the plaster to dry.
3. Provide props to use when camping.
4. Invite the children to pretend they are camping.

Adapt "Camping in Nature"

 Sing "The Happy Wanderer" and change the words to, "I love to go a-hiking, along the mountain trail, and as I go I love to sing, my backpack on my back. Valderi, valdera, valderi..."

 Encourage participation in the echo portion of the song.

 The tent with sleeping bags can be a calming space for children to enter when they are over-stimulated by their environment.

 If the child is using a mobility device or has difficulty walking around the environment, make sure that the floor area is clear of props. Place these props on a table in the center.

 Place a floor or table lamp in the tent for more light.

Plants in Nature

Materials

- plants that grow in your area
- aquarium or small fish tank
- gravel or small stones
- sand
- foil or laminated color paper
- potting soil
- mist/spray bottle
- piece of plastic or tray
- large rubber band or coated wire
- clip-on light

Procedure

1. Create a terrarium of plants that live in your area (see page xxx in Chapter 5 for directions).
2. Children can help build the terrarium.
3. Provide a chart of the steps for creating the terrarium, including pictures:

---

1. Begin with placing a layer of gravel on the bottom of the aquarium or small fish tank.
2. Add a layer of sand.
3. Create a stream or pond by placing foil or a small clear plastic bowl in the terrarium.
4. Cover the ground area with potting soil.
5. Add plants, moss, and stones.
6. Water the soil and plants.
7. Tightly cover the top with plastic or a tray.

---

4. Add miniature people or animals.
5. Make sure the terrarium is getting indirect light. A clip-on light can help in a poorly lit area.
6. Once a week, open the terrarium so plants do not get too moist.
7. New plants can be added, as needed.

Adapt "Plants in Nature"

 When creating the terrarium, talk about each step. Label the materials you are using. Encourage the child to echo the labels.

 To fill the terrarium, the child can use scoops or spoons with tape around the handles to make them easier to hold.

  One child can hold the terrarium while the other child fills it with pebbles or sand.

  Decrease steps in the process to three or four.

The Essential Literacy Connection

Books

Bartlett, Richard; Frye, Fredric & Bartlett, Patricia. 1999. **Terrarium and Cage Construction and Care.** New York: Barron's Educational Series. *Basic instructions on how to build a terrarium and how to take care of it.*

Carle, Eric. 1999. **Rooster's Off to See the World.** New York: Aladdin Library. *Rooster decides he wants to explore the world; one by one, the other farm animals join him. When they get hungry, they decide that they want to go home.* *

Fleming, Denise. 1991. **In the Tall, Tall Grass.** New York: Henry Holt. *Caterpillar goes on a safari to explore what can be found in the backyard grass.*

James, Simon. 2003. **Little One Step.** Cambridge, MA: Candlewick Press. *Lost in the woods, the two older ducklings help the younger duckling take one step at a time until they find their mother.*

Roca, Nuria. 2004. **Fall.** New York: Barron's Educational Series. *Brightly colored illustrations show all the fun that fall brings.*

Root, Phyllis. 2001. **One Duck Stuck.** New York: Scholastic. *In this counting book, duck is stuck in the marsh, while the other animals use teamwork to get him out.* *

Williams, Sue. 1996. **I Went Walking.** New York: Harcourt. *A boy goes for a walk in nature and sees a colorful parade of animals.* *

(*Available as a board book)

Other Literacy Materials

- brochures about nature in the area, camping, and national parks
- chart detailing pet care
- pen, pencil, and journal for recording information
- steps for building a terrarium

Adding Spark to the Nature Center

Play a tape of rain falling in the *Nature Center*. Provide raincoats and ponchos to wear in the center when it is "raining."

A bug container adds new interest to the nature center.

Evaluation of the Individual Child

Is the child:

1. Examining the natural materials in the center?
2. Using tools? Which tools and how?
3. Using new vocabulary? What words or phrases?
4. Demonstrating creative problem solving as she participates in the center?

Giggle Center

Overview

Humor is an effective way to support the development of young children. All children benefit from opportunities to deal with emotions in a positive way and find appropriate methods to deal with stress. The *Giggle Center* provides a place for young children to be silly, to laugh, and to use words to describe their feelings. Participating in this process helps develop social skills and effective ways of working with others. Children can use the humor that they frequently enjoy, such as playful interactions, symbolic humor (visual/slapstick), and verbal humor. The *Giggle Center* provides an environment that nurtures the social-emotional development of children with special needs.

Learning Objectives

The child with special needs will:
1. Enjoy funny things and being silly.
2. Identify positive emotions and feelings.
3. Interact with other children as they share humor.
4. Improve creative thinking and problem solving.

Time Frame

This unique center can be added to the classroom for two to three weeks, depending on the interest of the children. It will be especially enjoyable during the winter season, when children are not able to go outside and have limited light. The *Giggle Center* will provide comic relief for those winter days.

Letter to Parents or Guardians	Dear Parent or Guardian, We are adding a very special center to our classroom next week—the *Giggle Center*. It is designed to bring humor and fun to our young children. A good laugh or a giggle can improve the way we feel and help us find positive ways to deal with emotions. Your child can experience funny things and act silly. It will lighten up our wintry days. In the *Giggle Center*, we will have humorous books, funny clothes, and silly hats to wear, music that moves children to laughter, and enjoyable activities. While all this fun is going on, the children will be learning about language and developing motor skills. They will also have many opportunities to enhance their social skills as they share humor and laugh together.

Layout of the Giggle Center

This center will produce lots of laughter, so it should be placed in an area with other noisy centers. The area will need good lighting and mirrors so children can see the humorous clothing and activities. A low table for a workspace is also helpful. Use shelves and hooks or pegs to display items that children can use or wear.

Vocabulary Enrichment

clown

feelings

funny

happy

joke

laugh

share

silly

smile

Teacher- and Parent-Collected Props

- funny glasses, with a nose, with decorations, and in big sizes
- funny hats
- interesting clothing, such as T-shirts, dress-up clothes, and gloves
- masks that cover only a portion of the face (not the nose)
- rabbit ears, reindeer antlers, and other headgear
- silly shoes, such as clown shoes, shoes that light up, brightly colored shoes, or shoes with wild designs
- toys that make funny or surprising sounds, such as a jack-in-the-box, pull toy with dog ears that flap, a ball that has unusual sounds, and a wind-up toy that jumps
- wigs

Web of Integrated Learning

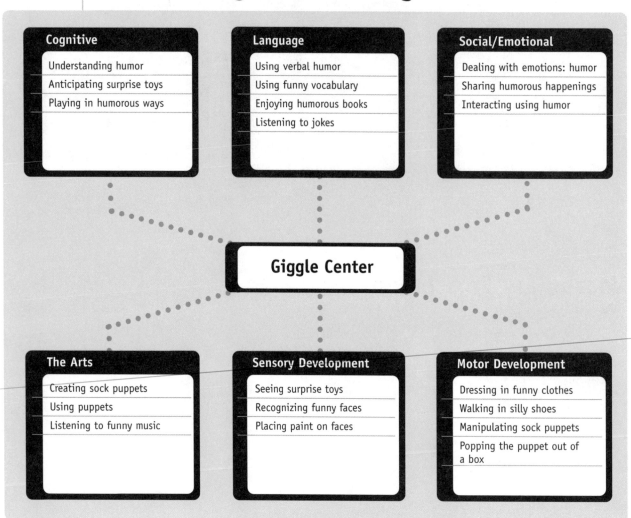

Cognitive
- Understanding humor
- Anticipating surprise toys
- Playing in humorous ways

Language
- Using verbal humor
- Using funny vocabulary
- Enjoying humorous books
- Listening to jokes

Social/Emotional
- Dealing with emotions: humor
- Sharing humorous happenings
- Interacting using humor

Giggle Center

The Arts
- Creating sock puppets
- Using puppets
- Listening to funny music

Sensory Development
- Seeing surprise toys
- Recognizing funny faces
- Placing paint on faces

Motor Development
- Dressing in funny clothes
- Walking in silly shoes
- Manipulating sock puppets
- Popping the puppet out of a box

Activities

Sock Puppets

Materials

- collection of socks (bright colors, stripes, designs, with toes, and silly)
- materials to add to puppets, such as large buttons, yarn, ribbon, pieces of fabric, rope, pipe cleaners (glitter or bright colors), metal pot scrubbers, ping-pong balls, party hats, pieces of felt, pieces of cardboard, pieces of sponge
- glue

Procedure

1. Make four or five sock puppets with mouths that open and close.
2. Place the sock on your hand with the heel between fingers and thumb.
3. Stuff the extended toe portion of the sock into the space between index finger and thumb. Tack this part inside so the puppet's mouth will open and close.
4. Invite children to select items to decorate the sock puppet.
5. Encourage the children to create puppets that look funny to them.
6. When several puppets are completed, have a silly puppet show.
7. Although young children do not need a puppet stage, turning a table on its side can make a simple stage; children can stand behind it with their performing puppets.

Adapt "Sock Puppets"

  Give the child a glue stick or glue pen to use, if she does not want to touch the glue or is unable to squeeze the bottle.

Model how to place eyes, ears, nose, and mouth on the sock puppet. Use words to describe the process. A pre-made puppet to model may help decrease a child's frustration and impulsiveness.

Puppets are great communication tools for children who talk very little. Encourage their use of the puppet. The child may talk through the puppet, when she otherwise might not speak.

 Puppets are also useful to act out emotions in appropriate ways.

  Child can sit in an adapted seat or chair, or kneel behind the puppet stage.

Activities

Pop, Spin, or Wag

Materials

- cardboard box with lid
- humorous wrapping paper
- collection of toys that do unusual things, for example:
  - bear that dances
  - wind-up toy that spins
  - jack-in-the-box
  - small push-and-pull toys
  - chicken that pecks

A frog mask and webbed feet make us laugh.

Procedure

1. Cover a cardboard box and lid with wrapping paper. (Make sure the box is easy to open.)
2. Place a collection of unusual toys inside the box.
3. Let children explore the contents of the box and experiment with the toys.

Adapt "Pop, Spin, or Wag"

 Before the child explores the items in the box, describe them to the child.

 Ask, "What is in the box?" Encourage the child to name the toy, make the sound of the toy, or laugh.

 Demonstrate or help the child with how to play with the toy in the typical way and then in an unusual way to expand the child's play skills.

 To help the child maintain focus on the task, she may lie on the floor or sit in a beanbag chair while manipulating toys in the box.

 Place only two toys in the box at a time to make it less overwhelming for the child.

Activities

Be a Clown

Materials

- pictures of clowns
- face paint
- unbreakable mirrors
- clown dress-up items, such as rubber noses, loud clothing, big shoes, wagon, funny hats, big gloves or plastic hands, and colorful wigs (can be made from yarn or mop)
- stuffed animals
- dance costumes
- inflated weighted punching clown

Glasses and a big nose are funny props.

Procedure

1. Decorate a corner of the *Giggle Center* with pictures of clowns.
2. Place face paint and unbreakable mirrors on a table.
3. Children can paint their own faces.
4. Clown dress-up items can be selected from the display.
5. Clown or funny music recordings inspire moving, shaking, and pretending.
6. Provide a wagon and stuffed animals for additional play and acting silly.
7. Visit the *Giggle Center* and laugh with the children as they clown around.

Adapt "Be a Clown"

 Focus on the funny aspects of this center. Encourage the child to try on funny hats and clothing. Talk about what makes these items funny, such as a "big nose," or "big glasses."

 If the child does not want paint on her face, she may be able to paint a willing friend's face or a washable doll's face.

 Provide an unbreakable lighted and magnified make-up mirror.

  Large clothes with limited snaps or buttons are easier to get on and off.

Activities

Funny Box

Materials

- large cardboard box (large enough for one child to crawl inside)
- scissors
- bright color paint
- markers or tempera paint
- paintbrushes

Procedure

1. Cut a large round hole in one side of the box.
2. Turn the box so the top is open.
3. Let children paint the box a solid bright color.
4. After the paint dries, the children can add funny pictures or draw dots and designs on the other side.
5. Children can dress up in funny items and crawl through the circle of the box.
6. A child can pop up out of the box in funny clothing.

Adapt "Funny Box"

 Encourage the child to say, "pop" or make a funny sound when they appear from inside the box.

  Sing the song "Pop Goes the Weasel" as the child pops up out of the box.

  Cut buttonholes a bit larger to make it easier to button clothing, or use Velcro closures instead of buttons or snaps.

 Make sure the area is well let. Let the child enter the box at her own pace.

 Place a chair inside the box for sitting. Provide peer or adult assistance for the child to pop up, as needed.

Pop-Up Puppet

Materials

- small, plastic yogurt containers
- scissors
- small dowel rod ¼" or ½" thick
- saw (adult only)
- 3 socks
- hot glue (adult only)
- markers

Procedure

1. Cut a hole in the bottom of the yogurt container. The hole should provide a tight fit for the dowel rod.
2. Saw the dowel rod into 6" pieces.
3. Cut part of the leg off the sock.
4. Hot glue the sock into the inside of the container so when the dowel rod is pushed up through the hole, it goes inside the sock and pushes it up.
5. Children can decorate the sock puppet by adding eyes, hair, mouth, tongue, and other features. Allow to dry completely.
6. Place the dowel rod in the bottom of the container and up into the sock.
7. Children can experiment with making the sock puppet appear and disappear.

Adapt "Pop-Up Puppet"

 Increase the size of the dowel rod by applying foam or tape for easier grasping.

  Form children into a group to put on a puppet show. Give each child a simple role to play; for example, King, Queen, and Princess.

Demonstrate how to make the puppets talk.

The Essential Literacy Connection

Books

Barrett, Judi. 1988. **Animals Should Definitely Not Wear Clothing**. New York: Aladdin. *Funny illustrations of animals wearing clothes show children exactly why animals should not wear clothing.*

Barrett, Judi. 1982. **Cloudy With a Chance of Meatballs**. New York: Aladdin Library. *Food is raining and snowing in the town of Chewandswallow. However, what happens when the wrong foods fall or too much food falls?*

Davis, Katie. 2000. **Who Hoots?** San Diego, CA: Harcourt Brace. *In this sequel to* Who Hops, *giggles will abound when guessing what sounds animals make.*

Davis, Katie. 2001. **Who Hops?** San Diego, CA: Harcourt Brace. *Davis tickles children's funny bones with this repetitive guessing game of how animals move.*

Many, Paul. 2002. **The Great Pancake Escape**. New York: Walker & Company. *When Dad, who is a magician, makes pancakes for his children using the magic book instead of the cookbook, they have to chase the pancakes across town just to eat breakfast.*

Patricelli, Leslie. 2003. **Yummy Yucky**. Cambridge, MA: Candlewick Press. *Opposites are explored through a display of food that is yummy versus things that are yucky.* *

Yektai, Niki. 1989. **What's Silly?** New York: Clarion Books. *Unusual situations will have children thinking about what is wrong with each silly page.*

(*Available as a board book)

Other Literacy Materials

- funny songs with word charts
- "Joke-of-the-Day" written on paper and displayed in the *Giggle Center* (The joke could be read in Circle Time when children are choosing their center.)
- programs from the circus

Adding Spark to the Giggle Center

Have a surprise visit from a clown. This can be a teacher, aide, or parent. With young children, it is best to keep the clown costume very simple—a funny wig, loud shirt, and big shoes. It helps to let the person put on or take off the items in front of the children so the children can see that the clown is really a familiar person dressed up.

Evaluation of the Individual Child

Is the child:

1. Finding things that are funny to her? What are they?
2. Using props in a humorous way?
3. Using words or gestures in play? Which ones?
4. Improving in large and small motor skills?
5. Sharing humor with others?

Hat Center

Overview

A *Hat Center* is a unique place for young children to play and pretend. In this space, they can try on hats, create hats, and purchase hats. These experiences will enhance their motor skills, nurture their creativity, and provide experiences that relate to their world. In this center, children can enjoy role-playing and cooperating with others as they wear their hats. They develop self-confidence as they design and wear their own creations.

Learning Objectives

The child with special needs will:
1. Develop motor skills while manipulating and constructing hats.
2. Expand vocabulary related to hats.
3. Enrich imaginative and creative thinking.
4. Enjoy working with others.

Time Frame

The *Hat Center* will be in the classroom for two to three weeks. During this period, a collection of hats will serve as the props that encourage play and enjoyment. After the center is used, store the hats together in a labeled container and continue to add unique hats to the collection throughout the year. This expanded collection can be reintroduced later in the year with opportunities to revisit favorites and recognize new hats.

Letter to Parents or Guardians

Dear Parent or Guardian,

We are developing a new center for our classroom—the *Hat Center*. We are currently collecting interesting hats that the children can try on, admire, and use in their play. Please look in your garage or attic to find any interesting hats you can donate to our new center. It would be helpful for you to bring hat(s) to our classroom and give us information about them. What is the "real" name for the hat? It would be interesting to know who wore it or if there are special stories related to the hat.

We will take pictures of the children in their special hats. These photos will be displayed in the *Hat Center* for all to enjoy. Please come by with a hat and see your child enjoying a special hat.

Layout of the Hat Center

The *Hat Center* will be designed as a store. Hats will be displayed on a wall, hanging on hooks or pegs so the children can see their choices. A large mirror should be close to the display area and at a height that allows all children to see what they are wearing. A standing unbreakable mirror can provide another view. A low table can hold a cash register that includes play money and a receipt book for purchases. Hat boxes can be placed on the floor where children can put hats into them and take them out. Decorate the store with draping fabric, sale signs, and pictures of hats from magazines and newspaper advertisements.

Vocabulary Enrichment

buy/purchase

cash register

colors of hats in the center

fancy

hat

head

mirror

money

sale

specific names of hats in the center, such as baseball, band, cap, bonnet, baby, and firefighter helmet

store

Teacher- and Parent-Collected Props

- decorations for hats, such as netting, feathers, trim, ribbon, yarn, artificial flowers, leaves, glitter, lace, felt pieces, stickers, pipe cleaners, and ribbons
- fabric for decoration
- fashion magazines and newspaper advertisements
- glue
- old newspapers
- play money
- variety of hats, such as baseball, winter, baby, firefighter, soldier, fancy hats, scarves, and funny hats

Web of Integrated Learning

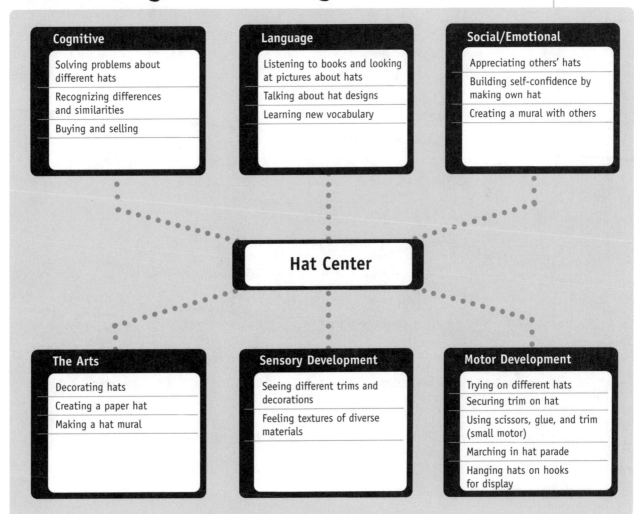

Cognitive
- Solving problems about different hats
- Recognizing differences and similarities
- Buying and selling

Language
- Listening to books and looking at pictures about hats
- Talking about hat designs
- Learning new vocabulary

Social/Emotional
- Appreciating others' hats
- Building self-confidence by making own hat
- Creating a mural with others

Hat Center

The Arts
- Decorating hats
- Creating a paper hat
- Making a hat mural

Sensory Development
- Seeing different trims and decorations
- Feeling textures of diverse materials

Motor Development
- Trying on different hats
- Securing trim on hat
- Using scissors, glue, and trim (small motor)
- Marching in hat parade
- Hanging hats on hooks for display

Activities

Creating a Fancy Hat

Materials

- butcher paper, newspaper, colored construction paper, or poster board
- scissors
- markers
- decorative materials, such as foil, feathers, trim, flowers, lace, ribbons, and small pieces of fabric

Procedure

1. Create five or six paper hats that fit the children. A simple style to construct is a modified party hat. Roll a piece of construction paper or poster board into a cylindrical shape. Staple and tape the hat securely together. Cut the peak out of the cylinder. This produces a base for the hat so the children can decorate it.

2. Place these hat bases on a low table with a collection of materials that can be used to decorate the hats. Glue and tape can be used to attach the trim.

3. Children can select the color base they want to use and the decorations they will add to the hat.

4. When they have completed the decorating, the children can admire their hats in the mirrors in the center.

5. Take photos of the children wearing their creations and display them in the *Hat Center* for all to admire.

Adapt "Creating a Fancy Hat"

  Offer the child a limited choice of materials. "Would you like to use feathers or cotton balls?"

  Describe the hat the child made in positive terms. "I like the blue yarn you glued to your hat." "You worked very hard to make your hat beautiful."

  A peer can model how to make a hat for a child who has difficulty making choices or getting started.

 Pour glue into a pie pan or paper plate. Tape the plate to the table or on top of a non-skid mat so that it will not move as the child dips materials into the glue.

Activities

Giant Hat

Materials

- overhead projector
- large sheet of paper
- scissors
- tape
- markers
- glue
- collection of trim and decorations

Procedure

1. Use an overhead projector or draw a huge hat outline on paper.
2. Cut out the giant hat.
3. Attach the hat shape to a wall in the *Hat Center*.
4. Children can work together to decorate the giant hat.

Adapt "Giant Hat"

 Place a piece of mesh under the paper so the child can feel the texture as she colors the hat.

 When the child is decorating or has completed decorating her hat, use words to describe the creation. Encourage her to repeat some of your words.

 Allow the child to work alone on the project if drawing with other children is over-stimulating.

Hat Parade

Materials

- collection of hats
- recording of marching music and tape or CD player

A fancy hat is perfect for a parade.

Procedure

1. Each child in the center will select a hat to wear in the hat parade.
2. Play marching music.
3. Children can march in the parade, strutting with their hat.

Adapt "Hat Parade"

 Count the marching beat with the music, "1, 2, 3, 4, hats, hats, hats, hats."

 A peer or adult can pull the child in a wagon or on a riding toy with string attached.

 Demonstrate how to march and practice to music before beginning the parade. Use the words, "Step, step, step" to the beat.

 Let each child take turns leading the parade. Use this as a reward for positive behaviors. "Bryan, you can be the leader now, because you kept your hands to yourself."

Hat Sale

Materials

- poster board
- scissors
- markers
- paper
- sticky labels
- play money

Procedure

1. During Circle Time, announce that the store in the *Hat Center* is going to be closed to prepare for the big "Hat Sale."

2. Place a sign on the center entrance that reads, "Closed."

3. Children in the center will put the hats on sale.

4. They can make sale tags to place on the hats. (All levels of scribbles and/or numbers are acceptable "writing.")

5. Create signs that advertise the big sale.

6. Reopen the center for the big sale.

7. Children can buy the sale hats or work in the store taking the money.

A stack of hats reminds him of the book *Caps for Sale*.

Activities

Adapt "Hat Sale"

 Talk to the child about a sale. "What does it mean to buy a hat or get a bargain?"

  Discuss how much things cost. Show children coins and talk about their value.

 Mark the edges of the signs or tags with bright color markers, paint, or tape to provide boundaries for drawing.

 Place each child's own materials in a pie pan or on a tray to provide a sense of space and to keep objects nearby.

 Tape the sign or tag to the table or work area so that it will not move around as the child draws on it.

Wrapping Paper Hats

Materials

- variety of wrapping paper, such as print, foil, holiday, and stripe
- scissors
- masking tape
- decorations, such as ribbons, trim, artificial flowers, feathers, and foil

Procedure

1. Cut wrapping paper into pieces 12" x 12" or 10" x 10".
2. Place the pieces on the table with trim for decorating.
3. Children choose the wrapping paper they want for their hat.
4. Each child will put the paper on her head.
5. Use masking tape to go around the child's head and secure the hat base.
6. Children can decorate and wear their fancy hat.

Adapt "Wrapping Paper Hats"

  If the child is unable to make a choice, limit the selection of wrapping paper. "Would you like to use red or blue paper?"

Some children do not like the feel of a hat. They can make a hat for a favorite doll or stuffed animal.

Activities

The Essential Literacy Connection

Books

Berenstain, Stan, & Berenstain, Jan. 1997. **Old Hat, New Hat.** New York: Random House. *Bear cannot seem to find a hat to replace his worn old hat when he goes to the store, so he decides to keep his old hat.*

Hines, Anna Grossnickle. 2002. **Which Hat Is That?** New York: Harcourt. *A mouse uses her imagination to be many things each time she puts on a different hat.*

Katz, Karen. 2002. **Twelve Hats for Lena.** New York: Margaret K. McElderry Books. *Using art and craft supplies, Lena makes a hat for each month of the year.*

Miller, Margaret. 1988. **Whose Hat?** New York: Greenwillow Books. *Children explore the many occupations that require hats.*

Morris, Ann. 1989. **Hats Hats Hats.** New York: Lothrop, Lee & Shepard Books. *Hats worn by people from all over the world are shown.*

Slobodkina, Esphyr. 1968. **Caps for Sale.** New York: HarperCollins. *A peddler carries his caps that are for sale on his head. He sits under a tree to take a nap and when he wakes, he sees that monkeys in the tree are wearing his caps.*

Smith, William Jay. 1993. **Ho for a Hat!** Boston, MA: Little, Brown and Company. *A young boy and his dog take readers on a journey of hats.*

Volker, Kerstin. 2003. **Emma Goes Shopping.** Hauppauge, NY: Parklane Publishing. *In this book about opposites, Emma the zebra goes shopping for a hat.*

Other Literacy Materials

- magazines with pictures of people wearing hats
- pictures of hats with labels
- signs and advertisements about hats

Adding Spark to the Hat Center

Add an extremely silly hat to the center. For example, include a frog hat or a big fuzzy hat. These will encourage laughter as well as new play.

Evaluation of the Individual Child

Is the child:

1. Trying on the hats? Looking at herself in a mirror?
2. Using small motor skills in making or decorating a hat? Which ones?
3. Using words in play? What words are used?
4. Working with a peer?

I See: Vision Center

Overview

Between the ages of three and five, children develop advanced vision. Preschoolers become better skilled at visually scanning the environment, allowing them to search for objects. Preschoolers can discriminate visually, which means they notice similarities and differences between objects; this is a visual-perceptual task. They also learn how to make visually-guided movements, meaning that preschoolers are practicing activities that require them to maintain focus on an object while they are moving. An example of this skill is throwing a ball at a target while running. Preschoolers also develop visual memory. All of these skills are essential precursors to the very important life skill of reading.

Learning Objectives

The child with special needs will:

1. Visually scan the environment to find a specified object.
2. Maintain visual attention on a moving target.
3. Note visual differences between two similar objects.
4. Expand visual-perceptual skills.

Time Frame

The *I See: Vision Center* will work well for two to three weeks at a time. This center offers several activities that may be completed outside. You may want to consider the season when scheduling this center.

Letter to Parents or Guardians

Dear Parent or Guardian,

Reading is among the most important life skills. We believe that preschool is the time to begin working on what we call pre-reading skills, which include the development of several vision skills. We have opened an *I See: Vision Center* in the classroom where preschoolers can work on these important vision skills.

Some of the tasks the children will learn include how to maintain focus on a moving object while they stay still and how to focus on a stable target as they move. The children will work on using their eyes to decide the differences and similarities in objects. We will play games like "I Spy" in this center. You may want to try this game in the car or at home. Use simple words to describe an object you see nearby, and then let your child guess what object was chosen by saying, for example, "I spy something tall and green."

Layout of the I See: Vision Center

The *I See: Vision Center* will work well in a part of the room with good lighting. Natural sunlight is beneficial but not required. A table with chairs is useful for some activities. Keep objects for sorting in clear containers with labels so they are easily recognizable.

Vocabulary Enrichment

copy
different
eyes
find
match
same
shape
size
spy
target
vision

How do toys look on the light table?

Teacher- and Parent-Collected Props

- books and magazines
- card games like Old Maid and Go Fish
- items to sort such as buttons, beads, or small blocks
- light table (see page 308 in Chapter 5 for directions)
- paper
- plastic storage containers
- puzzles (simple jigsaw and foam board)
- small building materials, such as Legos®, Lincoln Logs®, or Tinker Toys®
- soft balls (beach, foam, Nerf®, and Nubby)
- templates for drawing
- writing utensils

Web of Integrated Learning

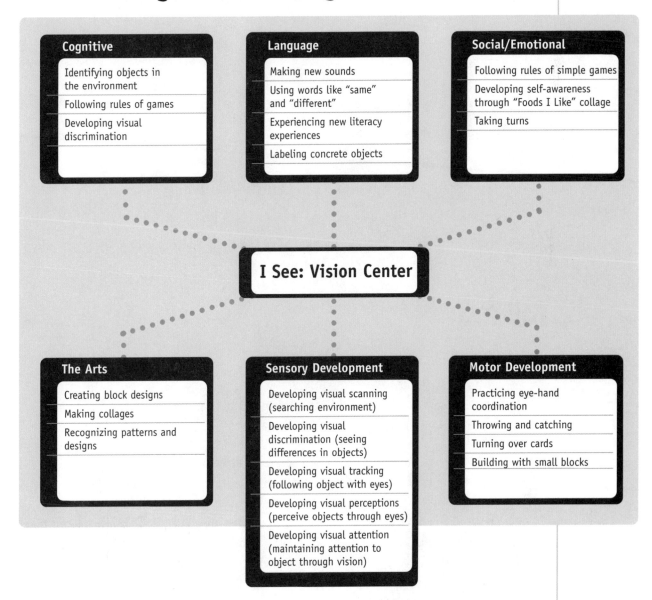

Cognitive
- Identifying objects in the environment
- Following rules of games
- Developing visual discrimination

Language
- Making new sounds
- Using words like "same" and "different"
- Experiencing new literacy experiences
- Labeling concrete objects

Social/Emotional
- Following rules of simple games
- Developing self-awareness through "Foods I Like" collage
- Taking turns

I See: Vision Center

The Arts
- Creating block designs
- Making collages
- Recognizing patterns and designs

Sensory Development
- Developing visual scanning (searching environment)
- Developing visual discrimination (seeing differences in objects)
- Developing visual tracking (following object with eyes)
- Developing visual perceptions (perceive objects through eyes)
- Developing visual attention (maintaining attention to object through vision)

Motor Development
- Practicing eye-hand coordination
- Throwing and catching
- Turning over cards
- Building with small blocks

Activities

I Spy

Materials

- simple, easy-to-find objects, indoors or outdoors

Procedure

1. This is a great activity for outdoors or indoors.
2. Start by choosing simple, easy-to-find objects that are nearby and then progress to items that are more difficult. You may start with a few items placed on a table.
3. Use a few physical (visual) descriptors for the object, such as color, shape, or size. "I Spy something that is brown, small, and round." Try to stay away from "purpose" descriptors such as "something you sit in."
4. To add a movement component, ask the children to touch or bring back the object you describe.

Adapt "I Spy"

 Select only two objects to choose from and describe one of the objects. See if the child can guess which one you spy.

Invite the child to manipulate the object in her hands and use shape and size descriptors, rather than color. "I spy something that is big and round." First place a large ball and then a small block in the child's hands to feel.

 "I Spy" is a great game for building language skills and expanding visual scanning.

Ball Toss

Materials

- different sizes of balls
- targets, such as clean trash cans, plastic containers, or Hula Hoops

Procedure

1. This activity works well in a large space or outdoors.
2. Place containers on the floor and ask children to toss balls into the target.
3. Children may count the balls as they go into the containers to keep score.
4. Hold a container or large ring in your arms and slowly move it while children try to throw balls inside or through. A Hula Hoop makes a great moving "target." Step farther and farther away from the children as they improve.
5. Make the game a race. Place targets on the ground and ask the children to throw balls into the target as fast as they can.

Adapt "Ball Toss"

Make containers larger and use smaller balls. Allow the child to drop, rather than throw their ball into or through the target.

Make a sound, such as "swoosh" or "boom" as the ball lands in the container.

Use solid, dark colored trash cans and red or yellow balls.

Use words such as "in," "out," "big," and "target" as the child participates in this activity.

Copy Cat

Materials

- small building materials or blocks
- paper
- markers

Procedure

1. Build a simple design from building materials. Start with a tower of six to eight blocks or a train of four or five blocks.
2. Give children the same materials and ask them to copy your design.
3. Allow each child time to work through this task before giving assistance. Some children will need to touch or manipulate your building before they can attempt it.
4. When the children have finished with their buildings, ask them to draw a picture of their building on paper. Remember, their one-dimensional picture may not look like their three-dimensional building.
5. As the children progress, make the buildings more difficult or bring out pre-made buildings for them to copy.

Adapt "Copy Cat"

  Start with only three to four block designs. Help the child copy the design. Transfer the block design to the top of the paper for the child to trace around the blocks.

  Use hand-over-hand assistance to make the building.

  Talk the child through the building process.

  Provide Velcro blocks or Legos® if the child has difficulty stacking or is easily frustrated.

Concentration

Materials

- card games such as Old Maid, Go Fish, or matching cards

Procedure

1. Begin with a few very different pairs. Place the pairs face down. Help the child find a match.
2. Use visual descriptors to talk about how the two cards are the same or different. For example, "These fish are the same, because they are both blue and wearing a hat" or "These fish are different, because one is green and the other is yellow."
3. As the child experiences more success, make the activity more challenging by adding additional pairs or pairs that are more difficult to tell apart.

Adapt "Concentration"

  Use over-sized playing cards or flash cards.

 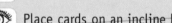 Place cards on an incline board (see pages 306–307 in Chapter 5 for directions) or a cardholder, if the child cannot hold cards or has difficulty seeing them.

 Cover the table with black paper and use a magnifying glass.

 Assist the child in turning over cards.

  Use flash cards with simple pictures of animals or objects to make this activity easier.

Use the words "same" or "different" when looking for a match.

The Essential Literacy Connection

Books

Brandenberg, Aliki. 1998. **My Five Senses**. New York: HarperCollins. *Children will discover all the ways they learn through their five senses.*

Geoghegan, Adrienne. 1996. **Dogs Don't Wear Glasses**. New York: Crocodile Books. *When Nanny Needles decides to clean the house and makes an even bigger mess, she blames it on her dog Seymour's eyesight. When she takes him to the eye doctor, she sees that he is fine and she is the one who needs glasses.*

Hoban, Tana. 1997. **Look Book**. New York: Greenwillow. *A circle die-cut in each page reveals a sneak peak at the everyday item on the next page.*

Hubbell, Patricia. 2000. **Bouncing Time**. New York: HarperCollins. *A young child enjoys bouncing like all of the animals she sees at the zoo.*

Lesieg, Theo. 1999. **The Eye Book**. New York: Random House. *A little boy and a rabbit use their eyes to see everything around them.*

Oxenbury, Helen. 1995. **I See**. Cambridge, MA: Candlewick Press. *A baby sees many things during her day.* *

Smith, Lane. 1991. **Glasses: Who Needs Them?** New York: Viking. *When a young boy needs glasses, he is afraid he will look like a "dork." The eye doctor shows him that many people wear glasses.*

Williams, Sue. 1990. **I Went Walking**. San Diego, CA: Harcourt Brace. *A boy asks, "What did I see," in a rhyming story similar to* Brown Bear, Brown Bear, What Do You See?

(*Available as a board book)

Other Literacy Materials

- card games
- magazines
- puzzles

Adding Spark to the I See: Vision Center

Ask children to sort through magazines to find pictures of a specific category such as "Foods I Like" or "Animals." They can tear or cut out pictures and glue them to paper to make a collage.

Evaluation of the Individual Child

Is the child:

1. Able to visually locate a specified object in her immediate environment?
2. Able to track a moving object that is several feet away?
3. Able to match objects by visual similarity?
4. Able to copy a simple block design?

Painting with a paintbrush is interesting to watch.

I Hear: Hearing Center

Overview

Sounds and music are an important part of every preschool program. Children use their sense of hearing to learn about the world around them. In the *I Hear: Hearing Center*, preschoolers can experience making sounds using both common and unusual noisemakers. This will enhance self-expression, while providing the children with opportunities to move their bodies in new ways. Activities in the *I Hear: Hearing Center* will be used to promote social development in all children. The *I Hear: Hearing Center* will also encourage young children to identify objects by the sounds they make.

Learning Objectives

The child with special needs will:

1. Listen to sounds produced by a variety of sources.
2. Explore sounds made by different objects.
3. Develop new methods for self-expression.
4. Interact socially in a positive manner.

Time Frame

The *I Hear: Hearing Center* is designed for two to three weeks of use at a time. This center may be set up in the early childhood classroom several times during the year.

Letter to Parents or Guardians

Dear Parent or Guardian,

Young children use the sense of hearing to learn about their world. During the preschool years, children can expand their knowledge of sounds and sound-making. We have an *I Hear: Hearing Center* in the classroom where the preschoolers have the opportunity to make sounds with many different types of materials. They will learn to identify objects by the sounds they make.

We are working on "Sounds From Home" and "Sounds From Outside" recordings. We have a tape recorder available for checkout. If you are willing to record sounds from your own home or sounds from your outdoor environment, we will share these sounds with all the children so they can learn about the sounds made by objects in their environment.

Layout of the I Hear: Hearing Center

The *I Hear: Hearing Center* can be easily rotated into the *Music Center* or another unique center. Consider the noise level of this center when choosing the appropriate environmental placement. Sound boards (see page 315 in Chapter 5 for directions), carpeting, and pillows will help absorb sounds.

Vocabulary Enrichment

ears	loud
fast	rhythm
hear	slow
hearing	soft
listen	sound

Teacher- and Parent-Collected Props

- easy-to-use cassette tape or CD player
- cassette tapes or CDs (include blank, marching bands, children singing, and environmental sounds)
- rhythm instruments, such as blocks, triangles, rhythm sticks, bells, shakers, and cymbals (see pages 309–311 in Chapter 5 for directions for making various musical instruments)

Web of Integrated Learning

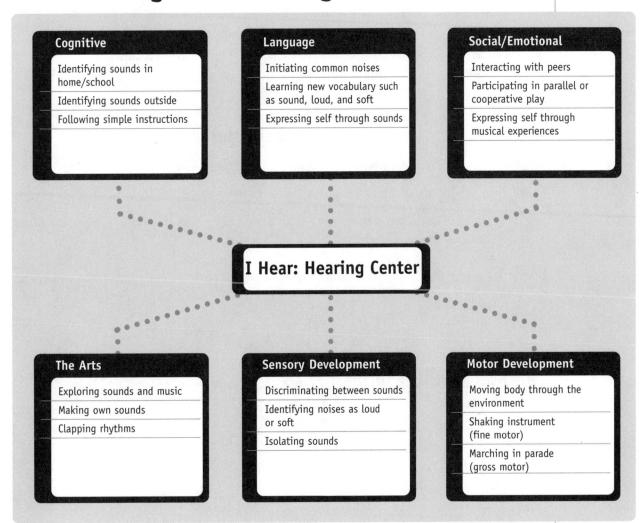

Cognitive
- Identifying sounds in home/school
- Identifying sounds outside
- Following simple instructions

Language
- Initiating common noises
- Learning new vocabulary such as sound, loud, and soft
- Expressing self through sounds

Social/Emotional
- Interacting with peers
- Participating in parallel or cooperative play
- Expressing self through musical experiences

I Hear: Hearing Center

The Arts
- Exploring sounds and music
- Making own sounds
- Clapping rhythms

Sensory Development
- Discriminating between sounds
- Identifying noises as loud or soft
- Isolating sounds

Motor Development
- Moving body through the environment
- Shaking instrument (fine motor)
- Marching in parade (gross motor)

Activities

Find the Music

Materials

- music box, or recordings and CD or tape player

Procedure

1. This activity is a nice way to introduce the *I Hear: Hearing Center* to the children.
2. Turn the music on and hide the music box, CD player, or tape player in the *I Hear: Hearing Center*.
3. Ask the children to "Find the Music."
4. Invite each child to take a turn. Alternate hiding the music box down low and up high to encourage a wide variety of motor skills.
5. You may give the child verbal cues, such as, "You're getting closer."
6. Give the child a moment to hold the music box after she has found it.

Adapt "Find the Music"

 Provide child with physical assistance to find the music box.

  The child can verbally direct you to the music box.

  To encourage taking turns, ask one child to hide the music box for the next child.

 Some children are particularly sensitive to loud music so you may need to keep the volume low.

Sounds From Home

Materials

- cassette tape player
- blank tapes

Procedure

1. Make a "Sounds From Home" recording, leaving several seconds between each sound.
2. Home sounds might include the vacuum cleaner operating, a baby crying, a phone ringing, water running, a doorbell ringing, a clock ticking, a fire alarm ringing, a washing machine running, a radio playing, a hair dryer blowing, a toilet flushing, and a cat meowing.

3. Discuss the sounds the children might hear in their home.

4. Play the recording one sound at a time and ask the children to identify what they hear.

5. Ask questions. "How did you recognize the sound?" "Was it loud or soft?" "Was it fast or slow?"

Adapt "Sounds From Home"

 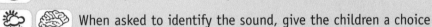 Show children pictures of the objects that made the sounds.

   When asked to identify the sound, give the children a choice between two or more pictures.

 Some sounds, such as a vacuum cleaner, may be unpleasant to some children. Be careful not to play these sounds too loud; you may choose to skip them entirely.

  Select only three or four sounds to play each day to decrease the chance of over-stimulating the children.

  Echo the sounds on the recording.

Sounds From Outdoors

Materials
- cassette tape player
- blank tapes

Procedure

1. Make a "Sounds From Outdoors" recording, leaving several seconds between each sound.

2. Outdoor sounds might include a dog barking, a lawnmower running, a car horn beeping, construction equipment running, a siren wailing, birds chirping, an airplane zooming, wind rustling, rain pouring down, thunder clapping, a cow mooing, a rooster crowing, crowds cheering, and the noises at a sports event.

3. Talk with the children about sounds they might hear outside.

4. Play a sound and ask the children, "What did you hear?"

Adapt "Sounds From Outdoors"

  Show children pictures of the objects that made the sounds.

   Give the children a choice between two or three pictures.

 Some sounds, such as a siren, may be unpleasant to some children. Be careful not to play these sounds too loud, or exclude them from the playback.

  Use three or four sounds each day so children will not be over-stimulated.

 Echo the sounds on the recording.

Sound Makers

Materials

- aluminum pie pans or aluminum cans
- oatmeal canisters with lids
- plastic bottles with lids
- buttons, beads, or small pebbles
- glue
- rubber bands
- yarn
- spoons
- hole punch

Different mallets produce interesting sounds on this African instrument.

Procedure

1. Punch holes around edges of pie pans or cans.

   Note: Smooth or cover all rough edges.

2. Place container collection on a table.
3. Allow each child to select which container to use.
4. Place containers of buttons, beads, or small pebbles on the table.
5. Allow each child to select the materials for filling a container.
6. Help the child fill her selected container with materials using spoons or hands.
7. Glue lids on containers and lace the cans or pie pans together by threading yarn through the holes. Leave extra yarn to make a loop for carrying. Allow the glue to dry completely.
8. Let children explore the noises their Sound Makers produce. Talk with the children about the sounds. "Is it loud or soft?"

Adapt "Sound Makers"

  Glue or lace the containers together for the child.

  Accompany the shaking with the words, "Shake, shake, shake."

  Fill and glue the containers for children who are likely to mouth or swallow non-edible materials.

Playground Parade

Materials

- books about parades, optional
- variety of child-made "sound makers" or other instruments
- dress-up clothes, optional
- portable CD player or tape player
- CD or tape recording of marching band music

Procedure

1. Talk about parades with the children. You may read a book about a parade.
2. Practice marching around the room to the rhythm of the marching band music.
3. Children select their Sound Makers or other instruments to play in the parade.
4. Children may dress up for the parade.
5. Carry the tape player with you and encourage the children to march through the playground, "making sounds" as they go.
6. This activity may be an indoor activity if weather or other circumstances prohibit marching on the playground.

Adapt "Playground Parade"

 Children may require mobility devices, such as a wheelchair, to move in the parade.

  Some children may not be able to walk and use their Sound Makers at the same time. You can pull these children in a wagon or cart.

  If a child becomes upset when accidentally touched or bumped by another child, place that child at the beginning or end of the line.

  Give the children praise as they march in their parade. "I like the way you are playing your music in the parade, Susan."

 Demonstrate how to march and count out the beat of marching feet. "One, two, three, four." Practice marching before beginning the parade.

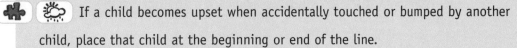

The Essential Literacy Connection

Books

Brandenberg, Aliki. 1998. **My Five Senses**. New York: HarperCollins. *Children will discover all the ways they learn through their five senses.*

Davis, Katie. 2000. **Who Hoots?** San Diego, CA: Harcourt Brace. *This funny story will inspire children to think about the sounds animals make.*

Moncure, Jane Belk. 1982. **Sounds All Around**. Chicago, IL: Children's Press. *Discover how sounds are made and why humans and animals use these sounds.*

Perkins, Al. 1968. **The Ear Book**. New York: Random House. *A boy and his dog learn about the sounds all around them.*

Showers, Paul. 1993. **The Listening Walk**. New York: HarperCollins. *A little girl and her father go on a walk and enjoy the sounds they hear.*

Wong, Janet. 2000. **Buzz**. New York: Harcourt. *Many sounds are distinct during the morning routine.*

Ziefert, Harriet. 2000. **Hats Off for the Fourth of July**. New York: Penguin Putnam. *The people who live in Chatham are excited to see the Fourth of July parade.*

Other Literacy Materials

- banner for parade
- sound recordings

What sound does a shell make?

Adding Spark to the I Hear: Hearing Center

Ask children to move to the sounds that they hear from the "Sounds From Home" or "Sounds From Outside" recordings. For example, they can "shake like a washing machine," "walk like a dog," or "jiggle like a telephone ringing." Observe the new movements the children can do while they are listening and identifying these sounds.

Evaluation of the Individual Child

Is the child:

1. Able to identify simple objects by sound?
2. Able to localize sounds (find where the sound is coming from)?
3. Using noisemakers to express herself?
4. Interacting with others during sound experiences?

I Touch: Tactile Center

Overview

Preschoolers use their senses to gather information about the world. The *I Touch: Tactile Center* will provide them with opportunities and experiences to develop their sense of touch. Unique textures and materials in the center expand their tactile sensation. Young children will be encouraged to touch with their hands, feet, face, and limbs. They will learn to label the things they touch, using words such as "hard," "soft," "sticky," and "wet." Preschoolers with special needs can be hypersensitive to different textures. The *I Touch: Tactile Center* should be stimulating and non-threatening, so even children who are touch-sensitive will want to experience the fun. Children should not be forced to touch or feel a texture. Instead, slowly introduce the texture and encourage the child to participate in the playful experience.

Learning Objectives

The child with special needs will:

1. Explore textures through the sense of touch.
2. Learn about different textures and materials.
3. Use tools to work with textures and materials.
4. Expand creativity in play.

Time Frame

The *I Touch: Tactile Center* can remain set up for a minimum of two to three weeks. The center can stay for a longer time if the preschoolers remain interested. Observe preschoolers in the center and add new textures as interest wanes. The center may be brought back later.

Letter to Parents or Guardians

Dear Parent or Guardian,

Young children use all of their senses to learn about their environment. Touch is one of their primary senses. We want to encourage children to use the sense of touch effectively, so we have set up an *I Touch: Tactile Center* where preschoolers will have the opportunity to explore and play with textures, materials, and tools that may be new to them. Textures will include smooth, sticky, bumpy, wet, hard, and rough.

We are looking for donations of materials for our *I Touch: Tactile Center*. Please bring in fabric scraps, such as fur, satin, lace, or leather. We also can use sandpaper, bubble wrap, and cotton swabs. With your help, we will have an interesting *I Touch: Tactile Center* that will expand the children's use of their sense of touch.

Layout of the I Touch: Tactile Center

The *I Touch: Tactile Center* should be located in an area of the room where cleanup is simple. The center may be used in an area where you do art projects or fine motor activities. A table and chairs are useful, along with a sand and water table, as this center is easily transformed into a *Sand Center* or *Water Center*. Store scrap materials in clear, plastic containers that are labeled for adult and child accessibility.

Vocabulary Enrichment

cold	smooth
different	soft
feel	sticky
hard	touch
rough	warm
same	

Teacher- and Parent-Collected Props

- clear plastic boxes (to store materials)
- construction paper
- cooking supplies, such as cornstarch, flour, rice, beans, and salt
- cooking tools, such as spoons, bowls, funnel, sifter, colander, and tongs
- fabric scraps, such as fur, satin, lace, leather, corduroy, cotton, wool, jersey, burlap, spandex, and denim
- glue
- household materials, such as cotton balls, cotton swabs, foil, plastic wrap, and yarn
- playdough
- sand and water table (or place large plastic containers on the floor)
- shower curtain liner or sheets of plastic (to cover the floor)
- small broom or vacuum
- stuffed animals

Web of Integrated Learning

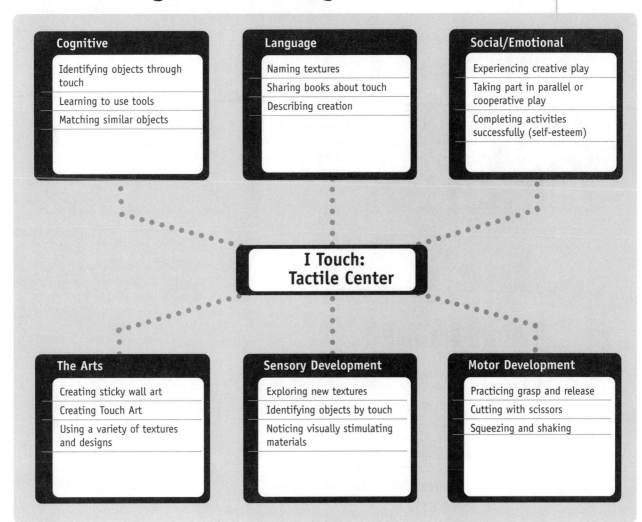

Cognitive
- Identifying objects through touch
- Learning to use tools
- Matching similar objects

Language
- Naming textures
- Sharing books about touch
- Describing creation

Social/Emotional
- Experiencing creative play
- Taking part in parallel or cooperative play
- Completing activities successfully (self-esteem)

I Touch: Tactile Center

The Arts
- Creating sticky wall art
- Creating Touch Art
- Using a variety of textures and designs

Sensory Development
- Exploring new textures
- Identifying objects by touch
- Noticing visually stimulating materials

Motor Development
- Practicing grasp and release
- Cutting with scissors
- Squeezing and shaking

Sticky Wall

Materials

- contact paper
- tape
- materials of various textures, such as fur, satin, cotton balls, bark, leaves, small sticks, sandpaper, yarn, newspaper, and foil
- child-safe scissors

Procedure

1. Tape contact paper with sticky side out to a large wall.
2. Place a variety of textured objects and materials on a table for selection by the children.
3. Let the children stick their selections onto the sticky wall.
4. Encourage the children to touch the sticky wall with other parts of their body, such as their feet, faces, or limbs.
5. Leave the wall in place so the children can come back to visit the textures or to add new items.

Adapt "Sticky Wall"

 Place contact paper on a table surface or on the floor if the child does not have the mobility needed to put materials on the sticky wall.

 Use white contact paper with dark materials for better color contrast.

 Ask the children to help you label the items, using vocabulary such as "hard," "soft," "bumpy," "sticky," or "rough."

 Write descriptors below the corresponding items.

Texture Box Match

Materials

- medium-size cardboard box or shoebox
- scissors
- piece of fabric
- variety of different textured items
- fabric pieces with different textures
- index cards
- markers

Procedure

1. Cut a small hole (big enough for a hand) in one side of the box.

2. Cover the hole with fabric, so the contents of the box cannot be seen.

3. When the children are not present, place several different textured materials or items inside the box.

4. Place other matching materials or items outside the box.

5. Place word labels with the textured materials or items outside the box.

6. Help the child feel a texture outside the box. Ask the child to name the texture, such as soft, hard, bumpy, fuzzy, and so on.

7. Invite the child to put her hand inside the box to find the same texture. When she brings a texture out of the box, ask her whether it is the same or different texture as the named material.

8. Place the chosen texture beside its match outside the box.

9. Continue until all matches have been made.

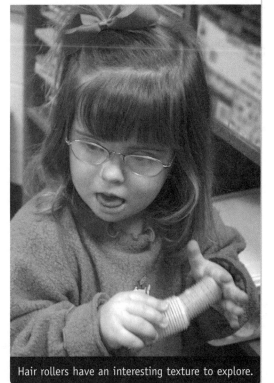

Hair rollers have an interesting texture to explore.

Adapt "Texture Box Match"

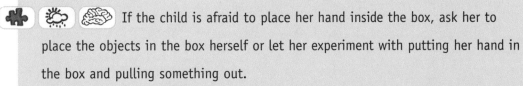 To simplify the game, have the child pull a texture out of the box and ask her to match it to a texture on the table; use only two or three textures to match.

If the child is afraid to place her hand inside the box, ask her to place the objects in the box herself or let her experiment with putting her hand in the box and pulling something out.

Use only textures that the child likes to touch rather than a new texture or something that the child is afraid to touch.

Use only a few distinctive terms to label the textures, such as *hard, soft, smooth,* or *rough.*

Activities

Touch Collage/Art

Wet paper has a unique feel.

Materials

- cooking supplies with a variety of textures, such as cornstarch mixed with water, flour, colored sugar
- materials with a variety of textures, such as corduroy, denim, leather, spandex, and satin
- construction paper
- glue or glue sticks
- child-safe scissors

Procedure

1. Place materials in a spot that is easily accessible for the children.
2. Give each child a piece of construction paper and child-safe scissors.
3. Ask the child to make a collage of her favorite textures.
4. Label the collage with the textures the child selected.

Adapt "Touch Collage/Art"

  To increase cognitive skill level, ask the child to complete a particular type of textured collage. "Jonathan, will you make me a soft collage?"

 Use positive words to describe the collage the child has made. "Your collage is full of soft textures."

 Place light-colored paper on a cookie sheet to provide boundaries for gluing objects.

The Essential Literacy Connection

Books

Brandenberg, Aliki. 1992. **My Hands**. New York: Perfection Learning Prebound. *The many uses of hands are explored in pictures of children with and without disabilities.*

Brandenberg, Aliki. 1998. **My Five Senses**. New York: HarperCollins. *Children will discover all the ways they learn through their five senses.*

Martin, Bill, & Archambault, John. 1998. **Here Are My Hands**. New York: Henry Holt. *Children learn self-awareness of their bodies while examining illustrations of children from various backgrounds.* *

Oxenbury, Helen. 1995. **I Touch**. Cambridge, MA: Candlewick Press. *Illustrations of a toddler touching various objects are shown throughout the pages of this book.* *

Thompson, Mary. 1996. **Andy and His Yellow Frisbee**. Bethesda, MD: Woodbine House. *Join these young children as they learn about autism and why Andy is preoccupied with spinning his yellow Frisbee.*

(*Available as a board book)

Other Literacy Materials

- eye-hand coordination in lacing
- labels for collage textures
- magnetic letters and shapes
- scissors and clippers

Adding Spark to the I Touch: Tactile Center

Add plastic animals, cars, trucks, and people to the *I Touch: Tactile Center* to stimulate sociodramatic play; for example, cars drive through the snow (cornstarch or flour).

Evaluation of the Individual Child

Is the child:

1. Exploring new textures or materials?
2. Able to identify a texture? Which textures are identified?
3. Using a tool to manipulate textures or materials?
4. Participating in new play activities, such as parallel play or sociodramatic play?

In and Out Center

● ●

Overview

The *In and Out Center* contains many materials and activities that stimulate young children's fine motor and problem-solving skills. In this center, young children experience the relational concepts of *in* and *out*. One of the best ways for young children to learn these and other important language and cognitive concepts is by moving their bodies into different positions. The *In and Out Center* offers preschoolers essential large movement experiences. Children learn *in* and *out* through manipulation of objects, using shape sorters, puzzles, and pegboards. The *In and Out Center* offers children opportunities to develop many different skills related to *in* and *out*.

Learning Objectives

The child with special needs will:

1. Develop fine motor skills.
2. Improve eye-hand coordination.
3. Use language to accompany *in* and *out* activities.
4. Develop problem-solving skills.

Time Frame

The *In and Out Center* is designed for two weeks of classroom use. Observe the children's involvement in this center and add new materials as interest wanes. This center may be brought back later.

Letter to Parents or Guardians	Dear Parent or Guardian,

Dear Parent or Guardian,

We have just set up the *In and Out Center* in our classroom. The center is designed to help our preschoolers learn the important concepts of *in* and *out*. The children will participate in small (fine) motor activities, such as putting together puzzles, lacing beads, and working with pegboards. We will provide large (gross) motor activities to help the children understand that they can move their bodies *in*, *out*, *over*, and *under*. When you are playing with your child, use words to label his or her position. You may say, "Look, you are *inside* the playhouse," or "You put the cup *in* the sink."

We are collecting small items for the children to sort and manipulate in the *In and Out Center*. We would appreciate donations of any of the following items—buttons, cotton balls, golf tees, Styrofoam pieces, plastic storage containers, empty plastic drink bottles, scrap cardboard, and empty cereal and/or cookie boxes.

Layout of the In and Out Center

This center will work well in a part of the room where both large and small movement activities may be executed. It can be organized in conjunction with the *Fine Motor Center*, as some similar manipulatives will be used. Store small items in clear plastic containers with pictures and labels that show the contents.

Vocabulary Enrichment

beside

empty

full

in

inside

out

outside

over

under

Teacher- and Parent-Collected Props

- beads and laces
- bowls, spoons, scoops, and funnels
- clear plastic bottles or containers to fill, such as a coffee can with a hole cut in the lid
- clear plastic storage containers for materials
- form boards to show shapes
- items for stringing, such as empty thread spools, curlers, cereal with holes, yarn, shoelaces, and pipe cleaners
- peg boards of all sizes, including a Lite Brite®
- puzzles
- small cardboard boxes with and without lids
- small items to put inside containers, such as buttons, large coins, cotton balls, straws, or large nuts and bolts.

Safety Note: Do not use small items with preschoolers who mouth objects.

Web of Integrated Learning

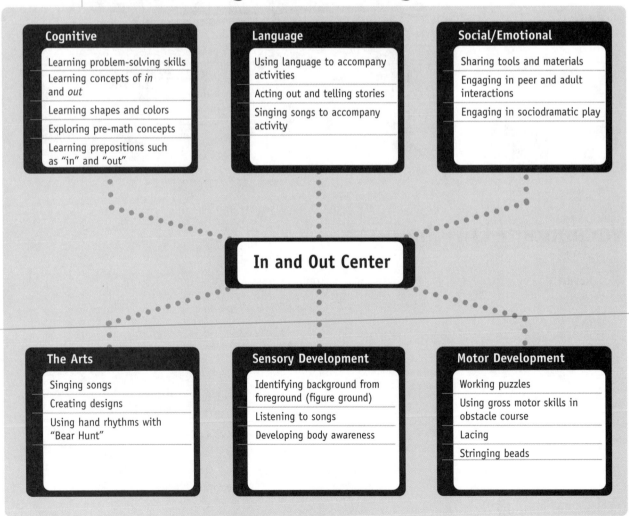

Cognitive
- Learning problem-solving skills
- Learning concepts of *in* and *out*
- Learning shapes and colors
- Exploring pre-math concepts
- Learning prepositions such as "in" and "out"

Language
- Using language to accompany activities
- Acting out and telling stories
- Singing songs to accompany activity

Social/Emotional
- Sharing tools and materials
- Engaging in peer and adult interactions
- Engaging in sociodramatic play

In and Out Center

The Arts
- Singing songs
- Creating designs
- Using hand rhythms with "Bear Hunt"

Sensory Development
- Identifying background from foreground (figure ground)
- Listening to songs
- Developing body awareness

Motor Development
- Working puzzles
- Using gross motor skills in obstacle course
- Lacing
- Stringing beads

Cardboard Sewing Cards

Materials

- pieces of scrap cardboard
- scissors (adult only)
- paint and paintbrushes, optional
- hole punch or screwdriver (adult only)
- string, yarn, shoelaces, or rubber string (round elastic cording)
- masking tape

Procedure

1. Use adult scissors to cut shapes, animals, letters, or characters out of the cardboard.
2. Paint the cards, if desired.
3. Use a hole punch or screwdriver to carefully punch holes around the edges of the cards. Be sure to space holes ½" to 1" apart.
4. Cut pieces of string, yarn, or rubber string into lengths twice the length of the cards.
5. Wrap the tip of the yarn or string with a small piece of masking tape. This creates a stiff end that is easier to thread through holes.

Yarn goes *in* and *out* of the lacing card.

Adapt "Cardboard Sewing Cards"

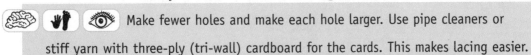 Make fewer holes and make each hole larger. Use pipe cleaners or stiff yarn with three-ply (tri-wall) cardboard for the cards. This makes lacing easier.

Paint cards in yellow or white. Circle the holes with a black marker to make holes easier to see.

Cut a lap-sized piece of cardboard and punch large holes through the thickness. Use macramé rope with ends taped to prevent unraveling for stringing.

Activities

Going on a Bear Hunt

Look at me *inside* the box!

Materials

- indoor tunnel
- inner tube
- large blanket
- Hula Hoops
- table
- stuffed bears

Procedure

1. Set up an indoor or outdoor obstacle course using items that require the children to step, crawl, or move into, over, or under.
2. Place stuffed bears inside or under objects.
3. Demonstrate how to move through the obstacle course. Crawl under a blanket or table. Step into Hula Hoops or inner tubes. Crawl through the tunnel, collecting bears as you go.
4. Talk the children through the obstacle course. "Spencer is crawling *inside* the tunnel." "Katherine is jumping *in* and *out* of the Hula Hoops."
5. When finished, invite the children to count the bears they found on their hunt.

Adapt "Going on a Bear Hunt"

 Make obstacles that children who use mobility aides, such as wheelchairs, crutches, or walkers can go *inside*, *over*, or *under* in tents, ramps, and doorways.

 Read the book, tell the story, or sing the song, "We're Going on a Bear Hunt."

  You may need to physically help the child move through the obstacle course while talking them through the process.

 Shorten the obstacle courses to three items.

Parking Garage

Materials

- cardboard boxes of various sizes, such as shoeboxes, cereal boxes, and milk cartons
- scissors (adult only)
- toy trucks and cars
- toy people or animals

Procedure

1. Make a garage out of the boxes. Cut out doors large enough for toy vehicles to go inside the garage.
2. Demonstrate how to park vehicles *in* or *on top of* the garage.
3. Use verbal descriptors for the children, as they put people *inside* the cars and trucks. Talk about how many cars can go *inside* or *on top of* the parking garage.

Adapt "Parking Garage"

 Draw black roads on a large piece of butcher paper, indicating how the cars can get inside the garage.

 Say the words "in" and "out" to accompany the activity of the child.

 Use a battery-powered car or truck with a switch adapter.

 Place vehicles and garages on top of a table for easy accessibility.

Fishing

Materials

- wooden dowel rods
- string or yarn
- scissors
- glue
- construction paper
- lamination or clear contact paper
- lightweight magnets or paper clips
- rocking boat or child-size chairs set up as a boat
- bucket

Procedure

1. Tie string or yarn to the end of dowel rods to make fishing poles. Glue the ends of the string or yarn so it will not unravel. Attach lightweight magnets to the end of the yarn.

2. Cut out fish shapes from construction paper. You may laminate the fish to make them more durable.

3. Attach magnets or paper clips to both sides of the fish.

4. Children can sit in the rocking boat or child-size chairs to fish. They should place each fish *in* the bucket.

5. Fish may be counted or sorted by color. Talk about the process, using the *inside* or *in* concepts. "You have three fish *in* your bucket." "Throw the fish back *in* the pond."

Adapt "Fishing"

 Shorten or lengthen the fishing poles and/or fishing line, as necessary.

 Wrap fishing rods with tape to make them easier to grasp, or assist child with holding the rod.

 Make larger fish out of red or yellow construction paper.

 Place larger magnets or several small magnets on the fish to make them easier to catch.

 Sing and chant, "Three Blue Birds" and adapt the words: "Three green fish swimming in the sea. Three green fish swimming in the sea. One jumped out. Oh! Two green fish swimming in the sea. Two green fish swimming in the sea...."

The Essential Literacy Connection

Books

Berenstain, Stan, & Berenstain, Jan. 1997. **Inside Outside Upside Down**. New York: Random House. *Brother Bear gets into a box; Papa Bear picks it up, turns it over, takes it outside, and puts it on a truck upside down.*

Hunter, Ryan Ann. 1999. **Dig a Tunnel**. New York: Holiday House. *All sorts of tunnels built by animals, insects, and humans are illustrated in this book.*

Kalan, Robert. 1989. **Jump, Frog, Jump!** New York: HarperCollins. *As the frog tries to catch a fly, other animals are trying to catch the frog. Each time he is close to being captured, the phrase, "Jump, frog, jump," is repeated.*

Lester, Helen. 2002. **Hooway for Wodney Wat**. Boston, MA: Houghton Mifflin. *His classmates tease Rodney Rat because he cannot pronounce his R's correctly. All the rats are afraid when a new rat, Camilla, starts school and announces she is bigger, meaner, and smarter than everyone else, until Rodney accidentally outsmarts her during a game of Simon Says and becomes the class hero.*

Rosen, Michael. 1989. **We're Going on a Bear Hunt**. New York: Simon & Schuster. *A father and four children go on a bear hunt, venturing through the field, into the river, and finding their way through the forest into a cave.**

(*Available as a board book)

Other Literacy Materials

- labels for parking garage
- puzzles
- signs for following roads and signs

Adding Spark to the In and Out Center

Place large pieces of Styrofoam and several golf tees inside the *In and Out Center*. Children will enjoy making holes in the Styrofoam with the golf tees.

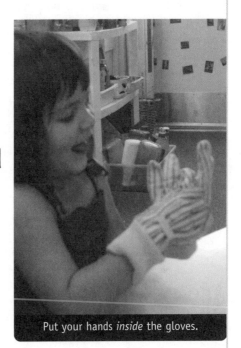

Put your hands *inside* the gloves.

Evaluation of the Individual Child

Is the child:

1. Able to place small objects into a small container?
2. Able to complete a 5-, 10-, or 20-piece puzzle?
3. Verbalizing or demonstrating an understanding of the concepts of *in* and *out* appropriately?
4. Able to lace a shoe or lacing card?

Ball Center

· ·

Overview

Balls are stimulating toys for preschool children. The *Ball Center* will provide opportunities for movement and language experiences. In this center, children can practice catching, throwing, and kicking balls of various sizes. Some preschoolers can catch a medium-size ball in their hands and kick a rolling ball. Other preschoolers may just be learning to throw a small ball or to kick a stationary ball. In the *Ball Center*, young children can explore concepts such as *in, out, over, under,* and *through*. They will play with their peers to develop interaction skills and turn-taking abilities.

Learning Objectives

The child with special needs will:

1. Develop eye-hand coordination.
2. Develop eye-foot coordination.
3. Improve ball throwing and/or catching.
4. Interact appropriately with peers.

Time Frame

The *Ball Center* will work best if it is set up for two to three weeks. It may be set up again and revisited later in the year if the children are interested. Some activities may work well outside, considering the season.

Letter to Parents or Guardians

Dear Parent or Guardian,

Children of all ages like to play with balls. In our *Ball Center*, the preschoolers will practice important motor skills, such as throwing, catching, and kicking balls. As the children play with balls in this center, there will be many opportunities for them to learn concepts such as *in, out, over,* and *under*.

Catching a ball is an eye-hand coordination skill that takes much practice. Some preschoolers can trap a large ball (such as a beach ball) against their bodies. Others can catch a medium ball (such as a Nerf® ball) in their hands. When you play catch with your child, start by standing very close and gently throwing a large, soft ball into his or her chest. As your child's skill improves, move back a few steps and toss the ball into his or her hands.

Layout of the Ball Center

The *Ball Center* requires room for the children to move, throw, and catch balls. It may be set up in the *Gross Motor Center* for convenience. Children in the *Ball Center* will be active and will make noise. Therefore, this center is best located away from quiet areas like the *Books/Library Center* or the *Private Place Center*. Carpeting or floor mats will also help decrease the noise level.

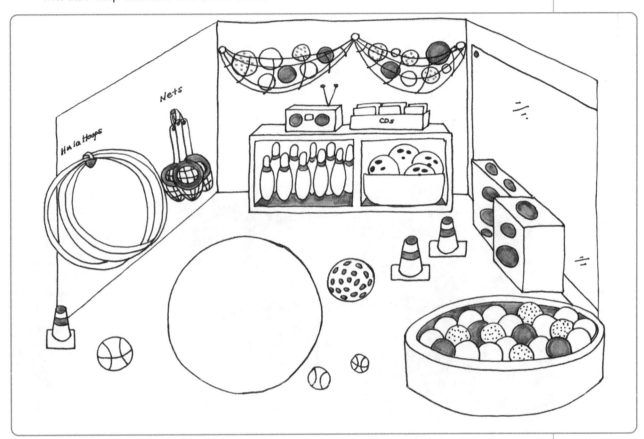

Vocabulary Enrichment

ball	roll
catch	through
inside	throw
kick	under
over	

Teacher- and Parent-Collected Props

- cardboard boxes of various sizes with an opening at the top and ball-size holes cut out of the sides
- carpet roll to roll balls through (see page 305 in Chapter 5 for directions)
- clean socks knotted into balls
- clean trash cans or plastic containers
- Hula Hoops
- large plastic cups
- large therapy or exercise ball
- medium balls, such as nubby, beach, Nerf®, and soccer balls
- net or large bag for ball storage
- plastic bowling pins
- plastic cones
- small balls, such as tennis, foam, and Koosh® balls
- tire inner tube

An exercise ball adds new challenges.

Web of Integrated Learning

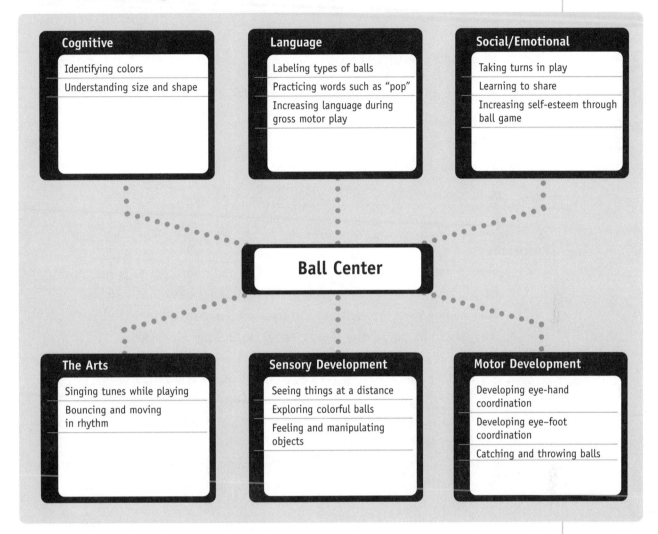

Cognitive
- Identifying colors
- Understanding size and shape

Language
- Labeling types of balls
- Practicing words such as "pop"
- Increasing language during gross motor play

Social/Emotional
- Taking turns in play
- Learning to share
- Increasing self-esteem through ball game

Ball Center

The Arts
- Singing tunes while playing
- Bouncing and moving in rhythm

Sensory Development
- Seeing things at a distance
- Exploring colorful balls
- Feeling and manipulating objects

Motor Development
- Developing eye-hand coordination
- Developing eye–foot coordination
- Catching and throwing balls

"(Children) gain knowledge from their interactions with objects...in their world. They learn about a beach ball by feeling and seeing it. They experiment with the ball to discover how it responds by throwing it in the air or rolling it on the floor. This experimentation helps them gather the information they want."

Activities

Beanbag Toss

Materials

- fabrics with a variety of textures and colors, such as corduroy, satin, denim, and fur
- scissors
- sewing materials, such as needle, thread, scissors, and sewing machine
- dried beans, rice, or cotton batting
- large piece of cardboard
- paints
- brushes

Procedure

1. Make beanbags out of various fabric textures and colors. Fill bags with beans, rice, or cotton batting. It is good to have beanbags of varying weights.
2. From a large piece of cardboard, cut openings large enough for the beanbags. You may choose to cut primary shapes, facial features, or plain circles.
3. Trim the edges of each opening in a different primary color.
4. Secure the cardboard piece in front of a wall with room for the beanbags to fall behind the board.
5. Encourage the children to take turns, allowing only one child at a time to throw beanbags. Another child can pick up the beanbags.
6. As the child improves in her throwing, you may ask her to aim and throw the bag into a specific hole. "Abby, can you throw the beanbag into the red circle?"

Adapt "Beanbag Toss"

 When introducing the *Ball Center*, label the type of ball, such as beach ball, Nerf® ball, and so on; use this label in the center as well.

 Paint the entire cardboard piece black and circle the opening with red paint. Place the painted cardboard against a white or light colored wall.

  Cut out only one or two very large openings.

 Allow the child to feel and manipulate the beanbags if she is unable to throw them.

 Cover the floor behind the cardboard and the wall with paper so that the beanbag will make a noise when it hits the wall or floor.

Ball Collecting

Materials

- butterfly nets or canvas bags with handles for catching balls
- small foam balls or other soft balls of various colors

Procedure

1. Give each child a butterfly net or canvas bag for catching the balls.
2. Toss balls to the child and let her catch and collect them. Remember to stand close to the children who have difficulty catching.
3. After each child has collected a ball, take turns asking each what color ball she has collected.

Adapt "Ball Collecting"

 Use large red or yellow balls for children with visual impairments.

  Children who are unable to hold nets or bags may be able to catch the balls in their hands or in a small container.

 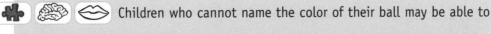 Children who cannot name the color of their ball may be able to match the color on a chart or card.

   Children who are good at throwing may throw balls to their peers, increasing peer interactions.

Bubble Pop

Materials

- bubbles (see page 304 in Chapter 5 for bubble recipes)
- bubble wands

Procedure

1. This is a great outdoors activity; put down a plastic mat if you are doing this activity indoors.
2. Blow bubbles and ask the children to pop them between their hands.
3. Demonstrate how to clap, popping the bubbles between your hands.
4. Each child can take a turn blowing bubbles for others to pop.

Adapt "Bubble Pop"

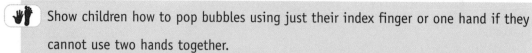 Show children how to pop bubbles using just their index finger or one hand if they cannot use two hands together.

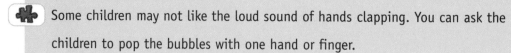 Some children may not like the loud sound of hands clapping. You can ask the children to pop the bubbles with one hand or finger.

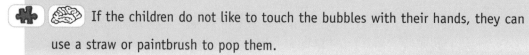 If the children do not like to touch the bubbles with their hands, they can use a straw or paintbrush to pop them.

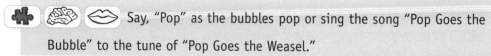 Say, "Pop" as the bubbles pop or sing the song "Pop Goes the Bubble" to the tune of "Pop Goes the Weasel."

The Essential Literacy Connection

Books

Allen, Marty. 1999. **Let's Play Ball**. Goleta, CA: Kid's Books. *Children will learn about different kinds of balls and what sport they are used for.* *

Dorling Kindersley. 2003. **Touch and Feel: Baseball**. New York: DK Publishing. *Children will learn to explore their environment by feeling the textures of the baseball, bat, baseball diamond, and so on.* *

Harrison, Peggy. 2003. **We Love Baseball**. New York: Random House. *Join a team of seven-year-olds as they get their baseball uniforms, practice playing, and then play a game of baseball.*

Loomis, Christine. 1993. **At the Mall**. New York: Scholastic. *A child finds many things, including balls, while shopping at the mall with his mom.*

Nelson, Mary. 2000. **Balls!** New York: Random House. *Peek under the flaps with Elmo as he finds balls of different sizes and uses.* *

Tafuri, Nancy. 1989. **The Ball Bounced**. New York: Greenwillow Books. *A small child follows the ball as it bounces many places.* *

(*Available as a board book)

Other Literacy Materials

- catalog with toys and balls
- pictures and labels for different balls

Adding Spark to the Ball Center

Place a small baby wading pool inside the *Ball Center*. Fill the baby pool with plastic balls, or leave it empty for the children to fill with balls of their choice.

Evaluation of the Individual Child

Is the child:

1. Improving in her ability to throw a ball (large, medium, or small size)?
2. Developing catching skills (large or medium-size ball)?
3. Improving in her ability to kick a ball (stable or moving)?
4. Interacting appropriately with her peers?

A child joyfully explores a big, soft ball.

Big and Little Center

Overview

Preschoolers visiting the *Big and Little Center* will have experiences that will expand their understanding of the world. The *Big and Little Center* offers activities that encourage the child's understanding of beginning math concepts such as *big*, *little*, *long*, *short*, *tall*, and *heavy*. Young children can develop math skills through the manipulation of tools, such as rulers and scales, during play. The *Big and Little Center* supports cognitive and language development during interactions with peers and adults.

Learning Objectives

The child with special needs will:

1. Expand language skills.
2. Learn simple math concepts.
3. Use tools to gain a greater understanding of the environment.
4. Use problem-solving skills to explore the environment.

Time Frame

The *Big and Little Center* is designed to work effectively for a period of two to three weeks. The center may be revisited to allow children to gain more experience with the learning objectives.

Letter to Parents or Guardians	Dear Parent or Guardian,

Dear Parent or Guardian,

We are preparing to open the *Big and Little Center* in our classroom. In this center, the preschoolers will have hands-on, playful experiences with basic math concepts such as *big*, *little*, *long*, and *short*. We will work with measuring tools such as scales, rulers, and measuring tapes. We would like to borrow a bath scale and food scale for the children's use in the center. If you have one available that we can borrow for two or three weeks, please let us know.

Cooking is a fun activity that allows children to experience measuring. Next time you are in the kitchen, invite your child to help you measure ingredients. Discuss the amounts as you go. Young children also enjoy looking in the mirror and comparing themselves to their family members. Use words to describe what you see, such as "You are smaller than Daddy" or "You are bigger than the baby," as they look in the mirror.

Layout of the Big and Little Center

The Big and Little Center needs minimal floor space, several chairs, a table, and a blank wall or a place to hang a sheet. A growth chart hung on a wall where children can measure themselves is a nice addition. An unbreakable, full-length mirror is also useful. Have paper (graph paper works well) and writing utensils available for the children to chart height or weight. Bring in big and little items that are not being used in other centers and label them as "big," "little," "long," "short," "heavy," or "light."

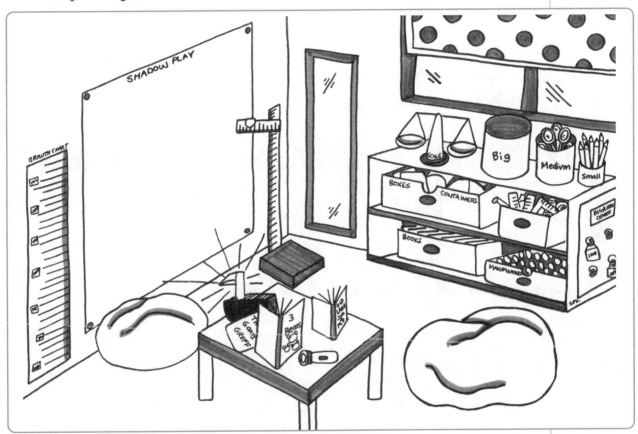

Vocabulary Enrichment

big	long
chart	measure
heavy	ruler
large	short
light	small
little	weigh

Teacher- and Parent-Collected Props

- bath scale
- food scale
- graph paper
- growth chart
- large and small measuring tapes
- large and small rulers
- paper and writing utensils
- unbreakable floor or wall mirror
- yardsticks

Web of Integrated Learning

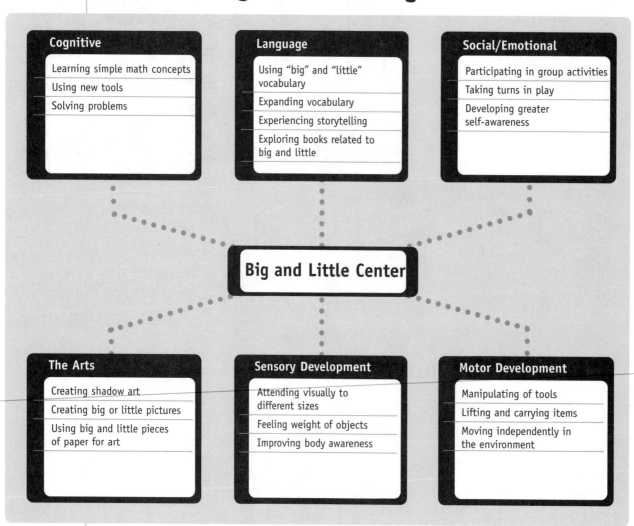

Cognitive
- Learning simple math concepts
- Using new tools
- Solving problems

Language
- Using "big" and "little" vocabulary
- Expanding vocabulary
- Experiencing storytelling
- Exploring books related to big and little

Social/Emotional
- Participating in group activities
- Taking turns in play
- Developing greater self-awareness

Big and Little Center

The Arts
- Creating shadow art
- Creating big or little pictures
- Using big and little pieces of paper for art

Sensory Development
- Attending visually to different sizes
- Feeling weight of objects
- Improving body awareness

Motor Development
- Manipulating of tools
- Lifting and carrying items
- Moving independently in the environment

Who Swallowed a Fly?

Materials

- paper and marker or copier
- scissors
- laminate or clear contact paper
- ½ gallon clear plastic storage bag
- stapler
- felt
- glue

Procedure

1. Draw or photocopy pictures of the following: an old woman, fly, spider, bird, cat, dog, cow, and horse. Make sure the animal pictures are of progressively larger animals.

2. Cut out and laminate the old woman's head, arms, and legs. Staple the head to one side of the opening of the bag and the arms and legs to the bottom of the bag. Be sure to leave a large opening in the storage bag so it can be filled with the animals. The finished product will allow the children to see the animals in the old woman's "stomach."

3. Cut out the animal shapes from felt or paper. If you choose paper, you may want to laminate them for durability. Glue a small piece of felt onto the back of the laminated animals.

4. Line up the animals on a felt board from smallest to largest.

5. Tell the story "There Was an Old Woman Who Swallowed a Fly." Allow a child to select the appropriate animal from the felt board and place it inside the old woman's stomach (storage bag), as you go.

6. Ask the children to identify each animal.

7. As you tell the story, note the size of each animal and the size of the old woman's stomach, as she swallows. "She swallowed a very small fly." "She swallowed a very large horse." "Is her stomach big or little?"

Adapt "Who Swallowed a Fly?"

  Give the child a special task, such as lining up the animals from smallest to largest on the felt board before you begin.

  Pass the animals around for the children to feel in their hands.

  Shorten the story to include only the fly, bird, cat, and horse and let the children help you tell the story.

 If the children have a good understanding of *big* and *little*, try using the words *heavy* and *light*. You can glue small weights to the back of the larger animals so that the children can feel the difference.

  If the child cannot sit on the floor during this activity, let her sit on a child-size chair, a therapy ball, or in a beanbag chair.

Activities

How Many Can Fit?

Materials

- large sheet of white paper
- markers
- 2 large, clear storage containers
- items of different sizes, such as large stuffed animals, small plastic animals, big balls, little balls, big cars, and little cars

Procedure

1. Make a graph for the wall with one horizontal column labeled "large" and the other labeled "small." Write numbers vertically up the left side of the paper.
2. Label one container "large" and the other "small."
3. Talk with the children about the words "large" and "small."
4. Place large and small items on the floor or table.
5. Ask each child to place a small item in the container marked "small."
6. Once the box is full, ask the children to help count how many small items are in the box.
7. Mark the graph on the wall, showing the children how many small items the box held.
8. Continue, sorting, counting, and charting the large items on the graph.

Adapt "How Many Can Fit?"

 If the child cannot bring you a specific item, ask her to point to or verbally describe the item she wants to choose.

 Give the children a choice between one large and one small item. "Which one is large?"

 Verbally praise children for their choices, right or wrong. "Thanks for making a choice, but this one is large."

 Let the child hold one large and one small item in her hands and help her to make a choice.

Paper Chains

Materials

- construction paper cut into strips measuring approximately 2" wide and 8" long
- glue or stapler
- yardsticks, rulers, or measuring tapes

Procedure

1. Assist children in making paper chains using glue or a stapler with supervision.
2. Discuss the concepts of *long* and *short*.
3. Help the child use a yardstick or measuring tape to measure the length of her link.
4. Line the links across a table or floor.
5. Ask the children to help decide which chain is longest and which chain is shortest.
6. Count the links in each chain and use a measuring tape or ruler to measure and compare the chains.

Adapt "Paper Chains"

 Help the children who do not want to touch glue use a stapler.

 Use large print rulers and measuring tapes or a magnifying glass.

 Children who cannot make a chain can help measure or count the links.

Activities

See My Shadow

Materials

- shadow screen (see pages 314–315 in Chapter 5 for directions)
- large flashlight, overhead projector, or floor lamp

Procedure

1. Turn off the lights in the *Big and Little Center*.
2. Place a large flashlight on a table or chair, directed toward the screen.
3. Preschoolers can stand in front of the light and watch their shadows on the screen.
4. Ask them to identify the shadows. "Whose shadow is that?" "Are you big or little?"
5. Help children observe how their shadows get bigger or smaller, as they move closer and farther away from the flashlight.
6. Have an adult stand beside a child. Compare who is bigger and smaller.
7. Preschoolers will enjoy watching their shadows move and dance!

Adapt "See My Shadow"

 Children can sit in a chair or adapted seating, such as a wheelchair, in front of the flashlight.

 Allow the child to hold the flashlight and stand or sit close to the screen so that they may see the shadow.

 You may also use words like "tall" and "short" or "near" and "far" to describe the children's shadows.

 Use an overhead projector or floor lamp if the children are unable to hold a flashlight or if they cannot use the flashlight appropriately.

Activities

Big and Little Pictures

Materials

- construction paper
- scissors
- crayons (big and little)
- markers (big and little)
- cardboard box or plastic file box

Procedure

1. Cut construction paper into two sizes—big pieces and little pieces.
2. Place paper and a collection of markers and crayons in the box.
3. Children can select the size of paper they will use—big or little.
4. Children can select the tool they will use—big or little.
5. After they have drawn a picture or made a design, label it "big" or "little" and display it in the *Big and Little Center*.

Adapt "Big and Little Pictures"

  Do not throw away small pieces of crayon. They can encourage children to use a better grasp while drawing.

  Place big and little paper and big and little crayons or markers in individual boxes, and label them. This may help some children make choices.

 Line paper with fluorescent glue and let it dry. This will provide a visual and tactile border on the paper for drawing.

The Essential Literacy Connection

Books

Bunting, Eve. 2003. **Little Bear's Little Boat**. New York: Clarion Books. *Little bear grows and grows until he no longer fits into his little boat.*

Ford, Miela. 1994. **Little Elephant**. New York: Greenwillow. *The concept of opposites is explained in short sentences and illustrated with pictures of a baby and mother elephant.*

Jenkins, Steve. 1996. **Big & Little**. Boston, MA: Houghton Mifflin. *This book illustrates the concept of big and little, showing similar animals that are different in size.*

McCurry, Kristen & Jackson, Aimee. 2004. **Ocean Babies**. New York: NorthWord Press. *Pictures of ocean babies and their mothers teach the concept of big and little while introducing children to ocean animals.*

Milne, Ellen. 1999. **Disney's Winnie the Pooh Opposites**. New York: Random House. *Simple rhyming text teaches children about opposites.*

Patricelli, Leslie. 2003. **Big Little**. Cambridge, MA: Candlewick Press. *Clever comparisons between big and little are displayed in cute illustrations and simple text.*

Taback, Simms. 1997. **There Was an Old Woman Who Swallowed a Fly**. New York: Viking. *This favorite folk tale has bright illustrations and a die-cut hole so children can see each animal in the stomach of the old woman.*

Other Literacy Materials

- graphs
- measuring tools with numbers/print
- signs to label the "big" and "little" activities

Adding Spark to the Big and Little Center

Bring a sand table into the center. Hide big and little objects in the table and send children on a treasure hunt for either big or little objects.

Children explore a container with different sizes of balls.

Evaluation of the Individual Child

Is the child:

1. Using appropriate vocabulary to describe concepts?
2. Demonstrating an understanding of the concepts of *big* and *little*?
3. Using tools effectively in the environment?
4. Able to utilize problem-solving skills within the environment?

Pet Shop Center

Overview

Young children and pets provide a unique center theme for the classroom. In the *Pet Shop Center*, children can learn about many different types of pets and about the care of these pets. Children can make collars, houses, sleeping mats, and other items needed by pets. When a child cares for a pet and learns to be kind and gentle, this supports the child's growing emotional development with both animals and people.

Learning Objectives

The child with special needs will:

1. Learn about the care of pets.
2. Discover the different kinds of pets that are available at the *Pet Shop Center*.
3. Learn new words and terms that relate to pets and their care.
4. Develop the skills needed to be kind and caring with pets.
5. Appreciate how pets respond to children and adults.

Time Frame

This center will be very interesting to young children and should remain in the classroom for three to four weeks. If possible, a trip to a pet store will expand the children's experiences and provide more information for their play. This concrete experience will expand the time the *Pet Shop Center* can be in the classroom.

Letter to Parents or Guardians

Dear Parent or Guardian,

For the next few weeks, we will have a *Pet Shop Center* set up in our classroom. We will bring stuffed animals and other materials to stimulate our children's play around this theme. Young children enjoy pretending to care for, feed, and groom pets. These experiences help them become sensitive to the needs of pets.

In the *Pet Shop Center*, they can create items that are needed by pets, such as collars, leashes, beds, toys, and houses. While your child is making these, he or she will learn about the animals and their toys. If you have a pet that is especially child-friendly, talk with us about a short visit to our *Pet Shop Center*. We would like a picture of a family pet (yours or a relative's) to be included in our Pet Book.

Layout of the Pet Shop Center

This area should simulate the inside of a pet store. It can include an area with cages where pets stay and a grooming area where pets are brushed and bathed. Another section should be provided where the "veterinarian" can check animals. The store will need a display area, with shelving for food, bones, beds, leashes, and toys. A scale and tape measure will add interest to the center. A check-out area should be set up where purchases can be made for the pets and pet-care products. Be sure to include printed materials that relate to pet stores, such as brochures about care, books about pets, and advertisements. If there is a class pet, move it to this area while the *Pet Shop Center* is open.

"Photographs of children playing in centers, building props, or working together clearly demonstrate their learning with concrete evidence of the process that is occurring."

Vocabulary Enrichment

bird

cat

checkup

collar

dog

feed and food

fish

groom: brush, comb, and clippers

guinea pig

leash

lizard

pet

pet toys

rabbit

shampoo

veterinarian

Two children examine and use a pet cage.

Teacher- and Parent-Collected Props

- animal travel cages or small pet houses
- books about pets, such as fish, dogs, cats, rabbits, and lizards
- empty cans or boxes of pet food
- grooming tools, such as a brush, comb, and clippers
- old bathroom scale
- old collars, leashes, and food bowls
- stuffed animals, such as cat, dog, rabbit, lizard, and fish
- veterinarian tools, such as stethoscope, small flashlight, and medicine bottle

Web of Integrated Learning

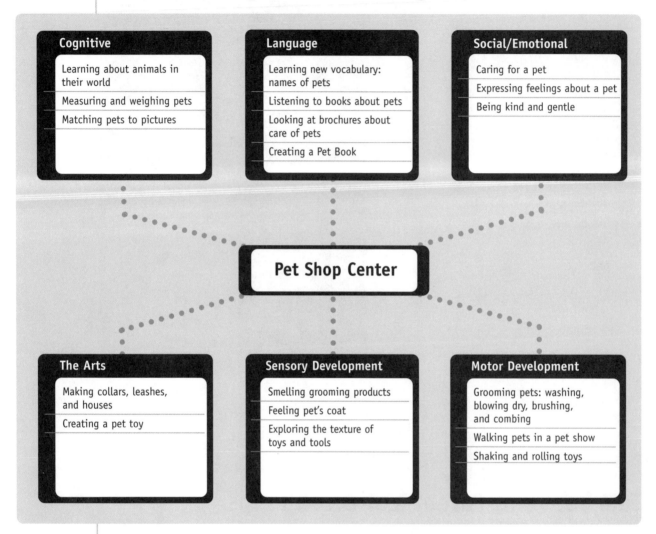

Cognitive
- Learning about animals in their world
- Measuring and weighing pets
- Matching pets to pictures

Language
- Learning new vocabulary: names of pets
- Listening to books about pets
- Looking at brochures about care of pets
- Creating a Pet Book

Social/Emotional
- Caring for a pet
- Expressing feelings about a pet
- Being kind and gentle

Pet Shop Center

The Arts
- Making collars, leashes, and houses
- Creating a pet toy

Sensory Development
- Smelling grooming products
- Feeling pet's coat
- Exploring the texture of toys and tools

Motor Development
- Grooming pets: washing, blowing dry, brushing, and combing
- Walking pets in a pet show
- Shaking and rolling toys

Activities

Grooming Dogs

Materials

- paper
- marker
- tape
- pet grooming props, such as empty shampoo bottles, brushes, combs, clippers, unbreakable mirror, leash, low table, blow dryer with cord removed
- pictures of different kinds of dogs and the grooming for each

Procedure

1. Set up a grooming area in the *Pet Shop Center*.
2. Place a large sign that identifies the grooming available, with prices for different sizes of dogs.
3. Provide all the tools needed for grooming in a plastic storage container on the table.
4. Children can select the stuffed dog they will groom.
5. They may also write up the bill for the cost of the grooming.

Adapt "Grooming Dogs"

  Sing the song "How Much Is That Doggie in the Window?" or "This is the way we groom our pet, so early in the morning..." to the tune of "Here We Go 'Round the Mulberry Bush" with the children as they work.

   Place a few grooming tools on a tabletop, with space between each item for easy viewing and selection.

 Label each grooming tool with its name.

Pet Show

Materials

- variety of stuffed animals
- poster board or construction paper
- markers
- materials to make props, such as poster board or construction paper, markers, rope, yarn, cording, ribbons, stickers, tape, glue, scissors
- rug with masking tape circle
- microphone, real or pretend

Procedure

1. Children can select the stuffed animal they want to show.
2. They can make and decorate the collar, leash, or other items that can be worn by their pet.
3. The announcer can introduce the child and the pet.
4. Children can walk around the circle on the rug to show everyone their pet.
5. Provide ribbons to all the children and their pets.

Adapt "Pet Show"

Pair each child with a peer who is good at pretend play.

If the child is unable to carry the pet while walking, she can put the pet in her lap or on a tabletop for display.

Make a sign that says "Pet Show" and place it in the center.

Ask the child to help announce her friends. "Here is Ellie and her dog, Buffy."

Making a Pet Toy

Materials

- socks: small and adult size
- bells
- ribbon, yarn, twine
- small toy
- masking tape
- small clear plastic bottles
- glue
- foil

Procedure

1. Children can design a toy for their family pet or for a pet in the *Pet Shop Center*.
2. They can combine materials to make the toy interesting for the pet.
3. Some possibilities include:
   - Socks with bells inside
   - Yarn with toy attached
   - Ball made from tape
   - Bottle roll: plastic bottle with materials that make a sound inside (cap taped or glued on securely)
   - Foil ball

Adapt "Making a Pet Toy"

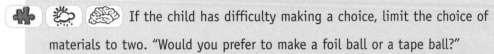 If the child has difficulty making a choice, limit the choice of materials to two. "Would you prefer to make a foil ball or a tape ball?"

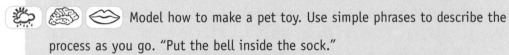 Model how to make a pet toy. Use simple phrases to describe the process as you go. "Put the bell inside the sock."

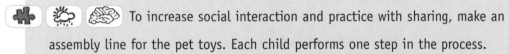 To increase social interaction and practice with sharing, make an assembly line for the pet toys. Each child performs one step in the process.

A child with physical limitations may be able to verbally direct an adult or another child in making the pet toy.

Big Pet Book

Materials

- several pieces of large poster board
- scissors
- pictures of pets from magazines and catalogs
- pictures of the children's pets
- markers
- glue or tape
- metal loops/rings

Procedure

1. Cut several large pieces of poster board in half to form the book pages.
2. Children can glue or tape pictures of pets to the big book pages.
3. Add the names of pets and children.
4. Children who do not have pets can add pictures of pets they like.
5. Use large metal rings or loops to hold the pages together.
6. Children can read the book and take pride in their pets.

Adapt "Big Pet Book"

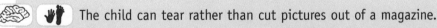 The child can tear rather than cut pictures out of a magazine.

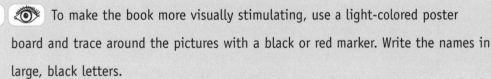 To make the book more visually stimulating, use a light-colored poster board and trace around the pictures with a black or red marker. Write the names in large, black letters.

Place the finished book on an incline board (see pages 306–307 in Chapter 5 for directions) for easier viewing.

The Essential Literacy Connection

Books

Bernthal, Mark. 2000. **Barney Goes to the Pet Shop**. New York: Scholastic. *Take a trip to the pet shop with Barney and Baby Bop.*

Dodds, Dayle Ann. 2001. **Pet Wash**. Cambridge, MA: Candlewick Press. *Two boys open a Pet Wash where they will wash any pet. When a friend brings his baby brother to be washed, they close the Pet Wash.*

Keats, Ezra Jack. 2001. **Pet Show!** New York: Puffin. *With the pet contest about to begin, Archie has to use some quick thinking skills because he cannot find the neighborhood cat.*

Namm, Diane. 2004. **Pick a Pet**. New York: Scholastic. *A young girl tries to choose a pet that will be her birthday gift. She and her parents visit a zoo, farm, and pet store. She finally finds an animal friend.*

Simon, Seymour. 1979. **Pets in a Jar: Collecting and Caring for Small Wild Animals**. New York: Puffin. *Learn how to build a terrarium in a jar.*

(*Available as a board book)

Other Literacy Materials

- brochures and books about pets
- grooming chart
- pad for writing bills

Adding Spark to the Pet Shop Center

Have a live pet visit the center. This should be a child-friendly family pet, such as a kitten or puppy, or a visitor from the Humane Society.

Evaluation of the Individual Child

Is the child:

1. Talking about the pets in the center? Which ones?
2. Demonstrating ways of grooming or playing with the pet?
3. Using new vocabulary in her conversations?
4. Demonstrating kind and caring behavior? In what way?

Evaluation of Centers

Classroom centers should be evaluated throughout the year to determine if they are functioning effectively. Traditional Centers, which are in the classroom for a long time, should be evaluated several times a year. Observe the centers to determine if they are actively engaging children in play and interactions. If the children are not choosing these centers or they are involved in repetitive play, introduce a new spark or prop to the center. Often, this new material will activate the children's involvement and expand their play.

Are these props being used creatively?

Observation of the children at play in Sociodramatic Centers and Unique Centers will help determine how long these centers should remain in the classroom. When children's interest is fading, pack up the center and bring it back at a later time. The rotation of these centers in and out of the classroom provides diverse choices and varied play. Some questions to consider when observing children's play in centers include:

- Are the children actively engaged in play in the center?
- Is language being used to accompany and support the play?
- Are props and materials being used in appropriate ways?
- Are play sequences and role playing occurring?
- Are materials and props used creatively?
- Are children collaborating in their play?

Observations: How and When

One of the best ways to determine young children's developmental levels and abilities is to observe them while they are involved in meaningful activities. In Center Time, you will be able to see and record children's use of language, motor skills, level of thinking, and social skills. These observations become the documented evidence of their learning and engagement.

Observations should be planned and systematic. Observe two or three children during Center Time each day, rotating the observations until all children in the classroom have been studied. It is important to develop the habit of writing down what is observed, including the date, time, and exact behaviors. It is essential to record observations in a manner that is easy for you. Some possibilities include a clipboard with pencils, sticky notes (to be placed later in the child's folder), or writing directly in the child's portfolio.

Record the child's actions, conversations, who they are playing with, what projects they are working on, and what skills they are using. Write down what the child is doing without judgment; interpretations can be made later. Observe the activity for five to seven minutes and then take a break. Afterwards, you can add details or other important information. Return to observe a different child or another activity. The information collected through planned observation can be added to a child's portfolio or file. This documentation will assist in the identification of the child's developmental progress and any areas of weakness.

Evaluation of the Individual Child

Center Time is a great opportunity to observe how children are developing and using their abilities. This collected documentation can be used to plan an individual child's program and to guide his learning. Each center described in this book has a section called Evaluation of the Individual Child, which includes questions to guide your observation of the child in that particular center. These questions can help you determine if the child has made progress or changes. These questions may also assist you in writing goals for the child as well as in documenting the child's achievements.

The checklists on pages 298–300 outline typical developmental milestones for preschoolers. These lists may aid in the evaluation of a child with special needs or provide ideas for goals. For a typically developing child, skills should be completed by the end of the year where they are listed. As you review these milestones, keep in mind that not all children can complete every task in their age group and that the sequence of developing skills may vary. If a child is not able to do at least 50% of the tasks in one or more areas, then he should be considered for further evaluation by a specialist.

Observe the child's skills in center activities.

"Each child develops at his own pace. What is considered 'typical' development covers a broad range of behaviors and skills."

Developmental Milestones for Three-Year-Olds

Cognitive

- ☐ Identifies action pictures
- ☐ Counts in rote to 10
- ☐ Follows two-step commands
- ☐ Matches several primary colors
- ☐ Identifies simple shapes
- ☐ Knows the concept of one
- ☐ Beginning to draw a person with a head

Language

- ☐ Vocabulary of at least 500 words
- ☐ Uses sentences
- ☐ Asks questions (Who? What? Why? Where?)
- ☐ Uses plurals and tenses
- ☐ Knows nursery rhymes
- ☐ Tells or shows the use of common objects

Gross Motor

- ☐ Walks and runs while swinging arms
- ☐ Stands on one foot for a moment
- ☐ Jumps high
- ☐ Jumps forward
- ☐ Throws large ball
- ☐ Catches large ball
- ☐ Alternates feet going up steps

Fine Motor

- ☐ Copies circle
- ☐ Imitates a cross
- ☐ Makes tower of 10 blocks
- ☐ Uses scissors to cut along a 4" long straight line
- ☐ Strings large beads

Social-Emotional

- ☐ Begins to share and take turns
- ☐ Associative play (no division of labor) begins
- ☐ Realizes own gender
- ☐ Likes to dress up

Self Care

- ☐ Undresses and dresses with minimal assistance
- ☐ Unbuttons 1" buttons
- ☐ Feeds self using spoon and fork
- ☐ Dry diaper during the day and usually dry at night

Developmental Milestones for Four-Year-Olds

Cognitive

- ☐ Draws a person with at least three parts
- ☐ Follows two- or three-step commands
- ☐ Identifies at least four colors
- ☐ Understands simple math concepts, such as *heavy* and *light*, *big* and *small*
- ☐ Understands one-to-one correspondence when counting up to three objects

Language

- ☐ Understands conversation
- ☐ Carries on conversation
- ☐ Names more detailed body parts (neck, chest, wrist)
- ☐ Repeats words in sentences
- ☐ Knows the concepts *between*, *above*, *below*, *top*, and *bottom*

Gross Motor

- ☐ Stands on one foot for three to five seconds
- ☐ Hops on one foot
- ☐ Stands and runs on tiptoes
- ☐ Bounces ball
- ☐ Alternates feet going down stairs
- ☐ Throws ball one-handed

Fine Motor

- ☐ Holds pencil with fingertips
- ☐ Uses scissors to cut along an 8" long straight line
- ☐ Traces a square and triangle
- ☐ Copies cross figure (+)
- ☐ Strings small beads

Social-Emotional

- ☐ Exhibits emerging cooperative play
- ☐ Creates stories based on real or imaginary experiences
- ☐ Acquires real or imaginary friends
- ☐ Shows off dramatically
- ☐ Likes working on projects that may carry over to the next day

Self Care

- ☐ Undresses and dresses independently
- ☐ Laces shoes
- ☐ Chooses own menu
- ☐ Sets table and serves self
- ☐ Puts shoes on correct feet
- ☐ Buttons small buttons

Developmental Milestones for Five-Year-Olds

Cognitive

- ☐ Has number concept to 10 ("Give me 10 blocks")
- ☐ Can identify coins
- ☐ Names colors
- ☐ Defines objects in terms of use
- ☐ Can state name, address, and birthday

Language

- ☐ Speech is fluent
- ☐ Intact sentence structure
- ☐ Understands *morning, afternoon, and evening*
- ☐ Understands *yesterday* and *tomorrow*
- ☐ Understands opposites

Gross Motor

- ☐ Walks with adult-like pattern
- ☐ Skips
- ☐ Runs with adult-like pattern
- ☐ Hops on one foot for 10 or more steps
- ☐ Catches ball in cupped hands

Fine Motor

- ☐ Cuts out large shapes
- ☐ Copies triangle shape
- ☐ Copies diamond shape
- ☐ Draws a recognizable person with several parts
- ☐ May print name

Social-Emotional

- ☐ Understands and cooperates with rules of simple games
- ☐ Role plays in a group
- ☐ Tends to play with same gender

Self Care

- ☐ Begins to tie shoes
- ☐ Unbuttons back buttons
- ☐ Independent in toileting
- ☐ Independent in washing hands

Centers and Individualized Education Programs (IEPs)

An Individualized Education Program (IEP) is a document required by the Individuals with Disabilities Education Act (IDEA). An IEP is to be completed for any student, ages three through 21, who is eligible for special education services. An IEP has several components, including annual goals and short-term objectives for the student. A team of professionals who work with the child write the IEP.

Teachers working with a child who is receiving special education services should participate in the development of the IEP. Center-based goals are appropriate to include in a preschooler's IEP. Many areas of development may be observed and facilitated in centers. In centers, a child can learn fine motor skills, gross motor skills, social-emotional skills, language skills, cognitive skills, and self-care skills. For example, a child in the *Art Center* may be working toward the objectives of cutting paper with scissors, copying circles

Writing down observations helps in developing IEPs.

with a marker, and folding paper in half. In the *Restaurant Center*, a child could be working on literacy objectives, such as writing on paper, handling a book, and recognizing environmental print.

A few simple guidelines will help you write effective goals and objectives for children with special needs. Goals are usually bigger and longer-term than objectives. Goals may be met in one year and objectives may be met in six to 12 weeks. Both goals and objectives should be functional and child-focused. They should be measurable and observable. Be specific when describing the tools or methods to be used. Ask yourself, "Could someone else read this and decide if the child has achieved the goal?" An example of a good objective would be, "Caroline will independently snip paper with child-safe scissors, 90% of the time."

IEP Goal: Carli will improve self-care skills.

IEP Objective #1: Carli will independently put on a shirt or jacket without fasteners, 90% of the time, per teacher observation.	**Centers Where This Objective May Be Observed**: *Home Living, Beach, Art, Nighttime, Giggle*
IEP Objective #2: Carli will pour a liquid, with little spillage, 80% of the time, per teacher observation.	**Centers Where This Objective May Be Observed**: *Water, Bakery, Restaurant, Sand, Gardening*
IEP Objective #3: Carli will independently wash her hands, 100% of the time, per teacher observation.	**Centers Where This Objective May Be Observed**: *Doctor's Office, Art, Pet Shop, Home Living, I Touch: Tactile*

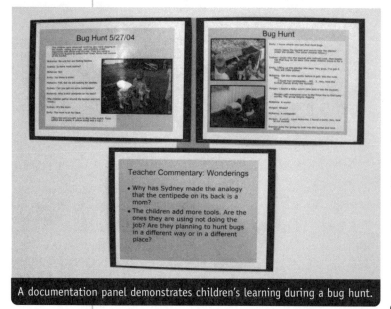

A documentation panel demonstrates children's learning during a bug hunt.

Documentation of Learning

It is important to document a child's performance in centers to monitor what he is learning and how he is developing. Start by recording what each child does in the centers at the beginning of the year. This will be a reference point to compare how the child is changing or progressing throughout the year. You may choose to write a brief description of what the child did or you may use the child's own words. The child's progress can also be documented by taking photographs or by collecting the products the child has made in the centers. A good way to organize documents is to place them in a folder as a portfolio. No matter what type of documentation is used, always record the date of the observation or the date the child made the product. Use these forms of documentation when re-evaluating IEP goals and objectives at the end of the year.

Unique Centers provide interesting additions to early childhood classrooms. Their design encourages creative thinking and playing with unusual materials. Here, children are challenged to think about new ideas and possibilities.

Building and Creating Items for Children With Special Needs

5

The props and recipes included in this chapter are easy to make, but are designed to be created by teachers or parents. In a few instances, children can help with some of the steps but, for the most part, adults should make these items.

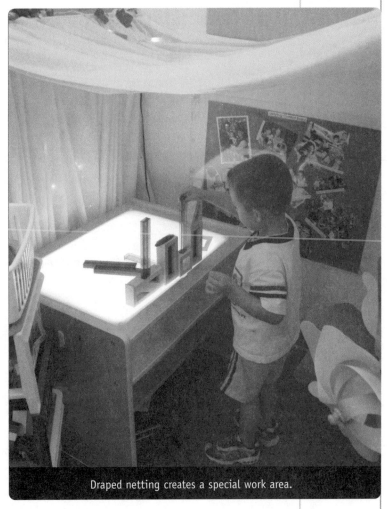

Draped netting creates a special work area.

Bubbles—Basic Bubbles

This simple recipe will provide a bubble mixture young children can use in their play.

Materials

- 6 cups water
- 2 cups liquid detergent (Joy or Dawn works best)
- ¼ cup sugar

Procedure

1. Mix ingredients and let stand for 4 hours.

Bubbles—Hardy Bubbles

This recipe creates bubbles that are stronger and will float longer in the air, allowing additional time for children to watch, touch, and enjoy bubbles.

Materials

- 1 gallon water
- 1 cup liquid detergent (Joy or Dawn works best)
- ¼ cup glycerin (to add strength)
- 1 teaspoon mineral oil (adds rainbow color)

Procedure

1. Mix ingredients and let stand for 24 hours.

Canopy Area

Preschoolers like areas that make them feel secure and safe. A canopy will help children with special needs feel secure and cozy, and will make a space like the *Block Center* even more inviting. Canopies lower the ceiling in an area and can be made very inexpensively with an old sheet or piece of fabric. Check fire codes in your region to determine how low from the ceiling the canopy may be hung, and spray the material with flame retardant (available at home improvement stores). A canopy hung low to the floor will also work effectively for children with special needs by making the large space feel smaller.

Materials

- colorful sheet or fabric
- heavy-duty rubber band
- strong fishing line or macramé rope

Procedure

1. Gather the center of the sheet or fabric and secure it with a heavy rubber band.
2. Hang the gathered fabric from the ceiling with fishing line or macramé rope.
3. Drape the corners of the fabric and attach them to the ceiling so the sheet resembles a canopy.

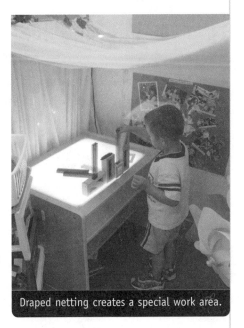

Draped netting creates a special work area.

Carpet Roll

A carpet roll can be used to climb inside, around, and over in the *Gross Motor Center*. The carpet roll can be a lot of fun for driving cars or rolling balls through in the *In and Out Center* or the *Ball Center*. Visit a local carpet dealer and ask for the cardboard roll that remains when the carpet is gone. The carpet dealer may also donate spare carpet to cover the roll. A good length for the carpet roll is 4' long; it may be cut into any size that fits the space.

Materials

- cardboard roll from inside roll of carpet
  Note: The cylinder must be large enough and sturdy enough for a young child to climb inside.
- utility knife or electric knife (adult only)
- durable carpet or vinyl to cover the cylinder (carpeting will cushion the cylinder, while vinyl protects and supports the surface for long-term use)
- glue
- heavy duty staples and stapler
- duct tape

Procedure

1. Cut the cardboard roll using the utility knife or an electric knife to make it 4' long (or a length that will fit the space).
2. Cover the roll with durable, washable carpet. Glue material to the inside of the cylinder; fabric on the outside is optional.
3. Staple carpet to the roll and cover the staples with duct tape.
4. Glue durable, washable carpet to the inside of the roll. Gluing fabric to the outside of the roll (over the carpet) is optional, but may make the roll more durable.

Documentation Panel

This is a visual representation showing what children are learning while working on a project. It includes photographs from the beginning of the activity through its completion. Educators in the Reggio Emilia Schools first demonstrated this type of panel, and it is now widely used in early childhood programs.

A documentation of learning panel for parents to read.

Materials

- camera and film or memory stick
- poster board or art board
- photographs of the young children

Procedure

1. Assemble the photographs in an attractive manner on the board.
2. Reading the panel will help adults understand what the children are learning.
3. An alternate method uses individually framed steps in the process arranged in an attractive manner.

Incline Board

An incline board provides a stable and elevated surface where children can draw and paint. An incline of 20° will help a child hold a writing utensil with an appropriate and functional grasp. Books and cards may also be placed on the incline board for easy viewing. The incline board may be placed on a table or the floor in centers such as the *Fine Motor Center* or *Art Center*. Tri-wall cardboard may be collected as scraps from a packaging company.

Materials

- tri-wall (3-ply) or heavy duty cardboard (at least 14 ½" x 19")
- utility knife or electric knife for cutting cardboard (adult only)
- hot glue gun and hot glue (adult only)
- solid color contact paper

Procedure

1. Cut cardboard into the following 4 pieces:

 - 1 piece measuring 15" x 14"
 - 2 triangle-shape pieces with a length of 14" and a height of 4" at the tallest point
 - 1 piece 15" long and ½" wide

2. Hot glue the pieces of cardboard to form an incline board.

3. Glue the ½" strip to the bottom of the board to keep paper from sliding.

4. Cover incline with solid color contact paper for greater durability.

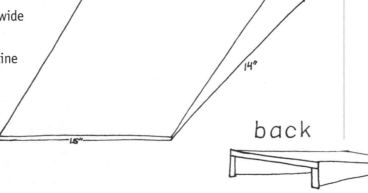

incline board (front)

back

Knob Hanger

Young children and those who are physically challenged can easily handle items with large knobs on the end. The knobs help them select and return items to the appropriate place as they develop self-help skills.

Materials

 - 1 piece of lumber 2' long
 - 8 wooden knobs (may be purchased from a home improvement store)
 - 10 screws and screwdriver

Procedure

1. Use wooden knobs like those found on furniture (available at home improvement stores).

2. Attach the knobs to the lumber and space them 3" apart, starting 1 ½" from the edge.

3. Screw the hanger to the wall.

4. The knobs work well for young children because clothes do not fall off after they are placed on the pegs.

5. Place the knob hanger at a height that is easy for the children to use.

6. This hanger helps children with special needs be independent as they select and return clothing.

Light Table

A low light table can be constructed for young children to use in their activities. This low and inexpensive light table works well with children with special needs.

Materials

- 1 – ⅜" thick piece of 2' x 4' plywood
- 2 – 4' long 1" x 10" boards
- 2 – 2' long 1" x 10" boards
- 1 – ¼" thick piece of 2' x 4' translucent (not transparent) Plexiglas
- 4 – 10" long 2" x 2" wood pieces
- fluorescent shop light with on/off switch and cord (adult only)
- hammer and nails or screwdriver and screws (adult only)
- saw (adult only)
- silver spray paint (adult only)
- nontoxic paint and paintbrush
- glue

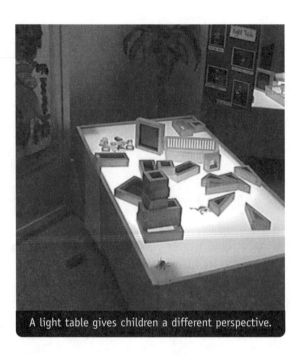

A light table gives children a different perspective.

Procedure

1. Assemble the 1" x 10" boards into a 2' x 4' frame.
2. Cut a notch in one of the 10" sides of plywood, large enough for the shop light plug and switch to pass through.
3. Nail or screw the plywood to the bottom of the box.
4. Glue the 2" x 2" supports into the corners of the box.
5. Spray paint the interior of the box with silver paint, which increases the reflection of the light.
6. Fasten the shop light to the inside bottom of the box. Pass the on/off switch to the exterior the box.
7. Attach the Plexiglas to the open top of the box.
8. Place molding strips around the edges to hold the Plexiglas in place.
9. Sand all rough edges and then paint the light table your choice of color.

Milk Carton Blocks

This lightweight block is easy for children with special needs to move and use in their constructions. The flat top makes the blocks especially easy to use.

Materials

- 10 to 15 cardboard milk cartons
- tape, such as duct or electrical
- materials to decorate the milk cartons, such as contact paper, paint, washable markers, and crayons

Procedure

1. Wash the milk cartons to remove all milk deposits.
2. After the cartons have dried, fold the tops down flat.
3. Tape the tops down.
4. Children can decorate the milk carton blocks.

Musical Instruments—Community Drum

The drum is a very popular musical instrument for young children. Several children can play together by hitting the drum. It is responsive to their actions, and it is easy to create simple rhythm patterns with this drum.

Materials

- 3-gallon galvanized steel bucket
- spray paint (adult only)
- tape, such as duct, electrical, and packing
- large piece of rubber roofing (scraps can often be obtained from a roofing company)
- scissors
- 6 to 8 grommets or eyelets
- polyester rope, nylon rope, or clothesline

Procedure

1. The galvanized bucket is the base for the drum.
2. Remove the handle from the bucket. Spray paint the bucket.
3. Put tape around the top edge of the bucket to preventing cutting.
4. Cut the rubber scrap in a circle that is 2" wider than the top of the bucket.
5. Make 6 to 8 evenly spaced holes around the edge of the rubber for grommets or eyelets.
6. Use the rope or clothesline to thread through the grommets and make the rubber fit tightly over the top of the bucket.

(continued on the next page)

7. Tie the rope together on the bottom of the bucket.
8. This community drum can be played with hands or a mallet.

Musical Instruments—Musical Shakers

Shakers are easy to make. They are very responsive to young children's movements, and can be used with many musical experiences.

Materials

- 5 metal cans with lids (coffee cans or snack food canisters work well)
- small pebbles, gravel, or bolts
- duct tape
- contact paper or spray paint

Procedure

1. Wash the metal cans and lids.
2. Place pebbles, gravel, or bolts inside the can.
3. Tape the lid securely to the top of the can.
4. Paint the cans or cover them with contact paper.
5. The shaker sound can be produced by rolling or shaking the can.

Musical Instruments—Rhythm Sticks

These simple-to-make sticks can be used by the children to accompany their singing, moving, and listening. The varied thickness and lengths will produce different sounds and add variety to musical experiences.

Materials

- dowel rods that are ⅛" to 2" in diameter
- handsaw (adult only)
- sandpaper
- nontoxic paint and paintbrushes
- plastic sheet

Procedure

1. Saw the dowel rods into 12" pieces (each length will make 4 rhythm sticks).
2. Sand all rough edges.
3. Paint each thickness a different color to help children discriminate differences in sounds.
4. Store together so children can select the sound they want to make.

Musical Instruments—Water Drum

Drums are an essential musical instrument for young children. They provide a great way to keep a steady beat for music and dancing. Large drums provide a deep and resonating sound that intrigues children.

Materials
- plastic water jugs (water cooler jugs, 3- to 4-gallon size)
- small smooth pebbles
- glue gun or epoxy glue (adult only)

Procedure
1. Clean the water jugs.
2. Add pebbles and glue the lids back on.
3. To play, tap the bottom with palm of hand.

Play Clay

This clay requires cooking and cooling before the children can use it. The clay can be different colors and can be painted when dry. This recipe makes about 1½ cups and is easily doubled.

Materials
- 1 cup baking soda
- ½ cup cornstarch
- saucepan
- ⅔ cup warm water
- hot plate or stove (adult only)
- cutting board
- food coloring
- airtight container

Procedure
1. Mix baking soda and cornstarch in a saucepan.
2. Add water and stir until smooth.
3. Place over medium heat and bring to a boil. Stir mixture constantly until it looks like mashed potatoes.
4. Remove saucepan from heat and pour clay onto a cutting board to cool.
5. For color, knead food coloring into the cooled clay until well-blended.
6. This clay dries well and is perfect for painting on when dried.
7. Store in an airtight container.

Playdough Formula

This playdough has an excellent consistency that children enjoy touching. It can be used for a long time if stored in an airtight container.

Materials

- 2 cups flour
- 1 cup salt
- 2 cups water
- 2 tablespoons oil
- 2 teaspoons cream of tarter
- food coloring
- saucepan
- hot plate or stove (adult only)
- plastic container with a tight-fitting lid

Procedure

1. Stir ingredients in a saucepan over low heat until mixture has thickened into a nice doughy ball.
2. Allow time for the dough to cool thoroughly.
3. Store in a plastic container with a tight-fitting lid.
4. This playdough has a smooth texture and will last a long time, when stored properly.

Plexiglas Display Area

Children's pictures and projects should be displayed so children can see and touch them. This design for the frame will make it possible for the teacher to slide work in and out without changing the frame.

Materials

- 2 – 12" to 24" long 1" x 1" furring strips that have been planed smooth
- ⅛" thick clear Plexiglas, cut to size for the display
- 4 to 6 screws and a screwdriver

Procedure

1. Use two pieces of wood furring to make the top and bottom of a simple frame. The pieces of wood should be the width of one or two pictures.
2. Fit a piece of Plexiglas between the two pieces of wood furring.
3. Screw the frame to the wall at the eye level of the children.

4. Leave both sides of the frame open with no wood frame on them.

5. Be sure to leave a ½" space between the Plexiglas and the wall.

6. With the sides of the frame open, pictures can be changed by simply sliding them in and out of either side. (Young children will not be able to remove the pictures.)

Photos covered with Plexiglas can be seen and touched.

Riser

The riser provides a safe place for preschoolers to stand, climb, or work. Preschoolers can sit on or place toys on the riser for play. The riser is useful in the *Gross Motor Center* to provide new motor challenges for preschoolers. It can also be used as a divider to separate different centers. The recommended size for a riser is 2' wide, 4' long, and 10" to 12" high.

A place to sit or work at a comfortable height

Materials

- 1 – ⅜" 4' x 8' plywood piece (this is enough plywood to make 4 risers)
- saw (adult only)
- 2 – 1" x 10" 4' long boards (or use 1"x 12" boards, for a taller riser)
- 2 – 1" x 10" 2' long boards
- hammer and nails or screwdriver and screws (adult only)
- durable, smooth carpet or vinyl (carpet remnants work well)
- heavy duty staples and stapler (adult only)
- 4 – 12" pieces of strong rope

(continued on the next page)

Procedure

1. Cut the plywood into four pieces; each piece should be 2' wide and 4' long.
2. Make the two sides of each riser from the 4' long boards.
3. Make the two ends of each riser from the 2' long boards.
4. Cover the risers with durable, smooth carpet or vinyl so the surface is soft and washable.
5. Staple the carpet or vinyl to the underside of the riser and cover staples with duct tape.
6. Attach a short rope handle to each side to help when moving the riser from place to place.

Sand Pillows

Young children like to snuggle up to pillows and stuffed animals. Sand pillows can be used in the *Private Place Center* for children to lie on and under. The heavy weight of a sand pillow can help children with special needs develop a sense of body awareness and can have a calming effect on them.

Materials

- 2 pillowcases
- 2 pounds of white sand
- thread and needle or sewing machine (adult only)

Procedure

1. Place the sand inside one pillowcase.
2. Sew the open end of the pillowcase.
3. Use the other pillowcase to cover the Sand Pillow so it can be removed and washed easily.

Shadow Screen

The shadow screen is easy to construct and use. It provides stimulus for children to move their bodies and to manipulate puppets, and observe immediate response to their actions.

Materials

- 1 full-size white bed sheet
- heavy duty stapler (adult only)
- 8 to 12 – 1" x ½" furring strips, 2' long
- 4 metal corner reinforcement pieces
- wooden stand to hold assembled screen
- floor lamp, clip-on lamp, or old overhead projector

Procedure

1. Staple the sheet edges to the furring strips.
2. Attach metal reinforcements to the corners of the frame.
3. Place screen on a stand that will hold it securely.
4. Shine light so the screen will produce shadows.

Sound Board

These inexpensive and easily constructed panels can provide sound absorption in centers or classroom. Place sound boards on the wall to capture the sounds in a noisy area.

Materials

- 1 sheet of 4' x 8' sound board 1" thick (available at home improvement stores)
- handsaw (adult only)
- loosely woven burlap or other fabric
- heavy duty stapler (adult only)
- duct tape

Sounds panels absorb sound in a specific area.

Procedure

1. Cut the sound board into two 4' x 4' pieces.
2. Cover each piece of the board with fabric on one side.
3. Staple the fabric to the backside of the board.
4. Cover staples and fabric edge with duct tape.
5. Attach to the wall in selected location to assist with noise reduction.

Terrarium

A terrarium provides an environment for plants to grow with a minimum amount of work. Because it is a closed environment it will stay moist, so plants will grow without additional watering. (Young children can help assemble the terrarium.)

(continued on the next page)

Materials

- large plastic 2-liter drink bottle with lid
- 1 piece of charcoal (without additives)
- gravel
- potting soil
- collection of small plants from outdoors or purchased from a greenhouse
- mister

Procedure

1. Cut the top off the drink bottle (keep the top to reapply).
2. Break the charcoal into several smaller pieces and place a few pieces on the bottom of the bottle.
3. Put a layer of gravel on top of the charcoal pieces. Add a layer of potting soil about 2" deep.
4. Place small plants in the soil.
5. Water the plants and mist the foliage.
6. Replace the top of the bottle with the lid of the container, and place the terrarium in a lighted area of the room.
7. If the terrarium seems to be getting too moist, remove the top or the lid. If the system is working, the terrarium will not need watering.
8. Children can enjoy their creation and watch the plants grow.

Wedge

Preschool children need a variety of new experiences to expand their motor skills. Foam wedges may be used as a ramp to roll down, climb up, or jump off.

Materials

- large piece of dense foam (thick enough to walk on)
- scissors or saw (adult only)
- sturdy fabric to cover the wedge, such as denim or corduroy
- heavy-duty stapler (adult only)
- duct tape

Procedure

1. Collect a large piece of dense foam that is thick enough to walk on.
2. Cut the foam into a wedge at least 2' long and 1' high (on the tall end).
3. Cover the wedge with thick, sturdy material. Secure with staples, and then cover the staples with tape.

Index

Children's Book Index

Index